Lean For Dummies®

F3

Cheat Sheet

Types of Waste

- **muda:** Waste; any activity that does not add value
  - Type-1 *muda:* Non-value-added, but necessary for the system to function
  - Type-2 *muda:* Non-value-added and unnecessary for the system to function; the first targets for elimination
- **mura:** Waste due to unevenness or variation
- **muri:** Waste caused by overstressing people, equipment, or systems

Lean Fundamentals

- Focus on the customer.
- Improve the value stream.
- Maintain flow.
- Pull through the system.
- Strive for perfection.
- Respect people.

Lean Japanese Terms

- **andon:** A signal to alert people to problems in a process
- **gemba:** Where the action occurs
- **genchi genbutsu:** Go and see
- **heijunka:** Smoothing; the technique of leveling schedules
- **hoshin:** A system of planning, forms, and rules
- **jidoka:** Stopping machines when an error has been detected, preventing defects from progressing through the process
- **Kaikaku:** Radical improvement.
- **Kaizen:** Incremental, continuous improvement
- **kanban:** A signal system used to trigger replenishment
- **poka-yoke:** A device to prevent defect production
- **sensei:** A master or teacher

The Seven

- **Transportation:** (non-value-added) movement of parts, materials, or information between processes?
- **Waiting:** Are people, parts, systems, or facilities idle, waiting for a work cycle to be completed?
- **Overproduction:** Are you producing sooner, faster, or in greater quantities than the customer is demanding?
- **Defects:** Does the process result in anything that the customer would deem unacceptable?
- **Inventory:** Do you have any raw materials, work-in-progress (WIP), or finished goods that are in excess or not having value added to them?
- **Movement:** Do you move materials, people, equipment, and goods unnecessarily or excessively within a processing step?
- **Extra processing:** Do you have work being performed beyond what is required to satisfy the customer standards or requirements?

5S of the Workplace

- **Sort:** Organize the workplace. Dispose of all unnecessary items.
- **Straighten:** Arrange all remaining items in standard locations that can be easily and readily accessed.
- **Scrub:** Keep all equipment and working areas neat and clean.
- **Systematize:** Create a system to maintain order in the area as a regular part of the daily activities.
- **Standardize:** Exercise discipline to maintain cleanliness in the workplace and find ways to enhance/improve the process.

The Definition of a Value-Added Activity

- It must transform the product or service.
- The customer must be willing to "pay" for it.
- It must be done correctly the first time.

D0470205

Lean For Dummies®

The Kaizen Project PDCA (or PDSA) Cycle

1. **Plan.**

   Create a plan for change, identifying specifically what you want to change. Define the steps you need to make the change, and predict the results of the change.

2. **Do.**

   Carry out the plan in a trial or test environment, on a small scale, under controlled conditions.

3. **Check (or study).**

   Examine the results of your trial. Verify that you've improved the process. If you have, consider implementing it on a broader scale. If you haven't improved the process, go back and try again.

4. **Act.**

   Implement the changes you've verified on a broader scale. Update the standard operating procedures.

Value Stream Mapping Icons

Icon	Icon Name	Description	Icon	Icon Name	Description
	Process box	Describes an activity in the value stream. Includes a title and description of the process, as well as data, like process time, setup time, and so on.		Finished goods movement	Indicates when materials in a finished state are moved along the value stream. This can be a supplier moving its product to a company or a company moving its product to its customer.
	Outside source	Indicates and identifies both customers and suppliers.		Material push	Indicates material being pushed through the process. The push is usually a production plan or schedule.
	Truck	Indicates an outside delivery — either to a customer or from a supplier.			
	Information	Describes information transmitted along the value stream.		Supermarket	Indicates in-process inventory stored in a controlled environment called a supermarket.
	Electronic information transmission	Indicates that the information is transmitted electronically.		Material pull	Indicates material movement via a pull signal (kanban).
	Manual information transmission	Indicates that the information is transmitted manually.		Operator	Indicates that one or more operators are present at a process step.
	Inventory	Identifies stored inventory — either raw materials, in process, or finished goods.		*Kaizen* burst	Indicates the need for and description of a *Kaizen* activity within the value stream.

For Dummies: Bestselling Book Series for Beginners

by Natalie J. Sayer and Bruce Williams

Wiley Publishing, Inc.

Lean For Dummies®

Published by
Wiley Publishing, Inc.
111 River St.
Hoboken, NJ 07030-5774
www.wiley.com

WILEY

About the Authors

Natalie J. Sayer began studying and applying Lean before it was formally known as Lean. Over her 20-year career in the automotive industry in the United States and Mexico, Natalie honed her skills applying Lean and Organizational Development methods across functional areas of Fortune 130 companies. In 1996, Natalie was an instrumental team member in the Lean transformation of a GM facility in Matamoros, Mexico. The team was awarded the 1996 GM President's Council Honors for the project. While working with General Motors, she had multiple opportunities to visit and learn from New United Motor Manufacturing, Inc. (NUMMI). Natalie has trained, coached, mentored, and rolled up her sleeves to implement Lean practices, whether working in a company or volunteering at a food bank.

She received a Bachelor of Mechanical Engineering from the University of Dayton in 1988 and a Master of Manufacturing Systems Engineering from the University of Michigan in 1992. She is a graduate of Coach University and Corporate Coach University. Natalie is also a Six Sigma Black Belt and a Global Leadership Executive Coach.

In 2003, Natalie founded I-Emerge, an Arizona-based global consultancy dedicated to the facilitation of people and processes experiencing significant change. The I-Emerge toolbox includes executive and personal coaching, group facilitation, Lean methods, public speaking, and Organizational Development tools and assessments. She is a passionate people person, who lives her life with the convictions that "there is always a better way" and "change won't happen without the people."

Beyond I-Emerge, Natalie can be found on stage acting in musical theater, teaching graduate school, traveling to exotic places, learning something new, working on causes advancing people and literacy, or spending time with friends and family.

Bruce Williams strives for perfection and added value as a scientist, educator, consultant, and entrepreneur. Leveraging the Lean principle of standardized work, this is his third *For Dummies* book in three years, having previously coauthored the best-selling *Six Sigma For Dummies* in 2005 and the *Six Sigma Workbook For Dummies* in 2006.

Undergraduate degrees in physics and astrophysics from the University of Colorado testify to his early pursuit of understanding the ultimate nature of root cause.

He was a sculler in the value stream of aerospace systems, where he shot the rapids in the tumultuous whitewater of the Hubble Space Telescope program. With graduate degrees in technical management and computer science from Johns Hopkins University and the University of Colorado, Bruce elevated his value-stream role to that of tugboat captain, leading and managing technical teams and projects.

A decade of personal *Kaizen* has inspired his continuous journey through technology, software, business development, and management. A *Kaikaku* moment unleashed his entrepreneurial self in 1999. He is now sea captain of Savvi International, charting the deeper value-stream waters of solutions for business performance improvement using Six Sigma, Lean, and Business Process Management.

He lives with his standard family in the rural desert foothills of North Scottsdale, Arizona, flowing just-in-time value in response to their continuous demand pull. He regularly suffers the *muri* of 5S'ing the house on weekends. His hobbies include mucking the *muda* of the family horses.

Dedication

Natalie J. Sayer: To Frank Cooney, Al Billis, and Pam Oakes, my first Lean teachers; to Jim, Patt, and Eric Sayer, my family who support all my endeavors; and to Anne Ramsey, Derek O'Neal, Lori Kobriger, and the rest of my inner circle. Thank you all.

Bruce Williams: To the Lean person within all of us. Recognize and nurture your Lean self. Every waste you eliminate today sets the stage for a better world tomorrow.

Authors' Acknowledgments

The authors acknowledge Craig Gygi for his expertise, dedication, and encouragement. You established the standard for us to follow; we hope we've done you proud.

We especially thank Frank Cooney for his mentoring, advice, and technical review. Lean can be a hard thing to pin down. Thanks, Frank, for bringing your tremendous body of practical experience to bear.

We'd also like to acknowledge our good friends and colleagues Janet Young, Vern Young, Dr. Deborah Peck, Eleanor Clements, Scott Kurish, and Dr. Kiran Garimella for your counsel, ideas, review, and support. Additionally, we'd like to acknowledge everyone at the Phoenix Think Tank, a place where great minds, ideas, and support meet to create "an exquisite shifting in thought."

Thanks to Ken Carraher of iGrafx and Debbie Rosen of webMethods for their unflinching support in providing whatever we needed. We could easily have filled the book with value-stream maps, process models, and dashboards. We'll just have to save them all for the *Lean Workbook For Dummies!*

As authors and researchers, we humbly bow to the miracle that is Google.

All people interested in Lean owe their ongoing gratitude to Mark Graban and his associates, who through their blog site translate Lean to the world around us.

As consumers, and on behalf of consumers everywhere, we acknowledge the uniquely groundbreaking contributions of brilliant pioneers W. Edwards Deming, Taiichi Ohno, and Shigeo Shingo, as well as U.S. Lean leaders Norm Bodek and Jim Womack. Through their achievements, we are all better off.

But most of all, we acknowledge the many thousands of Lean practitioners around the world, who regularly confront established structures, functional silos, arcane accounting practices, and entrenched procedures to cut the waste and find the real customer value. You make Lean thrive. You are our heroes.

Publisher's Acknowledgments

We're proud of this book; please send us your comments through our Dummies online registration form located at www.dummies.com/register/.

Some of the people who helped bring this book to market include the following:

Acquisitions, Editorial, and Media Development

Project Editor: Elizabeth Kuball

Acquisitions Editor: Michael Lewis

Technical Editor: Francis D. Cooney

Consumer Editorial Supervisor and Reprint Editor: Carmen Krikorian

Editorial Manager: Michelle Hacker

Editorial Assistants: Erin Calligan, Joe Niesen, Leeann Harney, David Lutton

Cartoons: Rich Tennant (www.the5thwave.com)

Composition Services

Project Coordinator: Heather Kolter

Layout and Graphics: Claudia Bell, Carl Byers, Shane Johnson, Stephanie D. Jumper

Anniversary Logo Design: Richard Pacifico

Proofreader: Techbooks

Indexer: Techbooks

Special Help
Tim Gallan

Publishing and Editorial for Consumer Dummies

Diane Graves Steele, Vice President and Publisher, Consumer Dummies

Joyce Pepple, Acquisitions Director, Consumer Dummies

Kristin A. Cocks, Product Development Director, Consumer Dummies

Michael Spring, Vice President and Publisher, Travel

Kelly Regan, Editorial Director, Travel

Publishing for Technology Dummies

Andy Cummings, Vice President and Publisher, Dummies Technology/General User

Composition Services

Gerry Fahey, Vice President of Production Services

Debbie Stailey, Director of Composition Services

Contents at a Glance

Table of Contents

Introduction

●●●

*T*he principles and practices of Lean organizations are recognized the world over as the most powerful and effective way to build and sustain continuously improving businesses and institutions. Following a Lean path, any business in any industry of any size or type can improve itself continuously over the long term. Led by advancements first pioneered at the Toyota Motor Corporation over 50 years ago, Lean is now established as the most consistently successful approach to organizing and operating any enterprise.

If you're in certain manufacturing industries, or public institutions like the U.S. military, you've probably heard about Lean. You may even have been through a *Kaizen* event or been part of implementing a pull system. If so, you've already experienced some of the power of Lean tools.

But if you're like most people, the term *Lean* itself may be unfamiliar to you, let alone its principles and practices. Even within those businesses and organizations that have adopted Lean methods, most people don't really understand the bigger picture of Lean. Organizations often implement Lean piecemeal, leaving some of the most important elements behind — and with much less than optimal results.

For decades, the whole system of Lean principles and practices was known only to specialized manufacturers, certain academic researchers, and quality gurus. The Toyota Production System (TPS) was the incubator where the methods, techniques, and tools of Lean were pioneered and refined. Its full potential has been a mystery to most organizations and professionals.

All that began to change in the late 1980s, as the term *Lean* was coined to describe the fundamentals of business systems like TPS to the rest of the world. As the understanding of Lean has spread across continents, industries, and organizations, it has become less of a mystery and much easier to understand and implement.

Simply stated, Lean is a philosophy and a proven long-term approach that aligns everything in the business to deliver increasing customer value. It's about orienting people and systems to deliver a continuous stream of value to the customer, and eliminate waste and deficiencies in the process. Lean is an everyday practice at all levels to perform consistently, as well as to consistently improve performance.

About This Book

This book makes Lean accessible to you. We wrote it because Lean is applicable everywhere — it's applicable in large and complex corporations, but also in small businesses and industries, as well as public-sector institutions — at all levels.

We wrote this book for you, the individual. You may be a small-business owner, an ambitious career person, or a manager who wants to know what Lean is and how to apply it. You may be a college student or job applicant who wants to have an edge in upcoming job interviews. No matter who you are, if you want to know more about Lean, this is the book for you.

Lean For Dummies is not just an overview or survey of Lean. It's a comprehensive description of the philosophies and principles of Lean, as well as the methods and tools to put Lean into practice.

This book is

- ✔ A reference book that's organized into parts, chapters, and sections, so that you can flip right to what you need, when you need it
- ✔ A comprehensive text that addresses both the common tools of Lean and the improvement principles and practices
- ✔ A guide for leading a Lean initiative, helping you identify and manage Lean projects, and using Lean tools and procedures
- ✔ Step-by-step instructions for Value Stream Mapping and the methodology of Lean projects
- ✔ Instructions on where you can go for additional help, because the field of Lean is much too large to fit in just a few hundred pages

Lean *is* different, and it contains Japanese terms and ideas that may be foreign to you. But we've taken this difficult subject and made it understandable through examples, simple explanations, and visual aids.

Conventions Used in This Book

When a specialized word first appears in our book, we italicize it, and provide a definition. We also italicize any foreign-language words, including the many Japanese terms that make up the lingo of Lean.

For terms and phrases that industry practitioners use as acronyms, we define the term first and then use it in its abbreviated form going forward.

We put any Web addresses and e-mail addresses in `monofont`, to set it apart from the rest of the text. When this book was printed, some Web addresses may have needed to break across two lines of text. If that happened, rest assured that we haven't put in any extra characters (such as hyphens) to indicate the break. So, when using one of these Web addresses, just type in exactly what you see in this book, pretending as though the line break doesn't exist.

We use some business-management and statistical concepts and language in the course of the book. To get extra smart on the statistical and problem-solving aspects, check out *Six Sigma For Dummies,* by Craig Gygi, Neil DeCarlo, and Bruce Williams; *Six Sigma Workbook for Dummies* by Craig Gygi, Bruce Williams, and Terry Gustafson. Also check out *Managing For Dummies,* 2nd Edition, by Bob Nelson, PhD, and Peter Economy; *Statistics For Dummies,* by Deborah Rumsey, PhD; and *Coaching & Mentoring For Dummies* and *Managing Teams For Dummies,* both by Marty Brounstein (all published by Wiley).

Foolish Assumptions

We assume you've heard something about Lean and are intrigued and compelled to find out more, for one or more of the following reasons:

- ✔ You're contemplating using Lean in your business or organization, and you need to understand what you might be in for.

- ✔ Your business or organization is implementing Lean, and you need to get up to speed. Perhaps you've even been tapped to participate in a *Kaizen* event or a Value Stream Mapping exercise.

- ✔ You believe Lean is the pathway to better performance in your job and can help you advance your career.

- ✔ You're considering a job or career change, and your new opportunities require you to understand Lean practices.

- ✔ You're a student in business, international business, operations, or industrial engineering and you realize that Lean is part of your future.

We assume that you realize Lean demands a rigorous approach to analyzing the value stream of business processes. We also assume that you accept that Lean practice calls for capturing data and applying analytical tools to discover the true nature of value creation and the causes of waste in your environment. In addition, we assume that you might be from any industry, including manufacturing, service, transactional, healthcare, or even government. For these reasons, we have devoted several chapters of this book to describing and defining the Lean toolset.

How This Book Is Organized

We break this book into five separate parts. Each chapter is written as an independent standalone section, which means you can move around the book and delve into a given topic without necessarily having to read all the preceding material first. Anywhere we expound upon or extend other material, we cross-reference the chapter or part of origin, so you can tie it together.

Part I: Lean Basics

Part I is an overview of Lean, including the pedigree, tenets, and language of Lean. In this part, we address the key tenets underlying the foundation of Lean practice. Chapter 1 is a comprehensive overview of Lean. Chapter 2 addresses the key tenets as well as the language and lexicon of Lean.

Part II: Understanding Flow and the Value Stream

Part II gets into the essence of Lean: understanding the way value is created and flowed to the customer. In four chapters, we thoroughly describe the flow of value. Chapter 3 defines value precisely, in terms of the customer and the end consumer. Chapter 4 introduces and explains the process of Value Stream Mapping, one of the key tools of Lean. Chapter 5 explains how to use a Value Stream Map to define where you want to go and how you'll approach getting there. Chapter 6 explains the principles and practices of *Kaizen* — the basis for continuous improvement.

Part III: The Lean Toolbox

In this part, we present a comprehensive listing and overview of the many customer, value stream, flow, pull, perfection, and management tools of Lean in four chapters. Collectively, these tools form the Lean toolkit.

Chapter 7 describes the many tools used to understand the value stream and customer needs and wants. Chapter 8 describes the flow and pull tools. Chapter 9 covers the perfection tools used within Lean to create standardized work, improve with *Kaizen,* visualization, and everyday improvements. Chapter 10 addresses the management tools of *hoshin, gemba*, and the growing suite of software applications that support Lean practice.

Part IV: The Lean Enterprise

Part IV contains five chapters and describes how Lean becomes part of the enterprise. In this part, we explain the issues and challenges with implementing Lean in an organization. Chapter 11 addresses organizational issues specifically. Chapter 12 focuses on the people elements of Lean — often the most overlooked (and risky) part. Chapter 13 addresses the life cycle of a Lean implementation, from strategy to startup and, finally, evolution. Chapter 14 explains how Lean works in the different functions and organization of a business. Chapter 15 addresses Lean in different industries.

Part V: The Part of Tens

This part, in the *For Dummies* tradition, is a compilation of key points of reference. Chapter 16 discusses ten practices for success. Chapter 17 addresses ten pitfalls to avoid. And in Chapter 18, we tell you about ten additional places you can go for help.

Icons Used in This Book

Throughout the book, you'll see small symbols called *icons* in the margins, and these highlight special types of information. We use these to help you better understand and apply the material. When you see any of the following icons, this is what they mean:

These are key points to remember that can help you implement Lean successfully.

When you see this icon, we're cautioning you to beware of a particular risk or pitfall that could cause you trouble.

This icon flags a detailed technical issue or reference. Feel free to skip right over these, if you don't want to dig deeper.

We use this icon to summarize information into short, memorable thoughts.

Where to Go from Here

The beauty of a *For Dummies* book is that you don't have to start at the beginning and slowly work your way through. Instead, each chapter is self-contained, which means you can start with whichever chapters interest you the most. You can use *Lean For Dummies* as a reference book, which means you can jump in and out of certain parts, chapters, and sections as you wish.

Here are some suggestions on where to start:

- ✔ If you're brand new to Lean, start at the beginning, with Chapter 1.

- ✔ Want to know about the basics of Value Stream Mapping? Check out Chapter 4.

- ✔ If you want to know all the tools of Lean, jump in at Chapter 7.

- ✔ Interested in the organizational and people elements of Lean? Go to Chapters 11 and 12.

- ✔ If you want to understand all the Lean lingo and terminology, flip to the glossary.

Lean is a journey. Like any journey, it is exciting and exhilarating, stretching and life altering, challenging and unexpected. But it *is* worth it. We wish you well on this journey. With this book by your side, you have what it takes to live Lean and thrive!

Part I
Lean Basics

In this part . . .

Think of Lean as a fitness program for your business. Like a diet and exercise regime for your body, Lean is a way to get your business fit for life, through a focus on your customer, the implementation of new business practices, and the ongoing commitment to continuous improvement. In this part, we fill you in on the foundations, philosophy, and basics of Lean.

Chapter 1

Defining Lean

*W*hen you first hear the word *lean*, it conjures up an image. Most likely, you're seeing a mental picture of thin people — like long-distance runners, or those aerobics junkies who somehow don't seem to have an ounce of extra fat on them. Or maybe you're thinking about lean food — the foods that are lower in fat and, of course, much better for you. *Lean* also implies lightweight, in the sense of speed and agility, with a sort of edge or underlying aggressiveness that recalls the rhyme "lean and mean."

That's because the word *lean* suggests not only a physical condition, but also a certain discipline — a mental toughness. The notion of Lean carries with it a commitment to a set of principles and practices that not only *get* you fit, but *keep* you fit. People who are lean seem to be that way not just temporarily, but continuously. Lean people are committed to being lean; they act a certain way in their habits and routines. Lean isn't a fad or diet — it's a way of life.

Now take this concept and apply it to a business or organization. What do you see? What does *lean* mean, business-wise? Back in 1988, a group of researchers working at the Massachusetts Institute of Technology (MIT), led by Dr. James P. Womack, were examining the international automotive industry, and observed unique behaviors at the Toyota Motor Company (TMC). Researcher John Krafcik and the others struggled with a term to describe what they were seeing. They looked at all the performance attributes of a Toyota-style system, compared to traditional mass production. What they saw was a company that:

- ✔ Needed less effort to design, make, and service their products
- ✔ Required less investment to achieve a given level of production capacity
- ✔ Produced products with fewer defects

- ✔ Used fewer suppliers
- ✔ Performed its key processes — including concept-to-launch, order-to-delivery, and problem-to-repair — in less time and with less effort
- ✔ Needed less inventory at every step
- ✔ Had fewer employee injuries

They concluded that a company like this, a company that uses less of everything, is a "lean" company.

And just like that, the term *lean* became associated with a certain business capability — the ability to accomplish more with less. Lean organizations use less human effort to perform their work, less material to create their products and services, less time to develop them, and less energy and space to produce them. They're oriented toward customer demand, and develop high-quality products and services in the most effective and economical manner possible. (See Table 1-1 for a comparison of mass production and Lean.)

The practice of *Lean* — from here on capitalized because, in this context, it's a proper noun — is, therefore, a commitment to the set of tenets and behaviors that not only gets your organization fit, but keeps it that way.

Table 1-1	The Lean Enterprise versus Traditional Mass Production	
	Mass Production	**Lean Enterprise**
Primary business	A product-centric strategy. Focus is on exploiting economies of scale of stable product designs and non-unique technologies.	A customer-focused strategy. Focus is on identifying and exploiting shifts in competitive advantage.
Organizational structure	Hierarchical structures along functional lines. Encourages functional alignments and following orders. Inhibits the flow of vital information that highlights defects, operator errors, equipment abnormalities, and organizational deficiencies.	Flat, flexible structures along lines of value creation. Encourages individual initiative and the flow of information highlighting defects, operator errors, equipment abnormalities, and organizational deficiencies.
Operational framework	Application of tools along divisions of labor. Following of orders, and few problem-solving skills.	Application of tools that assume standardized work. Strength in problem identification, hypothesis generation, and experimentation.

Lean has become a worldwide movement. Lean concepts aren't new; the techniques, in various forms, have been practiced in companies large and small around the globe for decades. But the term *Lean* has crystallized a particular set of ideas and concepts:

- ✔ Maintaining an unrelenting focus on providing customer value

- ✔ Adopting a philosophy of continuous, incremental improvement

- ✔ Providing exactly what's needed at the right time, based on customer demand

- ✔ Keeping things moving — in a value-added, effective manner

- ✔ Using techniques for reducing variation and eliminating waste

- ✔ Respecting people

- ✔ Taking the long-term view

Lean has been adopted across a broad range of industries, most notably automotive, but also aerospace, banking, construction, energy, healthcare, and government. Dozens of consulting firms, hundreds of training courses, and thousands of books and articles all chronicle the many aspects of Lean practice. Consulting firms have developed Lean implementation programs for every business function, including management, manufacturing, administration, supply chains, product design, and even software development. Lean has become a recognized methodology. It even has an award: The Shingo Prize, called "the Nobel Prize of Manufacturing" by *Business Week,* was developed to promote Lean practices, and has been awarded in North America each year since 1988. Honoring the renowned engineering genius Shigeo Shingo, its purpose is to "promote awareness of Lean manufacturing concepts."

This is all interesting enough, but what really matters is that the customers are the better for it — much better, in fact. It's been invisible to most people, but Lean has brought to everyone vastly improved products and services — and it's brought them faster, cheaper, and more reliably. Its successes have saved billions of dollars. Its competitiveness has forced previously bloated, self-absorbed organizations to retool themselves and focus on customer value. And it has equipped struggling companies and industries with methods and techniques to improve their performance.

The many dimensions of Lean — its tenets and philosophies, the methodology and techniques, the tools and applications, and the management frameworks — have evolved considerably since that day in 1988. Lean is now a science and a practice.

In this book, we fill you in on the origins and applications of Lean practice. But although Lean has a toolset, it is much more than a set of tools. Lean is a philosophy, an approach to your life and work. Lean is a journey, with no pre-defined path or end state. It's a way forward that guarantees continuous improvement. Lean isn't a diet or a fad, it's a way of life.

What Is Lean?

Lean is a broad catchphrase that describes a holistic and sustainable approach that uses less of everything to give you more. Lean is a business strategy based on satisfying the customer by delivering quality products and services that are just what the customer needs, when the customer needs them, in the amount required, at the right price, while using the minimum of materials, equipment, space, labor, and time. Lean practices enable an organization to reduce its development cycles, produce higher-quality products and services at lower costs, and use resources more efficiently.

Although the term *Lean* has been most directly associated with manufacturing and production processes, Lean practices cover the total enterprise, embracing all aspects of operations, including internal functions, supplier networks, and customer value chains.

Lean is a continuous, evolutionary process of change and adaptation, not a singular, idealized vision or technology-driven goal state. A central organizing principle is the long-term renewable enterprise, where the organization builds sustaining relationships with all its stakeholders, including employees, managers, owners, suppliers, distributors, and customers, as well as community, society, and the environment.

Lean means less of many things — less waste, shorter cycle times, fewer suppliers, less bureaucracy. But Lean also means more — more employee knowledge and empowerment, more organizational agility and capability, more productivity, more satisfied customers, and more long-term success.

Waste not, want not

What's the least possible amount of material, time, space, facilities, capital, energy, effort, or whatever else you need to develop and deliver a given product or service to your customer? You wouldn't want to use any more than you really need to get the customer what they require. Anything more than the absolute minimum is essentially waste.

The sources of waste are everywhere:

- ✓ **Using more raw material than necessary:** Not only are you buying, transporting, and storing the extra raw material in the first place, but you then have to pay to transport and dispose of damaged or obsolete goods.

- ✓ **Spending more time to develop and produce your products and services:** You're not just making the customer wait — you're also consuming energy, wasting people's time and using facilities to store and move around materials and work. And there's the opportunity cost of delayed payment.

- ✓ **Making mistakes:** Not only are mistakes frustrating to you, your coworkers, and your management, as well as the customer, but you have to spend more time and use more materials doing it over.

- ✓ **Overproducing and carrying excess inventory:** Excess inventory directly wastes space. Plus, it has to be handled and maintained. And what's the sense in making more than you're selling?

- ✓ **Using more space than necessary:** Space is facility and capital cost, as well as the energy and labor to maintain it.

- ✓ **Spending more money than necessary:** It doesn't take an accountant to know that spending more money than you should to get something done is wasteful!

- ✓ **Using more equipment and tools than necessary:** Not only are those extra tools and equipment expensive, but they also have to be stored, repaired, and maintained.

- ✓ **Involving more people than necessary:** People are extremely valuable and expensive, and they should be engaged in doing only what's most important.

- ✓ **Having incorrect or incomplete information or instructions:** It results in mistakes, rework, scrap, lost time, and missed deadlines — plus, it can be hazardous.

- ✓ **Having people work improperly:** This is the most wasteful of all. Not only is it a direct waste of time and effort, but it's damaging to the psyche and to morale. It's also potentially physically harmful and dangerous.

The logic of Lean

In Lean, you pursue understanding the source and rooting out the causes of waste. The practice of Lean as the root-cause eliminator of wastefulness is based on a core set of fundamental assumptions. Follow this logic:

✔ **You're in business to sell products and services to customers.** The customer has the need and defines the purpose. Everything begins and ends with what the customer requires. Everything else is fluff.

✔ **The customer is the only true arbiter of value.** The customer is willing to give you their money for your product or service only when they believe it's a fair exchange of value. It has to be the right combination of quality products and services, in the right place, at the right time and at the right price.

✔ **Value-creation is a process.** A combination of steps — such as marketing, design, production, processing, delivery and support — rightly performed, will result in the creation of products and services that the customer will properly value.

✔ **Waste diminishes the process of value creation.** Things that naturally creep in and prevent the steps in a process from flowing quickly and effectively will inhibit the creation of customer value.

✔ **A perfect process has no waste.** If every step in the process is fully capable, acts only when necessary, flows perfectly, and adapts to perform exactly as needed, the process will develop and deliver products and services without waste.

✔ **Perfect processes maximize customer value.** The closer to perfection a process becomes, the more effective the creation of value, the more satisfied the customers, and the more successful the endeavor.

No one has ever experienced the perfect process, but Lean continually strives for perfection. Lean is the strategy and approach, and it provides the methods and tools for pursuing the perfect process.

Where is Lean?

Lean is found wherever there is waste, and anywhere there is opportunity for improvement. In other words, Lean is found everywhere. It's not confined to any particular part of the organization or function of the enterprise. Although formal Lean practices began in manufacturing, they apply across the board.

It's in the enterprise

Lean is a business-improvement initiative, best applied enterprise-wide. A common misconception holds Lean as a sort of manufacturing quality program. Not so. The philosophy, principles, and practices of Lean are applicable anywhere, and they're most effective when applied across the entire organization. You may have heard jargon that implies certain groups or functions practice Lean, such as the following:

- *Lean Production* **or** *Lean Manufacturing:* Early in the formalization of Lean techniques, the practices were modeled after manufacturing and production approaches in companies like Toyota. Enormous successes ensued in other manufacturing companies as Lean practitioners applied the techniques in other manufacturing environments. As a result, these labels took hold.

- *Lean Office* **and** *Lean Administration:* These references note that the practices have been applied with great success in office environments, where the value streams are policy-based, information-oriented decision making and involve the effective management of transactions and data.

- *Lean Management:* This term is most often associated with the role of managers in the Lean enterprise. This covers the management of a Lean initiative, as well as the personal Lean practices of the managers themselves.

- *Lean Thinking:* Because Lean is more than just tools and techniques, people within an effective Lean organization apply Lean practices as a way of thinking — a way of approaching issues and challenges. After you've truly adopted the ways of Lean, you'll be a Lean thinker.

  Lean Thinking is also the name of a book by James Womack and Daniel Jones, first published in 1996, which stands as a milestone in Lean. It was in this landmark work that everyone began to associate Lean with more than just Toyota and automotive and began thinking of Lean as a movement of its own.

Each of these monikers represents an element of Lean in its own right, but only as a single facet or subset of the greater Lean enterprise. In fact, Lean is all of these and more.

Think of Lean in the enterprise not as a group of functional or departmental practices, but as a set of multidisciplinary practices that cross functional lines. Lean focuses on the processes that create customer value, which by their nature are cross-functional. Examples include the supplier-assembler process, the assembler-distributor-customer process, the marketing-design-development process, the company-shareholder process, and the company-government-regulatory process. In each of these cases, work is not aligned by classic Western-style functional departments. Instead, the process is facilitated by multidisciplinary teams — and in a Lean enterprise, the individuals on these teams are cross-trained as well.

It's in the people

Lean practice calls for a set of facilitating tools and techniques (covered in Part III) that focus the organization on eliminating waste and maximizing customer value. Although the tools are important, Lean is just as much about the people as the tools. This is a critical point — companies that have failed to recognize this have done so with disastrous consequences.

A successful Lean journey puts as much emphasis on the people in the organization as it does on the methods, tools, and techniques of Lean practice. The journey must engage everyone, continually educate and train them, challenge and empower them. Employees must be safe and feel secure in their work environment and job situations. They must be stimulated and incentivized, celebrated and compensated.

People are highly valued in the Lean organization. They are more important than tools and fixtures, equipment, material, or capital. Some Lean organizations have promised work for life, in return for an individual's commitment and dedication to pursuing perfection.

It's in the culture

In a Lean organization, the tenets and philosophy of Lean are fundamentally part of its fiber; Lean is very much embedded in the organization's culture. Everyone practices Lean techniques habitually. When you observe an organization practicing Lean, you will see that:

- People always look at activities as processes, and consider them in terms of customer value and eliminating the wasteful non-value-added steps.

- People naturally call for *Kaizen* events to brainstorm the elimination of waste, and implement Plan-Do-Check-Act (PDCA) or other projects to effect improvements.

- People regularly communicate through Value-Stream Maps, team meetings in the work area, process flow diagrams, communication centers, graphical analyses, control charts, and other explicit instruments.

- Everyone makes improvement suggestions — continually.

- Visual signs and cues are everywhere. People are in deliberate and decisive motion, performing standardized work. Meetings are short and crisp.

- People regularly take on new roles and tasks in order to be more complete team contributors. They embrace learning, share knowledge, and are open to changes and new ways of doing things.

- The business builds long-lasting relationships with employees, suppliers, providers, and customers.

What it's not

Lean is a lot of things — it's a philosophy; a set of principles; a language (complete with its own jargon and acronyms); a management strategy; a methodology; a set of techniques, behaviors, tools, and even specialty software — all of which support this notion of reducing waste and delivering long-term customer value. Lean is often associated with other process improvement programs and initiatives, and in particular it is frequently paired with Six Sigma (more on this later in this chapter). And Lean, as a way of thinking and behaving, can be part of many initiatives.

So Lean is a lot of things. But there are a number of things that it isn't:

- ✔ **Lean isn't consulting foo-foo dust.** It's not just a bunch of manager-speak, arcane mapping sessions, or feel-good teaming exercises sprinkled with hoity-sounding Japanese terms. Lean is a well-grounded, mature, and very real framework for developing and sustaining performance excellence.

- ✔ **Lean isn't onerous.** Unlike most other process improvement initiatives, Lean does not require large investments in training or expensive software; nor does it call for a prescriptive, one-size-fits-all formulaic rollout. It requires top-down senior-management support, but Lean can begin in a small group and expand naturally as it grows and as the business needs it. This ease-of-adoption is why Lean has been so successful in small and medium-sized companies, and in operating units of large companies.

- ✔ **Lean isn't overly analytical and statistical.** Certain difficult challenges will always require deep analysis to characterize, understand, and solve. But the vast majority of Lean improvements are brought about by very simple and straightforward exercises, observation, and activities that anyone can understand and apply.

- ✔ **Lean isn't a flash in the pan.** It emerged from longstanding practices, characterized and understood by researchers who were observing what makes certain businesses work better. Although some Lean concepts might sound counterintuitive at first — and are very much counter to how many organizations are run — the tools and techniques of Lean have been around for decades and are fully complementary to longstanding proven methods.

- ✔ **Lean isn't a Western-style system.** Take note of this key point: Lean may be very much different from what you're used to. Unlike most Western-style tools and techniques, Lean is not a quick-hit, big-bang, upside-the head, technology-enabled, silver-bullet solution to fix yesterday's problems right now, today. In fact, it's quite the opposite. Lean is a continuous, long-term, everyday approach to building the flexibility and adaptability that enables you to address tomorrow's challenges as they happen. *Kaizen* events and Lean projects often reap significant near-term benefits, but don't look to Lean as an overnight sensation. Lean is very much a long-term deal.

What makes Lean so special?

Organizations worldwide have a plethora of choices when considering approaches to both their tactical and strategic pressures and challenges. Lean is one of many, many options. Why is it so popular?

Companies, organizations, and government entities all know that they must do something — they can't just sit still. Gone are the days of doing things the same old way and being successful regardless — or of just being smart and hoping for the best. Aggressive, unrelenting global pressures are forcing everyone to embrace some type of approach and strategy for performance management and improvement. It's now a given that you're going to do something to improve — so what's it going to be?

The Lean approach is increasingly popular, because it offers organizations a sensible, proven, and accessible path to long-term success. Unlike so many of the alternatives, Lean is something that everyone can understand, everyone can do, and everyone can benefit from:

- ✔ **Lean is proven.** The principles and techniques of Lean have been practiced successfully by thousands of organizations of every type and size in every industry worldwide, spearheaded by nearly 50 years of continuous improvement by one of the world's most successful corporations.

- ✔ **Lean makes sense.** In an era of mind-boggling complexity, Lean is a solid foundation for addressing all kinds of challenges — simply. Lean is broadly applicable in any situation, combining old-world logic and reason with new-world tools and constraints.

- ✔ **Lean is accessible.** Make no mistake: The performance improvement industry is big business. All those pundits, purveyors, and progenitors out there aren't motivated by strictly altruistic intentions. Most of the performance improvement alternatives in the marketplace are big-ticket items, tailor-made for big wallets — and the big egos that carry them. Not Lean. Lean is accessible to anyone, with any budget. Lean is a serious commitment but isn't particularly expensive, exclusive, or difficult.

- ✔ **Lean is inclusive.** The Lean framework is purposely open and embraces tools and techniques known to solve problems. Lean is fully complementary with the tools of TQM, TPM, Six Sigma, and BPM, for example, so it's not an either/or decision (see "Lean and Its Continuous Process Improvement Cousins," later in this chapter, for more on these tools). Using Lean as a foundation, all the quality, performance, and technology tools still apply.

> ✔ **Lean is for everyone.** Many performance improvement solutions are strictly tailored for specialty disciplines, requiring advanced skills and knowledge. Not Lean. Lean is so powerful in part because it is so easily learned and applied by everyone. No one is excluded.

The Lean Pedigree

While the specific assembly of principles and practices known as *Lean* date from the late 1980s, the origins of Lean are much older. Lean has a deep pedigree. Historians cite King Henry III of France in 1574 watching the Venice Arsenal build complete galley ships in less than an hour using continuous-flow processes. In the 18th century, Benjamin Franklin established principles regarding waste and excess inventory and Eli Whitney developed interchangeable parts. In the late 19th century, Frank and Lillian Gilbreth pioneered the modern-day understanding of motion efficiency as it related to work. In the early 20th century, Frederic Winslow Taylor, the father of scientific management, introduced the concepts of standardized work and best-practices. (The legendary Shigeo Shingo cites Taylor's 1911 seminal work *Principles of Scientific Management* as his inspiration.)

However, it was in Henry Ford's revolutionary mass-production assembly plants where many practices first emerged. In 1915, Charles Buxton Going, in the preface to Arnold and Faurote's *Ford Methods and the Ford Shops,* observed:

> Ford's success has startled the country, almost the world, financially, industrially, mechanically. It exhibits in higher degree than most persons would have thought possible the seemingly contradictory requirements of true efficiency, which are: constant increase of quality, great increase of pay to the workers, repeated reduction in cost to the consumer. And with these appears, as at once cause and effect, an absolutely incredible enlargement of output reaching something like one hundred fold in less than ten years, and an enormous profit to the manufacturer.

Ford also explicitly understood many of the forms of waste and the concepts of value-added time and effort.

New practices were later developed during the industrial buildups that preceded and then supported World War II, both in the United States and Japan. In the United States, quality leaders like W. Edwards Deming and Joseph Juran refined management and statistical concepts in support of war production. The Training within Industry (TWI) Service formalized practices in management, training, and production, while emphasizing methods and relationships. In postwar Japan, Deming and Juran worked with Japanese industrial leaders to apply these practices to reconstruction.

Toyoda and Ohno

The Toyoda Automatic Loom Works was founded by Sakichi Toyoda in 1926, where he pioneered the practice of *jidoka* (see Chapter 2). Ten years later, the company changed its name to Toyota and Toyoda's son, Kiichiro, and engineer nephew, Eiji, began producing automobiles with parts from General Motors. Japan's entry into World War II in 1941 diverted its efforts to truck production; during postwar reconstruction, the company nearly went bankrupt.

Meanwhile, Ford regularly invited managers and engineers from around the world to visit Ford plants and observe his mass-production systems. In the spring of 1950, Eiji Toyoda participated in an extended three-month visit to Ford's famed Rouge plant in Dearborn, Michigan. At that time, the Rouge plant was largest and most complex manufacturing facility in the world. Toyota was producing about 2,500 cars a year; Ford was producing nearly 8,000 a day.

Eiji returned to Japan, and with Toyota's production manager, Taiichi Ohno, concluded that Ford's system of mass production would *not* work for them in Japan. The domestic Japanese automotive market was too small and too diversified — ranging from compact cars to luxury executive vehicles and a variety of trucks. In addition, the postwar native Japanese workforce was not willing to work under the same substandard conditions as the immigrant force in the United States. And the capital outlay for facilities and equipment was too high. Toyoda and Ohno set out to develop an entirely new means of production, including engineering, manufacture, supply, assembly, and work-force management.

The Toyota Production System

The Toyota Production System is so famous that it's referred to simply by its abbreviation: TPS. TPS is perhaps the most studied system of production and operations management in the world. Countless companies have visited Toyota and observed TPS in action. Dozens of books have chronicled its successes and hailed its methods.

TPS is the birthplace of Lean. Lean Manufacturing, in particular, is essentially a repackaging of the Toyota Production System. Most of the philosophy and tenets, as well as the methods, techniques, and tools of Lean are all found within TPS. What those MIT researchers examined in 1988 and called Lean was, basically, TPS. The terms *Lean Manufacturing* and the Toyota Production System are effectively synonymous.

TPS was principally architected by cousins Eiji and Kiichiro Toyoda and Taiichi Ohno. History credits Ohno as the Father of TPS. He led its development, extension to the supply base, and integration with global partners from the early 1950s through the 1980s. By the time Lean was introduced to U.S. manufacturing, Toyota had been evolving and applying TPS successfully for over 40 years.

Toyota built the first model House of TPS (see Figure 1-1), depicting graphically that Toyota's quality sets on the combination of just-in-time, built-in quality, and highly motivated people. All of this stands on a foundation of operational stability and *Kaizen,* bolstered by visual management and standardized work.

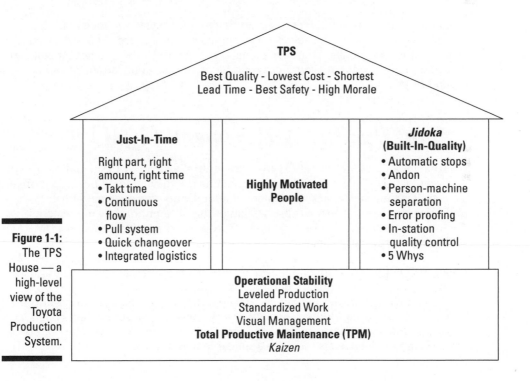

Figure 1-1: The TPS House — a high-level view of the Toyota Production System.

Most of the concepts presented in this book — and *any* book on Lean — are based on TPS implicitly. You won't necessarily know when some Lean principle or practice is based on TPS, but it's all there. As examples, the just-in-time concepts were developed at Toyota; *jidoka* was invented by Sakichi Toyoda; the seven forms of waste is a Toyota creation. So is Value-Stream Mapping. So, if you assume that everything in a Lean treatise is basically TPS, you'll be mostly right.

Lean and Its Continuous Process Improvement Cousins

We've been awash in business and process improvement programs for decades. It's been an alphabet soup of initiatives. Remember TQM, BPR, MBOs, and QITs? Well, now we also have the likes of TPM, TOC, GMP, QRM, ISO, Six Sigma, and BPM. They're all part of continuous process improvement (CPI). It's all very confusing — somewhat on purpose!

Because all these initiatives, methodologies, and "systems" focus on the same basic issues, they have a lot in common. They share some of the same tools and techniques. They claim similar results. But they also have significant differences — critical differences — in focus, scope, application, investment, and return.

Total Quality Management (TQM)

Total Quality Management (TQM) is an umbrella strategy for a quality-driven organization. TQM calls for quality to act as the driving force behind an organization's entire leadership, design, planning, and improvement efforts. Developed in the 1970s as an amalgam of the different quality movements and approaches in the United States, Europe, and Japan, interest in TQM peaked in the early 1990s.

Total Quality Management focuses on culture and organization. The cultural element demands a quality perspective in all aspects of the company's operations. Like other initiatives, TQM emphasizes a customer orientation, commitment from top management, continuous improvement, fact-based decision making, fast response, and employee participation. All the quality and statistical-analysis tools are applicable under TQM.

TQM has been applied in manufacturing, education, government, and service industries, with mixed success. As a broad culture-oriented initiative, it is challenged by the lack of a focused implementation methodology and direct measurable results.

Lean, like TQM, can act as the umbrella strategy for a corporation. Lean incorporates TQM principles and practices.

Six Sigma

Six Sigma emerged in the mid-1990s, self-proclaimed as "the world's greatest problem-solving methodology." With a well-defined implementation, training, and management framework, Six Sigma gave form and focus to the application of quality tools and techniques — and has delivered staggering bottom-line results.

Six Sigma was first developed as an internal quality initiative at Motorola, which won the inaugural U.S. Malcolm Baldridge National Quality Award in 1988 as a result. Six Sigma hit the national stage following its successful adoption by General Electric in 1996. Ten years later, over two-thirds of the global *Fortune* 500 companies practice Six Sigma in some form, and the estimated combined savings now well exceeds $100 billion!

Six Sigma is a way to identify and control variation in the processes that most affect performance and profits. Following a prescriptive methodology, trained practitioners known as *Black Belts* analyze root cause and implement corrective action. (Many of the tools of Six Sigma are common to Lean.) Black Belt projects typically take four to six months and can return hundreds of thousands of dollars in value — and more. Six Sigma techniques, and its famous Define-Measure-Analyze-Improve-Control (DMAIC) problem-solving methodology, are applicable within a Lean framework as a subordinate toolset for eliminating waste from defects and reducing process variance. (Read *Six Sigma For Dummies,* by Craig Gygi, Neil DeCarlo, and Bruce Williams, and the *Six Sigma Workbook For Dummies,* by Craig Gygi, Bruce Williams, and Terry Gustafson [both published by Wiley], to find out everything you need to know about Six Sigma.)

You may have heard of the terms *Lean Six Sigma* or sometimes *Lean Sigma.* Be careful here. These purport to be a natural combination of the two methods, to bring you the best of both worlds. What many of the Six Sigma consultants have done, in fact, is to cherry-pick a few Lean tools — particularly pull techniques and waste-reduction tools — and subordinate them into the Six

Sigma deployment framework. Although this certainly extends the power and capabilities of Six Sigma, it's not Lean. In particular, these other methods tend to neglect the people and cultural elements, the accessibility and inclusiveness, and the everyday *Kaizen*.

Theory of Constraints (TOC)

Theory of Constraints (TOC) is based on the premise that *productivity* (or the rate of revenue generation) is always limited at the point of at least one constraining process — a bottleneck. Only by increasing throughput at the bottleneck process can overall throughput be increased. TOC is sometimes referred to as constraint management.

TOC focuses on removing the constraints that limit an organization's performance from achieving its full potential. TOC, with its emphasis on process flow and waste reduction, is an effective toolset for Lean practitioners in examining bottlenecks in the value stream. TOC is particularly useful with its focus on throughput.

Total Productive Maintenance (TPM)

Total Productive Maintenance (TPM) is a value-added maintenance concept. TPM has been implemented as a standalone process in manufacturing environments, as a foundational strategy of TPS, or as the maintenance component of a TQM program. TPM focuses on maintenance as an integral part of the business. The goal is to minimize emergency and unscheduled maintenance by converting to planned maintenance activities. TPM evolved from TQM and is proven as an effective foundational methodology within a Lean framework.

ISO-9000

ISO 9000 is a family of standards for quality management systems. ISO 9000 was developed from the British Standards Institution's BS 5750 and is now maintained by the International Standards Organization (ISO) and administered by accreditation and certification bodies. Interest in ISO 9000 peaked in the late 1990s.

ISO 9000 does not guarantee the quality of end products and services; rather, it certifies that consistent business processes are being applied. Standardized work defined in Lean organizations becomes the basis upon which ISO 9000 procedures are defined.

Business Process Management (BPM)

The term *Business Process Management* (BPM) refers to activities performed by businesses to optimize and adapt their formal processes — particularly those processes controlled by automated systems. BPM is often most directly associated with technology and software systems that implement extensive integration and management of process data and information. BPM includes process modeling, data integration, workflow, and business activity monitoring (known as BAM). BPM is a significant enabler for Lean, and directly facilitates Lean goals and practices. BPM practices include:

✔ Modeling tools help define and categorize standardized work.

✔ Data-integration capabilities capture critical supplier, inventory, cycle time, status, delivery, and other value-stream characterization parameters.

✔ Activity-monitoring tools regularly check the performance of processes against control limits, alerting people or other processes if key indicators trend improperly.

BPM is the systems counterpart to Lean, facilitating Lean solutions in technology.

Chapter 2

The Foundation and Language of Lean

*I*f you've ever sojourned to a foreign place, you've experienced culture shock first hand. At first the new land seems strange — the food, the customs and the language, even if they speak your native tongue. Delicacies in one land may not be so delectable in another. Greetings can be confusing: Do you bow, kiss, or shake hands?

If you ask for directions, the natives may look at you as though you're crazy or give you seemingly nonsensical information. Part of the issue is that you have no context for the foundations and language of the culture. With time, and information, you assimilate into the new place. You start to learn some basic greetings and phrases, practice daily customs, and, eventually, with persistence and diligence, become more like a native.

When you undertake a Lean journey, at first it may feel this foreign. The terms are new. The business practices may seem strange or counterintuitive. But with time, education, application, and understanding, you'll become a Lean native.

In this chapter, we fill you in on the basic principles of Lean, and tell you all about the seven forms of waste. This chapter provides a high-level view of Lean — like the travel guide you may read on the way to that exotic destination.

Understanding Lean Basics

Chapter 1 explains how Lean has evolved over time, and how closely aligned it is with the Toyota Production System (TPS). The various experts and different practitioners of Lean don't necessarily agree on a fixed set of standard principles or tenets. But there is a generally accepted framework for Lean practice and the related TPS elements, as well as the underlying foundational wisdom. Collectively, they form a broad framework that includes everything from principles to methods and tools, leadership models, and even Lean thinking.

Creating the foundation

Commonly held tenets of Lean include Customer Value; Value-Stream Analysis; and Improvement, Flow, Pull, and Perfection. Lean always starts and ends with the customer. The customer is the one who defines and determines *value* of the product and service. The *Value Stream* is used in Lean to describe all of the activities that are performed and information required, in order to produce and deliver a given product or service. To create value in the most effective way for the customer, you must focus on improving flow, applying pull, and striving for perfection.

Understanding customer value

The fundamental premise for all Lean organizations, and the first step of any Lean undertaking, is to identify the customer and what the customer values. What does the customer really want? What does the customer want today? What will the customer want tomorrow?

Customers are always changing — today's wants become tomorrow's needs. Technology, markets, and demographics all change customer behavior. Can you imagine living without your mobile phone, the Internet, or e-mail? Little more than a decade ago, these things didn't even exist (at least not in a form that was usable by your average consumer) — now they've become a necessity. All you have to do is take a trip on an airplane and listen for the chorus of phones being turned on the instant the plane touches the ground, and you'll know how true this is.

When you provide a product or service, you need to be tightly in step with (and even slightly ahead of) what your customer wants. Tools like Quality Function Deployment (QFD) help capture customer wants and translate them into standards that you can implement in the stream of activity that creates customer value — the value stream.

In Lean, the customer defines what behaviors in the value stream are *value-added.* To be deemed value added, any process or activity acting on the product or service in any way must meet three key criteria:

✔ **The customer must be willing to pay for it.** Payment is generally thought of in monetary terms, but it could include time or other resources.

✔ **The activity must transform the product or service in some way.**

✔ **The activity must be done correctly the first time.**

You can find more about customers, consumers, and value in Chapter 3.

Analyzing the value stream

When you pop into your local supermarket to buy groceries, have you ever stopped to think about all the activities that had to occur, in just the right sequence, in order for you to readily buy what's on your list? Consider produce. You can now find just about all fruits and vegetables year-round. Look in the produce section and you'll find products from around the globe. The apples may have more frequent-flier miles that you do! From the fields, through transport, to your store, and ultimately to your table, hundreds of events must occur precisely the right way and at precisely the right time in order for the product to be available to you at a price and a freshness level that you'll buy.

Value is delivered to customers through the value stream. In an ideal world, the value stream would consist only of value-added activities and the associated flow of support information. That is the ideal to aim for, but in reality, waste exists in some form in every process. (We introduce you to the various types of waste in the "Muda, muda, muda" section, later in this chapter.)

After you understand what the customer values, the next step in Lean is to identify and analyze the stream of activities that creates that customer value. In this analysis, you identify all the activities and events that occur to get the product or service to your customer. You also identify the information flow that supports the value-stream activities. These activities and events may occur at your facility, or they may be upstream in supplier facilities or downstream in distribution or delivery. Generally, a business begins its improvement efforts with what it controls directly, and later expands beyond its organizational boundaries.

In Lean, you use a tool called the *Value-Stream Map* to capture and specify the activities, information, timing, and events in the value stream. (Value-Stream Mapping is an important activity, and we cover it extensively in Chapters 4 and 5.) First, you identify the value stream in its current state: How does it all work today? Then you identify the *ideal state:* How would the value stream look if you could do it all perfectly? This ideal-state Value-Stream Map enables you to visualize what the value stream might look like with no waste — only value-added activities.

After the current and ideal-state Value-Stream Maps are defined, a Lean team works to close the gap between the two states. The team conducts *Kaizen* (continuous improvement) activities that bring the two states closer together. Everyone in the organization is involved in *Kaizen,* both as individuals and as part of teams. In a Lean organization, *Kaizen* is performed as part of regular business practice. (Chapter 6 addresses Kaizen in detail.)

In order to design, develop, or deliver any product or service, there is an associated supporting flow of information. This information is captured in the Value-Stream Map. When you buy something, for example, inventory is decreased. In order to replenish the inventory, information must flow from the retail outlet to all the suppliers. Some retailers, like Wal-Mart and Ahold, have implemented Business Process Management (BPM) systems so that from the minute you check out, the information is sent upstream and triggers reorders.

Maintaining flow

When you turn on your tap, you expect to have a clean, consistent flow of water. As the customer, you're assuming that the water is disease-free, safe to drink, and fully available when you want it, at a reasonable price. If a pump breaks or a controller fails somewhere in the delivery system, that's someone else's problem. You, the customer, expect flowing water on demand. The water supplier must maintain its equipment, verify the water quality, and ensure that the delivery system is safe and reliable. The supplier has little or no room for mistakes. This is an example of a system of flow.

In the Lean world, this concept of flow is applied to everything, including, and especially, discrete products and services. Ideally, from the time the first action is taken in the value stream, products and services never stop until they reach the customer. From the moment the customer asks for it, products and services make their journey through a set of only value-added activities until they reach their destination.

Think about that: What it would it take for a product or service to never stop — ever — in the process of moving from creation to consumption? In a product manufacturing environment, this would require that products be processed one at a time, with no excess inventory, no defects or rework, and no equipment breakdowns. The only hope of coming anywhere close to this ideal is to apply standard methods for production with minimal variation. All the equipment must be readily available in the same area, instead of being organized by functionality in separate departments. Manufacturing processes must be synchronized precisely to the customer's rate of consumption. In Lean, this pace of value-stream production is known as the *takt time* (a calculated rate that marries the value of the customer demand with available work hours).

Flow is not the natural way humans think. We tend to organize things in batches — not flow. And it's the way most people have been trained. Take a simple activity like bulk mailing, for example. What type of process would you use? Figure 2-1 shows a flow chart for a batch process. Now look at Figure 2-2, which shows that same process in as a single-piece flow. In single-piece flow, the documents are handled less, use less space, and are finished and able to be sent more quickly. Yet most people think it's faster to process in batch.

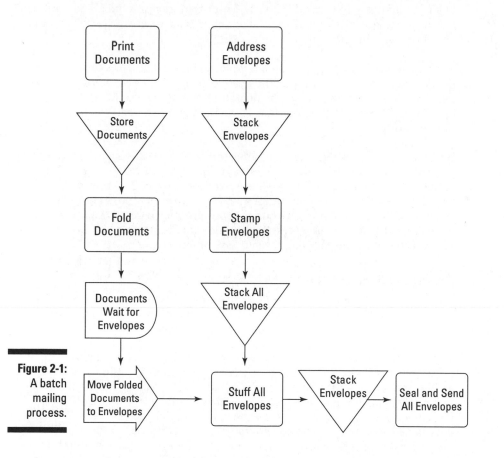

Figure 2-1: A batch mailing process.

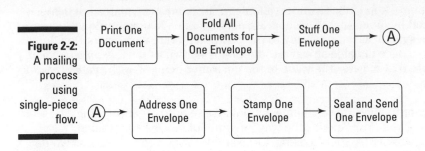

Figure 2-2:
A mailing process using single-piece flow.

Print One Document → Fold All Documents for One Envelope → Stuff One Envelope → (A)

(A) → Address One Envelope → Stamp One Envelope → Seal and Send One Envelope

TIP

Flow is one of those counterintuitive principles of Lean. You actually take less time, use fewer resources, and tie up less money in inventory producing your products when you operate from a flow perspective.

REMEMBER

Lean requires you to think differently. Throw out any preconceived notions about job boundaries, departmental organizations, or any other blocks that could prevent the implementation of Lean.

For flow to work, you must eliminate defects, equipment breakdowns, back-flows, and outages of any type. These are the impediments to flow, and they exist whether you're running a manufacturing, service, medical, or support operation. The key to your success is identifying these barriers in the context of your world.

When you look at things from the perspective of the value stream, you don't organize things functionally. Instead of grouping things by similar functional activities, you group them as families of value creation. In a manufacturing world, you look at common operations that parts would pass through, and organize modules of common equipment to produce a given family. In a lab environment, you may form testing modules according to common batteries of test types. How might you reorganize your environment?

Pulling through the system

Products and services can be *pulled* through a system as a result of action by the customer, or they can be *pushed* through by virtue of an upstream process. In a Lean enterprise, you use a pull system.

The classic candy-factory scene from *I Love Lucy* is a perfect example of an unbalanced push system. At first, the chocolates arrive at the workstation at a slow enough rate that Lucy can place them in the packages. But then the belt speeds up, going faster and faster. The inventory has no place to go. Lucy, a worker who wants to do her best, tries to stay on top of it. But when it gets to be too much, she begins stuffing the candy down her shirt, in her mouth, wherever she can, all in an effort to not let them pass her station. Why the belt sped up, the audience never knows. Did the demand from the customer increase? Or was it the whim of the scheduling department? Was it a test for the workers? Who knows? What we do know is that this was *not* a Lean process!

Lean utilizes *level scheduling* practices to keep the system operating at a steady and achievable pace. Scheduling occurs with the process closest to the customer. As the customer consumes a product or service, the rest of the system is triggered to replenish what the customer has used.

One of the most common examples of a pull system is the local supermarket (in fact, the supermarket was the source of inspiration for the pull system). A shelf space is labeled with a tag that contains information for a given product. A specified amount of the product will fit into the allocated space. When the product level runs low, the empty space acts as a signal for the stockperson to replenish the product. The tag contains the information about the product that belongs in the space.

This same idea governs Lean manufacturing. Instead of building up an excess of what's called Work-In-Process (WIP) inventory, the customer's demand for the product or service pulls finished goods through the system. The key notion is that work is performed only after the part is required downstream — after the space is created. Think of it as "take one, make one." A pull signal or *kanban* is used to trigger replenishment. *Kanbans* can come in various forms — a card, container, or empty space. Regardless of the form, the *kanban* signal contains the product information and quantities required for the replenishment of inventory. Figure 2-3 shows an example of a *kanban* system.

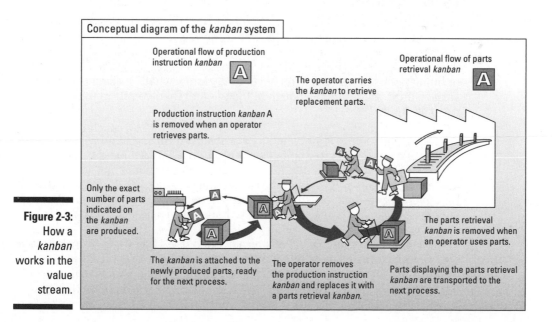

Figure 2-3: How a *kanban* works in the value stream.

Lean thrives on simplicity, because complex systems tend to be expensive, unwieldy, and error-prone. Manual solutions are often preferred over automation, because they're simpler. The goal is to identify the level of technology and complexity that is appropriate for the need — that which will only add value to the information flow or the value stream. Lean companies have "unplugged" parts of their large MRP systems in favor of manual pull signals. This causes the need for what's known as *back flushing* in order to relieve inventories. More recent technological advancements better support Lean practices. For example, *kanban* cards are now printed at supplier locations as inventory is relieved through point-of-sale systems.

A general rule for equipment availability in a pull system is that the equipment should be available for production 90 percent of the time and down for changeovers and maintenance 10 percent of the time.

When successfully implemented in conjunction with flow and perfection, pull systems result in higher inventory turns, reduced floor space, faster customer response, and improved cash flow.

Traditional sales and marketing practices need to be in step with the steady-state flow of the Lean enterprise. Sales incentives and seasonal campaigns, like inventory clearance sales or President's Day sales, drive up demand and cause products to be sold at lower prices. This artificially bull-whips the supply chain. The concepts of level selling and steady-state pricing support a more effective enterprise.

Striving for perfection

Lean is a never-ending journey. Although this may sound onerous, especially in a goal-driven society, the reality is that there is and always will be something to improve. As you uncover waste, you'll discover wastes that you didn't know existed, because they were masked by bigger wastes. It's like draining ponds or swamps: You never really know what's lurking beneath the surface until you're brave enough to look — and then you have to do something about it.

Constant incremental improvements are achieved through *Kaizen.* (We cover Kaizen in depth in Chapter 6.) In its simplest form, *Kaizen* means that you improve something every day. It is both a philosophy and a methodology. *Kaizen* improvements are generally not intended to be radical, earth-shattering improvements — instead, they're regular incremental improvements that eliminate waste, here, there, and everywhere, bit by bit.

Companies just beginning a Lean journey often use what are known as *Kaizen events. Kaizen events* most often begin with workshops that offer a significant opportunity for the organization. This opportunity could be a visual impact through the use of what's known as the 5S methodology (see Chapter 8), or it could be a customer-related opportunity like a significant reduction in a specific quality defect. A *Kaizen* event could also take on an "it can't be done" challenge to break through a barrier, like a reduction in equipment changeover time from hours to minutes.

When improvement is on a radical scale it is known as *Kaikaku*. When you think *Kaikaku,* think "Throw out all the rules." It may come in the form of multiple, simultaneous *Kaizen* events (also known as a *Kaizen blitz*). Alternatively, the term *Kaikaku* may imply a complete change in technology or process methodology.

Whether it's through *Kaizen* or *Kaikaku,* the aim is the same: Strive for perfection through improvement. Eliminate waste in all that you do. Create a sustainable, thriving business for the long haul. Continually seek ways to better serve the customer.

Learning from TPS

Because Lean evolved from the study of the Toyota Production System (TPS), you might expect that the principles of Lean and TPS are similar. They *are* similar, but they're organized in a different way. Because of the close interrelationship, you need to understand a little about TPS.

Keep in mind that Lean and TPS are absolutely applicable across many industries, well beyond the automotive manufacturing environments that form their heritage. (This is the subject of Chapters 14 and 15.)

Highly motivated people

More traditional organizations operate to a "shut up and do your job" mentality. This is not the case in the TPS environment. People are expected to engage fully, not only in their daily job functions, but also in the daily improvement activities. People are strongly encouraged to use their creativity, and provide important and useful suggestions to eliminate problems and improve the value stream. It is through the people — workers and managers alike — that improvement happens. The people use the tools, the people devise solutions, and the people implement improvements — it's all about the people!

People work in their individual job assignments and as part of broader teams. The teams may be natural workgroups or may be formed for special projects. As part of natural workgroups, team members are routinely cross-trained in order to expertly perform multiple job tasks across the team's span of responsibility. Whether acting as individuals or as part of a team, people are expected to regularly and routinely eliminate waste as part of their normal work.

The approach of man-and-machine interfaces is philosophically different in the TPS than in traditional western-style environments. In TPS, machines are always subordinated to man. This means that processes are designed so that man doesn't wait on machines — machines wait on man. Western approaches might value the resource costs of people versus equipment and conclude that the equipment might be more valuable than the person, but this is never so in TPS. People are always most important.

Operational stability

The foundation of the TPS is *operational stability*. Operational stability means that variation within all aspects of the operations is under control. In order to have unobstructed flow, orders must be timely and accurate, schedules must be stable and leveled, equipment must run as planned, qualified staff must be in place, and standardized work must be documented and implemented.

Does this mean that you can't do Lean without these things? No, but it does mean that your level of success will be reduced. One of the common mistakes that companies adopting TPS make is to not understand how TPS is a complete system, and how important holistic practices are to overall success. They think that implementing *kanban* is the answer — but without level and stable schedules, *kanban* doesn't work very well. The other common mistake is not paying enough attention to the people side of implementation.

Visual management

Visual management enables people to see exactly what's going on and respond to issues very rapidly. One method of visual management is known as *andon* (a signal to alert people of problems at a specific place in a process). The organization responds according to the signal shown; the response follows the documented standardized work practice.

Other aspects of visual management include cross-training boards, production tracking, customer information stations, communication displays, and tool boards. (We cover the tools of Lean in depth in Part III.)

Just-in-time

Just-in-time (JIT) is probably the most well known pillar of the TPS house. JIT means making only what is needed, when it is needed, and in the amount needed — no more, no less.

In order for JIT to function, several techniques and practices uphold and strengthen the system. These practices include

- **Producing to takt:** Takt connects the rate of production to customer demand.

- **Quick changeover:** Quick changeover provides the flexibility to produce a broader range of products over a short timeframe, such as a single day or a single shift.

- ✔ **Continuous flow:** Continuous flow creates a steady stream of products or services to the customer.

- ✔ **Pull:** Pull triggers the replenishment activities within the system. Pull systems and continuous flow in TPS map directly to the concepts of pull and flow in the Lean framework.

- ✔ **Integrated logistics:** Integrated logistics is the process of not only viewing all aspects of the supply chain as a system, but also managing them as a whole. Pull signals are used throughout the entire chain to trigger replenishment. Delivery schedules, *milk runs* (a method of consolidating material shipments that includes the routing of trucks to collect materials from various suppliers based on *kanban* signals, fixed routes, and fixed times) for material, and container strategies are all coordinated to provide the most effective solution for the JIT system.

Jidoka

Jidoka means that quality must be built in at the source. Quality cannot be "inspected in" — after the work has left its station, it's too late. When practicing *jidoka,* defects never pass to the next step in the process.

The broader definition of *jidoka* includes root cause analysis techniques like the 5 Whys and problem-prevention techniques like *poka-yoke,* where process mistakes are prevented physically. An example of *poka-yoke* can be found at filling stations that sell both diesel and unleaded fuels. The size of the nozzle for the diesel fuel is larger and will not fit into a vehicle that uses unleaded gasoline. Visual management techniques like *andon* boards are also part of a *jidoka* practice.

The philosophy of *jidoka* says the person producing work, within a given step, has the responsibility for the quality of job they are performing. If a problem exists, the person is responsible for resolving it. If the person can't resolve the issue, then he is responsible for stopping the process in order to get it fixed.

Foundational wisdom

Woven throughout Lean are a set of axioms. This wisdom is the foundational essence of Lean. These axioms are invariant and inviolate, and they give rise to all the methods, toolsets, and techniques. When you truly get this wisdom, you get Lean.

It's all about the customer

The underlying reason for being in any business endeavor is to serve a customer. Your customers are your focus: Without the customers, your business effectively doesn't exist. Your customers define what they value and what they don't. The customers set the expectations, and they respond to your offerings with their wallets and their feet.

Everything you do in a Lean organization is ultimately focused on serving the customer in the best possible way. The organizations that comprise the value stream must understand what the customers want, translate that into a product or service that the customers will buy, and provide it at a price they are willing to pay. Tools like *Kano modeling* and QFD help organizations better understand customer wants and needs and translate them into the language of the value stream. (Chapter 3 explores the customer-consumer value relationships and related tools.)

Eliminate waste — in everything you do

Sounds simple, doesn't it? It's like taking out the garbage. The tricky thing about this piece of wisdom is that waste is everywhere and it's never-ending. It is like the "Whack-a-Mole" carnival game, just when you think you've got 'em all, a gopher pops up someplace else.

Your ability to effectively provide value to your customer is directly related to your ability to eliminate waste and keep it away, permanently. But if waste is never-ending, how can you eliminate it permanently? This may sound contradictory, but it's not. Lean divides the broad category of waste into seven categories and three classifications (we cover these in the "Getting into Shape" section, later in this chapter). Within each category are millions of things that cause every form of waste. And, though the sources of waste are never-ending, you can get closer to an ideal world by permanently resolving waste one cause at a time.

Respect for people

Inherent in Lean is a respect for people that does not exist in more traditional systems. Lean organizations are learning organizations. They reward improvements to the system. They support their members through safe work environments, effective communication, extensive training, and, in some cases, employment guarantees. Employee cross-training develops the employees, while at the same time adding depth to the organization. Having teams of people who are knowledgeable about multiple aspects of the value stream enables the organization to minimize variation due to absenteeism and turnover.

In a Lean environment, employees are expected to use their brains for the betterment of the customer, the value stream, and the organization as a whole. They are expected to engage in the environment, learn from their mistakes, and expand their knowledge base.

People are seen as having more value than machines. In traditional manufacturing environments, it isn't uncommon to see a person standing at a machine, watching while the machine cycles. Lean views this as a waste of the precious resource — a human being. The Lean view is to implement appropriate technology, so that people can do more valuable work. This is part of the practice of *autonomation* (automation with a human touch). It isn't the belief that people can be replaced with machines. Rather it's the practice to add intelligence to machines to detect defects, prevent issues from being passed along the value stream and automatically unload, so people don't have to waste their time and brain power watching a machine function.

Make it visual

Transparency eliminates waste. When you can quickly see what's going on, you don't waste time, energy, or effort trying to figure it out. If there is a place for everything, you can quickly see when everything is not in its place. The old adage "a picture is worth a thousand words" cannot be truer in Lean. Through a picture, a graph, a trouble light, or other visual techniques, you can quickly and easily understand information in order to act on it. (We cover more about visual management in Part III.)

Another aspect of visual management (or management by eye, as it's also called) is the ability to see and respond to trends in data. The New York City Police Department uses maps with pushpins to identify where crimes are being committed. They have maps for robbery, murder, and other types of crime. By tracking where the problems happen, they can assign the right amount of officers to the right area. They can focus resources on solving all sorts of crimes — and since the 1990s, the city's crime statistics have reflected the results of their efforts.

After an article about the murder maps appeared in the *New York Times,* one automotive supplier applied this concept to product quality in its facility. It had a layout posted on the wall near a communication station. Every time a customer complaint or return was received, they placed a pin on the workstation that produced the defect. If one area or station proved to be the source of many complaints, then the company was able to focus its resources to investigate and resolve the problem, whether it stemmed from equipment failure, operator training, product design, or the need for *poka-yoke* (the practice of mistake-proofing). They found that the quality performance improved for two reasons:

- The maps brought awareness to the broader organization.
- The concentrated efforts to specific areas eliminated the causes of the problems.

Annually, countless thousands of trees give their lives to become large reports that few people read — but not in Lean. Thick reports are instantly seen as waste. On a single page (also called *A3 reporting,* in a reference to the international paper size), a description of the issue, actions, data, and resolution are documented. The purpose of reporting is to provide information for people to actually use. In one A3 format, the truly critical and necessary information is presented, so the reader can invest more time into action, rather than digestion of data.

Long-term journey

Lean does, in fact, produce instant results; you see immediate improvement. But to sustain that improvement, you must be in the game for the long haul. Lean is not a fad diet for your business. Instead, it is a lifestyle change that requires vigilance. If Lean were a race, it would be more like the tortoise, not the hare. Steady incremental improvements win over the long term. This is not to say that you don't experience a burst of speed along some stretches; this will happen when you conduct multiple improvement workshops simultaneously (known as the *Kaizen blitz*). Anyone with some data, analysis tools, and control charts can always improve something in the short term; the key to Lean is the sustainability and incorporation of the changes into the normal daily business routine for the long term.

Simple is better: The KISS principle

Life has become so complex that you practically need an advanced degree to change the oil in your vehicle or program the TV remote. Does all this complexity actually add value? When everything is working well, it seems to — but when it isn't, well, that's a different story. Because everything is so complex, it doesn't always work so well.

The easier something is, the easier it is to learn and the easier it is to deal with when problems occur — whether that something is a product, a service, or the process that creates it. Simplicity is one of the beauties of Lean. It doesn't mean that you don't solve complex issues, but it does mean that you strive to find simple solutions to them. Lean improvements don't have to cost a lot of money. If you can error-proof something equally well with a block of wood and duct tape versus a computer-controlled apparatus, Lean would tell you to go with the wood and duct-tape solution. The solution is quicker, faster and cheaper, both in the short term and the long term.

Keep it moving

Takt time sets the pace for movement. Working to takt time, everyone keeps the system moving at just the right speed to deliver the right amount at the right time to the customer. This notion of smooth, continuous flow is one of Lean's central axioms.

The customers want a finished product or service. They don't want a bunch of in-process, partially finished anythings. They don't care about what's in process! The ideal state of the value stream in Lean is single-piece flow, with no stoppages, in every process. Multitasking, inventory stoppages, broken equipment, and batching are all inhibitors to flow.

Quality at the source

You can't inspect quality *into* a product — ever. Many companies use inspectors to try to catch defects before they're released to the market, but the act of inspection doesn't change the quality of the product. Also popular is the process of containment, which is the excuse to inspect after the fact, while you keep producing suspect product. In Lean, you create a quality product at each step of the value stream. If defects occur, they don't leave the current process step, either because the person doing the job caught the error, the operation was *error-proofed* or there was autonomation that detected the issue. Key characteristics of a product may be checked by the next operator in the process. If they find an issue, they send the product back to the previous operation. The person who performed the transformational step owns the responsibility for the quality of his work. Now everyone is an "inspector," and quality at the source becomes more realistic.

If you've ever filled out an online form with required fields, you've experienced a form of quality at the source. If information is missing, the system will not let you proceed. Some forms are even intelligent enough to recognize incorrect data, like credit-card numbers and expiration dates. These forms contain *poka-yoke* or error-proofing "devices" (in this case, the device is computer language) to prevent errors from passing to the next step in the process.

Not all inspection is necessarily bad, but all inspection is, by definition, non-value added. Inspection does nothing to transform the product or service. Inspection is deemed necessary when the risk of the product or service advancing beyond that stage of the value stream will put the customer at risk or have a great financial impact; it could be a point of no return for repairs, for example. When separate inspection stations are required, they follow a standardized work process.

At the New United Motor Manufacturing, Inc. (NUMMI) factory in California — a joint venture between Toyota and General Motors — inspection stations are built into the line. The inspector is highly trained and has a set work flow and order to inspect the specific items — even the position on the floor is marked where the inspector should be standing to see parts of the vehicle. This inspection routine is built into the flow or takt of the line.

Measurement systems reinforcing Lean behaviors

People respond to how they're measured. If the measurement system supports a change in behavior, the change happens. One of the main challenges in Lean implementations is that the existing measurement systems do not support Lean practices.

One common example of a measurement system that does not support Lean is a traditional cost accounting system. Traditional accounting for equipment, inventory, and direct labor actually encourages waste. Under such systems, equipment absorbs overhead, so supervisors run equipment to make their numbers look better, whether they need to produce or not. This leads to the waste of overproduction, which we discuss in the "Muda, muda, muda" section, later in this chapter.

Additionally, the impact of direct labor in a cost-accounting environment is actually overemphasized. When cost-accounting systems were originally established, labor made up the majority of actual costs; now direct labor can be as little as 20 percent of the cost. Companies have purchased automated equipment to eliminate direct labor, only to find that they have the same number of bodies supporting the equipment as they used to have performing the work! The difference is that those bodies are now *indirect* labor, usually more skilled and, therefore, working at a higher pay rate. However, the accounting system still sees this as a benefit because of the measurement system.

In addition to changing business practices, successful Lean organizations know that they need the right measurement systems to reinforce Lean behaviors. One tool that these organizations use is a Balanced Scorecard (see Chapter 10). The Balanced Scorecard tracks aspects of the business beyond the traditional financial measures. Areas like safety, people, quality, delivery, and cost are measured to show the overall health of the business and identify where the opportunities for improvement exist.

No perfect organization exists. Even Toyota, the pinnacle of Lean success, has had its issues from time to time. Although Toyoda and Ohno are gone, they left behind for all of us a legacy of reflection, learning, and unrelenting quest for improvement. The new leaders have the charge to continue that legacy by learning from issues and addressing inconsistencies and challenges with the TPS foundations.

Learning lasts a lifetime

Learning happens thousands of times a day in a Lean organization. Learning and improving through observations, experiments, and mistakes are fundamental to *Kaizen*. In Lean, after a lesson is learned, the knowledge is institutionalized via updated work standards. And then the cycle repeats: Observe, improve, institutionalize. Individuals learn; teams learn; collectively, the knowledge of the organization increases. Every instant of every day is the right time to learn and grow.

Getting into Shape

As an individual, if you've ever tried to get in shape, you know that you have to change the way you diet, exercise, hydrate, and rest in order to have long-term success. In your diet, you have to take out the empty calories and highly processed food that do not add nutritional value. When you start paying attention to what you put in your mouth, you realize how much garbage has been unconsciously passing your lips.

When you start on a Lean journey, one of the key ways to improve the health of the value stream is to eliminate waste. Like the empty calories of junk food, you'll find that a lot of non-value-added activities have crept into your value stream. Waste in Lean is described by the three Ms of *muda* (waste), *mura* (unevenness), and *muri* (overburden). Muda is divided into seven forms of waste, which we cover in the following section.

Muda, muda, muda

Waste is all around you, every day and everywhere. You waste your time waiting in line, waiting in traffic, or waiting because of poor service. In your home, you may have experienced walking into a room looking for something that wasn't where it was supposed to be — wasted time and effort. In your kitchen, you may have had to throw out science experiments from your refrigerator — again, waste.

By now, you may be wondering what exactly is and isn't waste. Taiichi Ohno identified seven forms of waste. These seven forms are: transport, waiting, overproduction, defects, inventory, motion, and excess processing. In his book, *The Power of Process: Unleashing the Source of Competitive Advantage,* Dr. Kiran Garimella of webMethods created an easy mnemonic for remembering the seven forms: TWO DIME. Table 2-1 provides a summary of the seven forms of waste, according to the TWO DIME mnemonic as well as their more traditional names.

Table 2-1	The Seven Forms of Waste	
Form of Waste	*Also Known As*	*Explanation*
Transport	Conveyance	Movement of product or materials between transformational operations is waste. The more you move, the more opportunity you have for damage or injury. Poor layouts and disorganization are also common causes of transport wastes. Conveyors in a Lean environment are not used unless there is a safety reason; even then, they're non-value-added. They take up floor space, cause inventory accumulation, disconnect operators from other parts of the value stream, and interrupt process flow.
Waiting	Waiting or delay	Waiting in all forms is waste. In a production environment, any time an operator's hands are idle is a waste of that resource, whether the operator is idle due to shortages, unbalanced work loads, need for instructions, or by design (when operators watch machines cycle).
Overproduction	Overproduction	Producing more than the customer requires is waste. It causes other wastes like inventory costs, manpower and conveyance to deal with excess product, consumption of raw materials, installation of excess capacity, and so on.
Defect	Correction, repair, rejects	Any process, product, or service that fails to meet specifications is waste. Any processing that does not transform the product is considered non-value-added. It does not meet the criteria of done right the first time.
Inventory	Inventory	Inventory anywhere in the value stream is non-value-added. Inventory may be needed, but it is still non-value-added. It ties up financial resources. It is at risk to damage, obsolescence, spoilage, and quality issues. It takes up floor space and other resources to manage and track it. In addition, large inventories can cover up other sins in the process like imbalances, equipment issues, or poor work practices.

Form of Waste	Also Known As	Explanation
Motion	Motion or movement	Any movement of people's bodies that does not add value to the process is waste. This includes walking, bending, lifting, twisting, and reaching. It also includes any adjustments or alignments made before the product can be transformed.
Extra processing	Processing or overprocessing	Any processing that does not add value to the product or is the result of inade-quate technology, sensitive materials, or quality prevention is waste. Examples include in-process protective packaging, alignment processing like basting in gar-ment manufacturing or the removal of sprues in castings and molded parts.

Beyond the seven forms of waste, *muda* is further divided into two classifications:

✔ **Type-1** *muda* include actions that are non-value-added, but are for some other reason deemed necessary for the company. These forms of waste usually cannot be eliminated immediately.

✔ **Type-2** *muda* are those activities that are non-value-added and are also not necessary for the company. These are the first targets for elimination.

All in the family

Beyond the general forms of *muda* are two other cousins of the waste family: *mura* and *muri*. As with the forms of *muda,* the goal is to eliminate this type of waste, too.

Mura (Unevenness)

Mura is variation in an operation — when activities don't go smoothly or con-sistently. This is waste caused by variation in quality, cost, or delivery. *Mura* consists of all the resources that are wasted when quality cannot be pre-dicted. This is the cost of testing, inspection, containment, rework, returns, overtime, and unscheduled travel to the customer.

Lean lingo

Because the foundations of Lean originated from the Toyota Production System, the language of Lean contains quite a few Japanese words. These words have come to represent Lean systems and concepts. In addition, Lean has unique English terms. The glossary at the end of this book contains a thorough list of terms that are critical to your understanding of Lean. Think of these terms in Lean as you would *please, thank you,* and *hello* when learning a foreign language. Pretty soon, you'll be speaking Lean like a native.

Also, you may hear the word *efficient* used in conjunction with the improvements in an organization's operations. However, the aim of a Lean organization is to provide value in the most *effective* way possible. The word *effective* is used rather than *efficient,* to avoid the traditional definitions of efficiency associated with batch and queue and other forms of mass production, such as *labor efficiency.* When you're operating *effectively,* you're providing the right thing, at the right time, through an engaged and motivated workforce producing the highest quality level, shortest lead times, and lowest cost.

Muri (Overdoing)

Muri is the unnecessary or unreasonable overburdening of people, equipment, or systems by demands that exceed capacity. *Muri* is the Japanese word for unreasonable, impossible, or overdoing. From a Lean perspective, *muri* applies to how work and tasks are designed. One of the core tenets of Lean is *respect for people*. If a company is asking its people to repeatedly do movements that are harmful, wasteful, or unnecessary, then the company is not respecting the people and, therefore, is not respecting the foundation of Lean. You perform ergonomic evaluations of operations to identify movements that are either harmful or unnecessary.

Part II
Understanding Flow and the Value Stream

The 5th Wave   By Rich Tennant

"We mapped our corporate value stream, Phillip, and your department was such a mud flat that we're going to eliminate everything but the clams and scallops."

In this part . . .

Now that you know the basics, it's time to get started. At the heart of Lean is a focus on the customer and a spirit of continuous improvement. In this part, you figure out how the customer defines value. You discover how to analyze your business today and create a vision of the future. You also find out how to eliminate waste through continuous improvement or *Kaizen*.

Chapter 3

Seeing Value through the Eyes of the Customer

*Y*ou may think the concept of value is pretty standard, but the reality is that each person has his own perception of what constitutes value. What people value and how they value it changes with circumstance and time. As mutable as the criteria for defining value may be, in Lean you have to understand what your customers and consumers value, and then provide that value in the most effective way. When you define what your customers value, you also define the very nature of your activities and actions: what you should be doing, how you should be doing it, and even *if* you should be doing it.

The definition of value is important, because it forms the foundation upon which Lean processes are built, and it guides you in assembling activities in a continuous stream of value creation. In this chapter, we provide the basic definition of value, and show you the Lean standard definition of value. You discover how value can be perceived by the immediate customer as well as the end consumer. Finally, you get acquainted with the concept of flow and the value stream.

What Is Value?

Simply stated, *value* is the worth placed upon something. That something can be goods, services, or both. The worth can be expressed in terms of money, an exchange, a utility, a merit, or even a principle or standard.

Who determines the value? Customers do. Globally, there are about six billion of them, and numerous more in various combinations (businesses, social groups, and other organizations).

Although the definition of value is straightforward, what is more difficult to understand is how value is created, applied, measured, and translated. What are the actions and activities that actually create value? How does a person or organization come to value a particular product or service? What determines how much a person is willing to "pay" for it — with their time, money, or other resources? And how is the value exchanged?

Value isn't absolute — it doesn't occur in isolation. Value is relative to such factors as location, place, time, timing, form, fit, function, integration, interactions, resources, markets, demand, and economies. But in all cases, *value is defined by the customer*.

The process of *value creation* — developing the worth that someone is willing to place upon something — is usually lengthy and complicated.

Consider the complexity involved in the process of creating value in something that many people regularly take for granted: autonomous, personal mobility in the form of the automobile. In this case, value creation involves not just the design and assembly of the thousands of parts in a car, but also the highway system, the petroleum refining and distribution system, the maintenance and repair industry, the insurance industry, and the knowledge and conventions enforced in the millions of other drivers out there that you have to interact with in order to move about with some degree of certainty. Every driver antes up, in the form of sticker prices and insurance payments, gasoline and maintenance fees, highway and other taxes, greenhouse gases and environmental damage, and, of course, lots and lots of time. Autonomous, personal mobility is an extremely high-value item, and each of the above elements contributes a critical piece to that total value.

Now consider something seemingly much simpler: the pre-made salad you buy at the grocery store. A few vegetables in a plastic carton — seems pretty straightforward, right? But consider for a moment what goes into that salad: all the different ingredients, sourced from places not just across the country but around the world, picked and transported quickly, sliced and diced just the right way, handled carefully so as not to bruise or damage, combined in just the right amounts, in the right order, and placed carefully in a container made of the proper materials that retain freshness, labeled properly for both the grocer and the consumer, and then transported and positioned in a cooler at just the right time so that it's sitting there waiting for you, fresh and wholesome, at a price you're willing to pay, when you're grabbing a quick dinner on the way home from work. Whew! Not so simple. Now consider that you're the salad-maker, and you have to do that thousands of times a day for different customers and tastes, at a competitive price. Every step in your process must add real value for you and your customer, because there's no room for waste.

In any endeavor — large or small — the many activities, actions, and steps in the process must lead to an end result that has value for the buyer. This value must be easily perceived, readily quantified, and willingly exchanged for the product or service offered. And the provider of the product or service must not only deliver on the customer's expectation, but also receive a fair exchange of value for it.

To Add Value or Not to Add Value, That Is the Question

Every activity in your organization either adds value or it doesn't. In Lean, you analyze each activity in every process for its contribution to value, as defined by your customer. In the ideal state, every activity directly meets your customer's criteria for value — and if it doesn't, you don't do it.

Makes you think, doesn't it? Everyone and everything in the process doing *only* what creates customer value? Well, that's what Lean is all about!

Think about this principle in the context of what you do for your customers — whoever or whatever they may be. How much of all the time, people, resources, capital, space, and energy being consumed around you and by you is directly creating value for your customers? Now put on the other hat, and think about it from the customers' point of view. When you're paying for the product or service — with your valuable time, money, effort, or otherwise — how much are you spending to get what you really want — and *only* what you really want?

In this section, we fill you in on the strict definition used in Lean for *value-added* and *non-value-added.* You will understand non-value-added according to the three *M*s — *muda, mura,* and *muri.* Some activities in your process do not add value according to the customer's definition, but they are unfortunately necessary for your processes to function. We will tell you what to do in those cases, too.

Defining value-added

In Lean, value is always defined from the customer's viewpoint. The customer is the one — and only one — who defines the value of the output of a process. In order for an activity to be considered *value-added,* three precise criteria must be met:

- ✔ The customer must be willing to pay for the activity.
- ✔ The activity must transform the product or service in some way.
- ✔ The activity must be done correctly the first time.

This strict definition applies to everything. To add value in a process, all actions, activities, processes, persons, organizations, systems, pieces of equipment, and any other resources committed to the process must meet these three criteria.

You can easily spot value-added activity:

- At the carwash, it's when someone actually washes the car.
- At the hospital, it is when the patient receives treatment.
- On the assembly floor, it's when someone is actually putting parts together.

In each of these cases, it's clearly what the customer is paying for; it's transforming the product; and as long as it's being done correctly, it's contributing directly to customer value (that is, it's *value-added*).

Defining non-value-added

In Lean, if an activity does not meet just one of the value added criteria (see the preceding section) then it is deemed *non-value-added*. Either the customer isn't willing to pay for it, or the activity hasn't transformed the product or service in any measurable way, or the activity wasn't done correctly the first time. In other words, from the customer's perspective it could be considered wasted time or effort. In Lean, you strive to eliminate waste in everything you do.

At the carwash, it's the order-taker, the car-mover, the cashier, the queuing time, the excess water, and the customer waiting lounge. At the hospital, it's the check-in time, the wait time, filling out forms, inconclusive tests, and hospital food. On the assembly floor, it's the parts bins, the travel time, the setup time, the inspections and testing, the conveyors, the supervisors, the bad-parts reject basket.

In each of these cases, the item or person wasn't something the customer wanted to pay for, or the activity didn't directly transform the product or service, or something wasn't done correctly.

Wait a minute, you say! Some of those things are important, even necessary. Customers have to pay for what they're buying. Employees don't know what to do without a supervisor instructing them. Forms convey important information. Customer lounges keep people happy — you can't just make them wait outside. And bad components have to be removed — after all, it's a good thing when you catch a failure and don't ship a bad product to the customer, right?

Sorry to burst your bubble, but if the activity in question doesn't meet all three criteria, it's just not adding customer value. The customer lounge is nice, but it doesn't transform the product. Filling out forms may get you admitted to the hospital, but it doesn't directly contribute to your treatment. The reject basket means you caught the failures, but they're a living example of something that wasn't done correctly the first time. None of this means that you might not want or even need to do these things based on your existing process model, but it *does* mean that those activities are not adding value for the customer.

In Lean, non-value-added activities are further described by the three *M*s — *muda, mura,* and *muri:*

- ✔ *Muda* **(waste):** *Muda* is an activity that consumes resources without creating value for the customer. (We define the seven standard forms of waste in detail in Chapter 2.) There are two types of *muda:*

  - • Type-1 *muda* includes actions that are non-value-added, but that are for some other reason deemed necessary for the organization.

  - • Type-2 *muda* are those activities that are non-value-added and unnecessary for the company.

- ✔ *Mura* **(unevenness):** *Mura* is waste caused by variation in quality, cost, or delivery. When activities don't go smoothly or consistently, *mura* is the result. *Mura* consists of all the resources that are wasted when quality cannot be predicted, such as the cost of testing, inspection, containment, rework, returns, overtime, and unscheduled travel to the customer. You apply variation reduction techniques to eliminate *mura.*

- ✔ *Muri* **(overdoing):** *Muri* is the unnecessary or unreasonable overburdening of people, equipment, or systems by demands that exceed capacity. From a Lean perspective, *muri* applies to how work and tasks are designed. *Muri* is caused by movements that are harmful, wasteful, or unnecessary. You perform ergonomic evaluations and detailed job analysis of operations to identify movements that are either harmful or unnecessary.

Lean strives to eliminate all non-value-added activities.

When non-value-added seems like value-added

By their very nature, processes are full of waste that masquerades as value creation. Many activities initially seem as though they're necessary or value-added, but upon closer examination, through the eyes of the customer — and according to the three criteria listed in the "Defining value-added" section earlier in this chapter — they're not.

Muda, particularly type-1 *muda* (see the preceding section), is usually created because of current facility or technology limitations, government regulations, or unchallenged company business practices. Oftentimes, *muda* is so insidious that the organization is blind to it. Identifying *muda* is particularly difficult when *muda* is programmed into computer systems.

Seeking out and eliminating *muda* takes effort — it requires someone to challenge the status quo. Sometimes people don't think they have the time or energy to do that level of work. Sometimes they don't feel like they have the tools or authority to change the current state. Sometimes they don't know where to begin. And sometimes, they just don't want to change. Yet the fact of the matter is that, when you put in the effort to identify the *muda,* you will find a gold mine of opportunity.

Common examples of type 1-muda include the following:

✓ Overhead activities, such as administration, accounting, and legal

✓ Bureaucracy, such as forms, reports, and approvals

✓ Product support, such as product testing, critical inspection, and transportation

Type-1 *muda* includes all the things around or supporting the value-added functions, but these things don't actually do any direct transformation themselves.

You may insist, "These activities are necessary for the business!" And you may even be right — maybe they *are* necessary. But whether they're necessary or not, it doesn't change the fact that they are non-value-added. Here are some examples:

✓ **The trimming of printed paper to a perfect size and edge contour in the printing industry:** That paper trimming surely *seems* like a value-added activity. The trimming transforms the product by creating a clean edge. The customer is willing to pay for the book, but how much do they care if the pages are perfectly trimmed? In any case, if the printing process had a better way to align the pages during binding, no trimming would be necessary. No paper would be wasted and the extra resources would not be required.

✓ **The in-line inspection station in the automobile manufacturing industry:** You need to ensure operations are done correctly. You must protect your customer. While this is may be true, you cannot transform a product through inspection, you can only mitigate risk. The most well choreographed inspection station, while seemingly necessary, is always non-value-added.

✔ **Staying late and pushing extra hard to get a job done and meet a deadline:** The job has to get done, and people will rise to the occasion, right? Yes, but consider the cost. Not only do people tend to make more mistakes when they drive too hard without a rest, but burned-out people will leave the company and take critical knowledge and experience with them. On occasion, working in this manner may seem necessary, but no matter how you look at it, it's a waste.

Understanding How the Customer Defines Value

Who's the customer? If you're like most people, you're thinking it's the person at the retail end of the line; the one who buys the product or service; the one who walks into a store, gets out his wallet, pays for something, and leaves with it. Actually, that person is a special form of customer known as the *consumer;* we cover the consumer in the "Understanding How the Consumer Defines Value" section, later in this chapter.

The *customer,* as far as Lean is concerned, is the person or entity who is the recipient of the product or service you produce. For many, the customer is another business. For others, the customer is someone inside their own business. Sometimes the customer is a specific individual; other times, the customer is a group or team. But in any case, the customer is the one who places the value on your output.

Uncovering the elusive customer

The world has grown so complicated that sometimes it's difficult to determine just who anybody's customer really is. So many functions, supply chains, outsourced providers, contract distributors, and channels are part of the mix. But in the Lean world, this question — "Who is your customer?" — is fundamental, because the customer is the one who matters. The customer is the *only* one who truly defines the value in what you produce.

Your customer is likely *not* the consumer — the end user of the product or service you provide. You're probably part of a supply chain or network for some set of designs, materials, products, or services that are combined in a complex series of processes to provide that end-item solution to a consumer somewhere. Your customer is therefore most likely an individual (or set of individuals) within a group who pays for the products and services you generate.

In Figure 3-1, we show you a SIPOC diagram. The SIPOC is a standard tool in process management that helps identify and characterize the key driving influences on a process. A SIPOC diagram lists the suppliers and inputs to a process on the one hand, and the outputs and customers on the other. Considering the process itself as a black box for the moment, focus on what outputs are produced and who receives them. This recipient is the elusive customer you're looking for.

Figure 3-1:
Identifying
your
customer
using a
SIPOC
analysis.

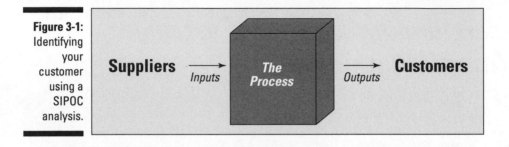

Every process — no matter how large-scale and all-encompassing, or small and focused — has a customer. Large-scale processes, such as order entry or production, have a broad spectrum of many types of customers. In small processes, such as RazRPhone Model V3 keypad assembly or the daily setup of a jewelry department in retail, the customer is much more narrowly and specifically defined. But in every case and at every level in any organization or endeavor, processes have customers.

As you consider who is the recipient of such process outputs in your own organization, consider these tips:

- ✔ **When you're looking at the improvement of a small portion of the overall process, recognize its role in the larger process.** Across an organization, there are many subprocesses — and, therefore, there are many customers — involved in the larger process of creating the total product or facilitating a complete service.

- ✔ **Your process may produce outputs for multiple customers.** If so, different customers will have different characteristics, and you'll need to regularly adjust the process according to the distribution of customer requirements, attributes, and situations.

- ✔ **Recognize how your process output serves the end consumer.** If your process does not directly supply the consumer, then your customer is a middleman. Your direct customer may be adding, filtering, interpreting, or changing how the consumer defines value. Your direct customer has different motivations and needs from the consumer. Make sure that you are meeting your direct customer's needs, but don't lose sight of the consumer's expectations and how they define value.

✔ **Don't become distracted by stakeholders.** A *stakeholder* is someone with a vested interest in a company; stakeholders may include managers, board members, stockholders, employees, suppliers, family members of employees, retirees, government, or the community. Although these entities are important, in Lean they aren't the customer. Stakeholders have an interest in company performance or results. But in Lean, the principle focus is the value-creation process and the elimination of waste in that process. When a business is distracted by the stakeholders, it may lose the focus on the process and take short-term actions that will actually increase *mura* (variation — see "Defining non-value-added," earlier in this chapter).

Sometimes the customer causes type-1 *muda* (see "Defining non-value-added," earlier in this chapter). Type-1 *muda* can come in the form of customer demands on you to accommodate their systems or processes. In the case of pre-made food, one grocery chain at one location may require double labels for a product to make their scanning easier, yet they are not be willing to pay for the extra label. So by definition, it's non-value-added, because the customer would not willing to pay for the added materials and resources for the label. In adding the label, the company producing the food will have to eat the cost as a goodwill measure. This is a case of the customer creating type-1 *muda*.

Considering customer value

The customer is the purchaser of your goods and services, and they are the recipient of the outputs from your process. The customer has many options, but the customer has chosen to buy these outputs from your process. Why? What goes into a customer's purchase decision? Why is the customer buying these specific outputs from your particular process? How does the customer determine what they're going to pay?

The answers to all of these questions come down to value. The customer chooses your option because it believes your option represents the best overall value for them. The customer places a worth on the process outputs and believes these outputs and this process best fulfill their requirements. The customer's requirements and decision criteria are many, and the customer's methods of assigning value may be formal or informal, but at the end of the day, you are the supplier the customer has chosen.

Understanding customer satisfaction

The customer assigns value based on the degree to which the process outputs fulfill their requirements. The greater the fulfillment of requirements, the higher the customer's satisfaction, and therefore the greater the customer's attributed value.

All customer requirements are not created equal. Some requirements are extremely important *must-have*s, other requirements are *nice-to-have*s, and still other requirements fall somewhere in the middle. How the fulfillment of these different requirements translates to customer satisfaction is not always obvious. Don't worry — in this section, we spell it all out.

In the 1980s, Japanese professor Noriaki Kano developed a visual way to understand customer requirements (see Figure 3-2). This model is a graphical plot of fulfillment versus satisfaction. What Kano recognized is that customer requirements naturally come in three flavors:

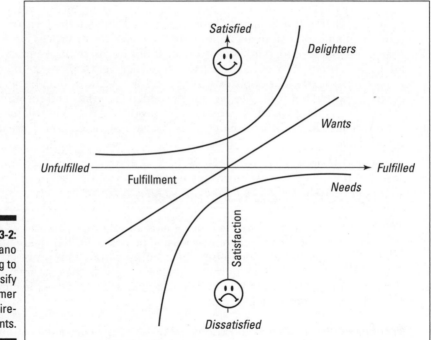

Figure 3-2:
Using Kano modeling to classify customer requirements.

✔ **Needs:** Needs are fundamental — they're absolute requirements. You must fulfill the needs of your customer. If your customer has unfulfilled needs, that very quickly translates to complete dissatisfaction. However, at best, fulfilling your customer's needs results in neutral satisfaction. In other words, meeting your customer's needs is a thankless job, but failing to meet your customer's needs is disastrous.

- **Wants:** Wants are expectations. If you don't fulfill your customer's wants, the customer will be dissatisfied; if you do fulfill your customer's wants, the customer will be satisfied. The relationship is linear: No lack of fulfillment of wants will ever create the dissatisfaction that unmet *needs* will, and likewise no degree of fulfillment of wants will ever have the satisfaction potential of the third type of requirement — the delighters.

- **Delighters:** Delighters are pure upside. No one really expects them, so there's no penalty if they're missing. But the level of customer satisfaction increases exponentially if the process fulfills these most whimsical of requirements.

The extent to which a process fulfills each type of requirement affects the level of customer satisfaction and perceived value.

One of the great applications of the Kano model is the wildly successful U.S. air carrier Southwest Airlines. When Southwest designed its business model, it fully understood the difference between these three types of requirements. Southwest began by recognizing that there is really only one fundamental customer need: Get me there safely. It realized that *unfulfilled* wants, like food, music, and first-class accommodations, wouldn't cost Southwest much customer satisfaction, as long as it offset those unfulfilled wants with *fulfilled* wants like the on-time consistency and cost savings from the single-aircraft fleet. But then Southwest threw in the big delighter: super-friendly flight attendants. By creating a near-party atmosphere, it exponentially increased customer satisfaction. Voilà! A huge winner — so much so that Southwest is now a new industry benchmark, imitated globally.

Take a moment to ponder the application of the Kano model to your business or organization. Of the many requirements you chase and manage, which fall into each of the three categories? How well do you fulfill them? How satisfied are your customers?

Breaking down customer requirements

Fulfilling the customer's wants, needs, and delighters is the path to customer satisfaction (see the preceding section). Kano modeling and Quality Function Deployment (QFD), covered in Chapter 7, are two tools that you can use to capture and understand customer requirements.

To really understand your customer's requirements, ask them! Talk to your customer extensively. Involve your customer in your planning and development.

After you identify your customer's requirements, you can analyze how effectively you're satisfying those requirements. And only *then* can you optimize value creation, ensuring the processes perform their transformations on the product or service properly and correctly the first time.

To create a solution and fulfill your customer's requirements, they are first translated into product or service *specifications*. Typically, these specifications are documented first at the highest level, known as the *top level,* the *system level,* or the *A level.* Then, the specifications are successively expanded into subsystems or subprocesses, each of which fulfills a specific role in achieving the overall objective defined by the top level specification. Within each of these levels, the specifications are categorized into the following types:

- **Functionality:** What are all the things that the product or service must do? How must it do them? How uniquely? The specifications are usually described through a set of action verbs, but they may also describe aesthetics and other physical or operational attributes.

- **Form and fit:** What are the shapes and sizes, the constraints and the tolerances of the way the product or service (or components thereof) must be designed, must align, or must interact?

- **Price:** What is the price that the customer will pay for the product or service? Is the price dynamic (will it or should it change over time)?

- **Purchase:** What are the various purchasing models and terms by which the customer will buy? What should the purchasing experience be?

- **Performance:** How quickly, how often, or for how long must the product or service perform its functions?

- **Reliability:** With what levels of reliability and dependability must the product or service perform its functions? What is the pedigree and what experience do you bring to ensure that reliability?

- **Maintainability:** What are the support and maintenance requirements? Is the customer or consumer required or able to maintain it, or portions of it, themselves? How will it be supported?

- **Scalability:** If the customer wants more, how readily should they be able to have more? Do any of the other requirements elements change with scalability?

- **Safety:** Are there safety aspects to the product or service — as related to the suppliers, consumers, maintenance groups, or even the general public?

- **Security:** Security concerns are a separate requirements element. Could the product or service pose a security risk in any way, either directly or indirectly?

✔ **Perception:** How are you perceived in the market? What is your brand identity? What has been the customer's past experience with your organization? Have you had any bad press that may affect a purchasing decision?

These categories of requirements apply during any phase of the product or service life cycle; they apply to the core processes of design, development, delivery, and service, as well as support processes, including sales, finance, legal, marketing, human resources, information technology, and facilities. Every process must attend to these elements to ensure the product or service the process provides will fulfill the customer's needs, wants, and desires. These categories apply not just to the end consumer, but also to your immediate customer and each successive customer in the chain. No matter where your process sits in the big picture, these categories of requirements apply to you!

From a Lean perspective, all processes can be improved and waste can be eliminated. Businesses often focus their Lean efforts only on the manufacturing or operational processes, sometimes losing sight of critically important places where their customer interfaces with them the most. Customer relationships are formed in the support processes like sales, accounts payable, and materials management. Oftentimes, companies neglect to eliminate waste in these processes, and the processes are often plagued with type-1 *muda*.

When you're focusing on your customers, understanding what is important to them, and then eliminating the wastes that prevent you from delivering what they want, how they want it, and when they want it, you put your company in a better position to compete.

Remember that what your customer values is not static. Customer interests and satisfaction change over time. The Kano model has a downward migration: Today's wants become tomorrow's needs. Having processes that connect you with your customers will help you stay agile and change with their changing demands.

Understanding How the Consumer Defines Value

The ultimate customer is the *consumer*. The consumer is defined as "one who obtains goods and services for his own use," rather than for resale or use in manufacturing. Consumers are the catalyst in the value chain; their buying action triggers the flow of activities on the part of the many product and service providers whose contributions ultimately fulfill the consumers' requirements and values.

As such, the consumer holds a uniquely important customer position, and it's incumbent on you — regardless of your position in the value chain — to be aware of consumer motivation and behavior. In most cases, you work directly for your immediate customer, because they specify your requirements and receive your outputs. However, consumer actions will ripple through the chain to affect you, so you must also understand how the *consumer* defines value.

Recognize, too, that although the entire stream of activity is ultimately oriented toward satisfying the consumer, the consumer's requirements and values do not necessarily align with the processes and agendas of all the many upstream players providing those goods and services. Your direct customer will likely represent the consumer's needs to you differently than the consumer would, so you must be in a position to understand and balance your direct customer's requirements with those of the end consumer.

Because Lean processes are customer focused, they respond to the requirements of the customer and refine their processes accordingly. Although each successive process may have a unique set of customer requirements, the starting point is with the consumer, because the consumer is the first point of requirements definition. The consumer is the first to assign value and first to vote with their wallet. The consumer kicks off the whole process.

Many organizations or businesses are agenda-centric, believing that they can foist their agenda on their consumer market. These organizations are not customer focused and do not practice the Lean art of customer-driven process definition. In recent years, it has become increasingly difficult for such companies to thrive. Customer-centric businesses fare far better.

Responding to the consumer

The Lean world begins with the consumer — the first customer to levy output requirements on a process. The consumer is where needs begin. All processes that support the consumer directly or indirectly are called into action. Theoretically, it is with the consumer's contemplation to buy that the entire value chain springs into action.

Organizations and businesses of all types strive to understand and anticipate the consumer. The better a business can predict consumer behavior, the more effectively it can fulfill the consumer's needs, wants, and delighters (see "Understanding customer satisfaction," earlier in this chapter). In some cases, you need to understand broad consumer behavior and then produce products in volume for the general consumer market. In other cases, you have to maintain the capacity to produce a product or deliver a service on demand. In most cases, it's a mix.

Most companies aren't fluid or flexible enough to wait for a customer-demand event to act across their entire supply chain, but many such demand build-to-order models exist at the direct consumer end of the market. Can you imagine a world where all companies operated that way? Can you think of a few who currently do? Here are a few:

- Many computer manufacturers no longer build systems and wait for customers to buy them. Their computers are built to the configurations and specifications ordered by the consumer — and shipped within days.

- Most fast-food restaurants now build your meal to order. They have the basic ingredients on hand (based on past consumer behavior), and when you order, they prepare your meal to your specifications and deliver it to you in a matter of minutes.

- Eyeglasses used to take days or weeks to arrive, but now some companies have moved the lab into the retail location. Your glasses are now ready in an hour.

- Business consultants wait for the call and then configure their consulting solutions based on the requirements. Consultants are extremely adept at forging new solutions in near real-time, based on the application of their latest knowledge, and quickly preparing a new solution for the client.

In these types of applications, the value stream is closely connected to the needs of the consumer. For example, the disk-drive manufacturer who supplies hard drives to the computer assembler follows the consumer demand market very closely. The food suppliers to restaurants know what the diner is ordering. (Remember how quickly menus changed when the low-carb diets were in vogue?)

Consumers further influence the market through a unique spin they have on requirements. In addition to the Kano profiles and formalized requirements flow, consumers exhibit specific behaviors and styles. These styles set the stage for how the entire value stream — and all the intermediate processes and customers — will act. Consumers largely fall into one of eight behavior style types, as defined by Sproles and Kendall's Consumer Style Inventory:

- Perfectionism; high-quality conscious

- Brand conscious

- Novelty-fashion conscious

- Recreational, hedonistic shopping conscious

- Price and "value-for-the-money" shopping conscious

- Impulsiveness

- Confusion over choice of brands, stores, and consumer information

- Habitual, brand-loyal orientation toward consumption

Consider an eyewear shop that makes the promise to deliver your glasses in an hour. What must that store do to live up to its promise? It must have all the materials, processes, and services on site to fulfill your needs. This includes having a sufficient variety of styles on hand to appeal to the variety of consumer interests — they need the designer section, the hip-and-trendy section, and the value section. They must also maintain the right level of inventory of frames and the lens blanks to go with them. Their equipment must be locally maintained. They must have trained technicians on site. And they must be conveniently located for consumer access (in shopping malls). All these elements come together to provide the consumer with glasses in an hour.

Not all consumers purchase the same way. Technology is changing the options for purchasing, but not everyone will adapt to the changes at the same rate.

Online purchasing has changed consumer behavior. Consumers see value in going online, both to check out and to check you out. They relish having the tools at their fingertips to research and make more educated purchases. More than ever, they know what they want, they're empowered by knowing how to get it, and they'll search until they find it. The convenience factor has become dominant, causing companies to become increasingly innovative in how they reach their existing markets, as well as penetrate new ones. Some consumers will do the research online, but still want to talk to a human or buy from a store — they're security minded and want to know that they can trust the person they're buying from. Other consumers are content to do everything online — from researching to buying.

Traditionally, Lean applications have neglected to focus sufficiently on many of the processes that the consumer touches directly. These processes include customer service, technical support, warranty, and more. Business reach can be improved dramatically by improving the processes that support these services. When a consumer is delighted by a product or experience, that consumer will be your biggest advocate. Conversely, when a customer is dissatisfied, he can be your biggest detractor!

Understanding what consumers value

Consumers are customers with a twist. In addition to the behaviors that business customers exhibit across the value chain (the so-called business-to-business, or B2B, group), the consumers have unique requirements and demands. The business-to-consumer relationship (B2C) must interpret these demands and properly manage them — directly or indirectly — back upstream to all the suppliers.

Understanding the distribution of styles in your market is a key step to understanding what your consumers value. Depending on the industry, the type of product or service, the magnitude of the purchase, and other factors, the relationship with the consumers through the pre- and post-buying phases ultimately determines the degree of success.

In simple terms, consumers want what they want, when they want it, at the price they're willing to pay for it, and if something goes wrong, they want accurate and friendly assistance or the ability to return it easily. These demands place tremendous pressure and constraints on each provider of the goods and services that combine to provide that end item to the consumer.

Companies are just now beginning to include the interface between the company and consumer as part of their Lean efforts. Processes from the point the consumer purchases through customer service and technical support are new frontiers for Lean implementation. These processes can make or break your relationship with consumers (not to mention their friends and families!), and are a new spring of improvement possibilities. Eliminating waste and creating a positive, value-added customer experience will increase your competitive edge.

The consumer is the ultimate customer. What the consumer values is ultimately what counts. Although you may have intermediary customers who have their own set of values, it is important to not lose sight of the consumer's wants and needs.

Introducing the Value Stream

After you understand value as it relates to your customers and consumers, you're ready to look closely at your processes to see how effectively you're satisfying their requirements (value creation). In Lean, you provide goods and services to the market through what is called the *value stream*.

If you've ever stood alongside a stream and watched the water flow, you probably noticed how the water runs and how the current changes. When there are no obstructions, and the volume is just right, the water moves freely and easily. But most streams have disturbances. Sticks, rocks, and fallen trees dam and disturb the flow. If there has been a storm, all sorts of debris drifts downstream. Where there are rocks, white water appears. Too much or too little water for the size of the riverbed, and there's more whitewater.

If you liken the stream to an operational process, the ideal condition is when the process flows unobstructed, like smooth, even water. The sticks and stones in a process are things like inventories, quality defects, and other forms of *muda* — non-value-added activities that block the flow of the product to the customer. In Lean, you strive to remove the debris and smooth out the flow.

Visualizing the value stream

The term *value stream* is used in Lean to describe how all the activities line up and work together to produce a given product or service. The activities combine to form a process of value creation. The process flow consists of activities that are both value-added and non-value-added.

The stream is always viewed from the customer's perspective, ideally from the ultimate customer's (the consumer) perspective. In viewing the value stream, you start where the stream ends with the consumer's view, and you track it all the way upstream to the smallest tributary — the sources of raw materials and labor, as depicted in Figure 3-3.

Figure 3-3:
The Value Stream: Each contributor adds value as products "flow" to the consumer.

The Value Stream

For any product or service, many activities and different types of materials and people contribute to make it happen. The materials are brought together — sometimes from all over the world — to make many products. Likewise, many services are provided globally. As consumers, we experience the end product or the last mile, because we're at the mouth of the stream, but a lot is happening upriver.

Think for a moment about all the things that have to happen for UPS or FedEx to deliver a parcel overnight. Consider all the events that must be coordinated perfectly and have to occur at precisely the right time in the value stream to deliver that parcel to the right address and in perfect condition. Sorting and handling, trucks, airplanes, tracking information — a staggering degree of logistical sophistication.

Now, visualize the value stream that is required to deliver a new automobile to the showroom. Literally tens of thousands of parts must arrive on the manufacturing line, in the right color, in the right order, at the right quality level, with the right orientation, for assembly to the right vehicle.

Consider again that ready-made salad at the grocery store. What does the value stream look like to make it available to you in a variety you desire, at a price you are willing to pay and a freshness level that you would expect? Figure 3-4 shows a high-level view of all of the activities that must occur in the value stream for you to have that salad available for your dinner. While the salad value stream might not be as complex as global package delivery or automobile manufacturing, it makes you stop to think about what it really takes to bring a product to market.

Looking at the flow of information

The creation of a product or service involves more than the direct flow of labor and materials — it also involves a flow of information. This information flow is exactly what it sounds like: It's all the information needed by all the processes and customers along the way to enable products and services to move through the value stream. The complete analysis of process and information flow within the value stream is what sets Lean apart from simple process analysis.

During the design and development phase, information flow includes requirements and design specifications, drawings, equipment specifications, manufacturing specifications, governmental filings. During the production phase, the information flow includes product orders, material releases, schedules, inventory, and quality data. During the post production phase, the information flow includes billing, collections, and banking functions.

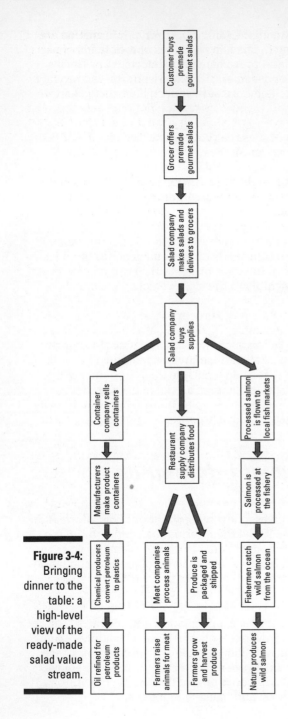

Figure 3-4:
Bringing
dinner to the
table: a
high-level
view of the
ready-made
salad value
stream.

For complex products like an automobile, millions of bits of information are created all along the value stream. Each of literally tens of thousands of parts have related design, production, and post-production information. Timely, complete and accurate information is required by many processes to ensure a smooth flow through to product delivery and support. If any kind of interruption or inaccuracies in the information flow occurs, not only may the consumer not receive his vehicle in a timely manner, but it could also be very costly to the manufacturing process — particularly if the interruption causes a safety or quality issue in the field.

Muda abounds in information processes, which is one reason that tracking the information flow is so important. If you can produce a product in minutes, but it takes hours or days to process the order, how lean is your process? And how well are you serving your customer?

In the ready-made salad example, the production information flow includes

- ✔ The grocery store sending an order to the salad company telling them what they need for the next day, based on sales

- ✔ A production schedule being prepared for each morning

- ✔ The salad company verifying the ingredients and container inventories for freshness and availability, based on the production schedule

- ✔ The company placing an order to its distributors for next morning delivery

- ✔ The distributors sending orders to their warehouse and shipping operations to meet the terms of the order

- ✔ The order cycles repeating all the way to the growers of the produce, wherever they're located in the world

Any issue with transmission or availability at any step in the process puts the company at risk of supplying the grocery with the product they need for the next day. And all this information is type-1 *muda:* It's required by the processes, but none of it is value-added from the consumer's perspective.

When introducing technology to the information flow, you have an opportunity to improve the business process and eliminate waste. An old Lean adage is "Simplify, eliminate, automate, then integrate." It applies to all areas of the business.

Chapter 4

A Resource Runs through It: Value Stream Mapping

All businesses and organizations are ultimately defined by what they produce. Not only do the most successful organizations produce goods and services that are highly valued by customers or consumers, but they also produce them in a manner that sustains the organization's viability over the long term. In the Lean enterprise, these capabilities are not an accident. They're the result of a very conscious awareness that every activity is really a *process* that adds some amount of measurable value. But how much value is a process adding? How productively? Within any given process, where are time, resources and efforts being wasted? And how do you make it better?

Think of a process as a place — a desk, a deli counter, a repair shop, a factory, or a hospital emergency room. Now think of the things that pass through those places — paperwork, sandwich materials, repair parts, raw materials, or patients. For everything that passes through those places, a transformation occurs: The paperwork is completed, the deli materials become a sandwich, the widget gets fixed, a consumer product is built, or the patient is treated. That transformation is the value-added result of the process. It all happens in a certain amount of time — at a certain rate — and it consumes various resources, such as space, energy, tools, and materials. It also takes a certain amount of applied effort and expertise to accomplish.

Now think of those things that pass through these places as a *flow* of materials and information. And consider precisely how and when the process added — or didn't add — value. How long did the paperwork just sit there before it was processed? How much scrap cheese or lettuce was thrown away in the making of the sandwich? How big of a mess was made on the workbench? How long did the customer have to wait? (We don't even dare ask about the emergency room!)

This flow of materials and information through a process to deliver a product or service to a customer is known as the *value stream.* A *Value Stream Map* is a graphical representation of the value stream. The Value Stream Map has an enterprise focus, instead of a functional one, because it covers all the activities required to bring the product or service to fruition. It depicts all the steps and highlights any ineffectiveness in the value stream.

As Lean has evolved out of the former incarnations of continuous-improvement initiatives, the Value Stream Map has moved to center stage. The Value Stream Map, combined with *Kaizen,* forms the heart of the continuous-improvement part of Lean.

In this chapter, we show you how to look at your value stream from a macro level; what the elements of a Value Stream Map (VSM) are; how to construct and read a Current-State VSM; how to validate the VSM that you've created; and how to measure and summarize the current state with a box score.

The Who, What, and Why of Value Stream Maps

A *Value Stream Map* is a graphical representation of how all the steps in any process line up to produce a product or service, as well as the flow of information that triggers the process into action. In the product world, the process may be about something physical, like making a car, creating a design, or authoring a report. In the service world, the process may be calling a help desk, buying pre-prepared food for dinner, or obtaining a driver's license.

A Value Stream Map plots the course from the input of raw materials through to the delivery of the finished goods or services to the customer. The *customer* identified at the end of a Value Stream Map is not necessarily the end customer or consumer who buys or consumes the final product or service; the customer may be another business or even someone or some other function within your own organization.

The first Value Stream Map that you construct shows the *current state* — the way things are now. Next, you identify the *ideal* Value Stream Map — the idealized notion of the process in a perfect world, where all steps are only value-added steps. As you conduct improvement activities, which refine the current state, you update the Value Stream Map to reflect the changes to the process. The goal is to be continually improving the process — constantly moving it in the direction of the ideal state.

A Value Stream Map flows from left to right with time — raw materials come in on the left, the process steps line up in order of occurrence, and the finished products or services exit to the right. The main flow is like the river channel, and the ancillary processes are like tributaries that feed the main process. In addition, the process steps are timed and then further categorized as value-added or non-value-added. A full Value Stream Map includes not just the flow of materials, but also the flow of the supporting information.

Figure 4-1 is a typical Value Stream Map, drawn with standard conventions. Don't worry — in this chapter, we explain everything you see in this figure, so if it looks like Greek to you now, just keep reading.

Value Stream Maps are often hand-drawn. However, software tools that enable the drawing, archiving, and e-mailing of VSMs are now available. These programs are useful, but you don't have to have computer software to create a fully functional VSM. You can draw one anywhere, on just about anything, including a dry-erase board, a pad of paper, or even the proverbial napkin. Anything will work, as long as it communicates!

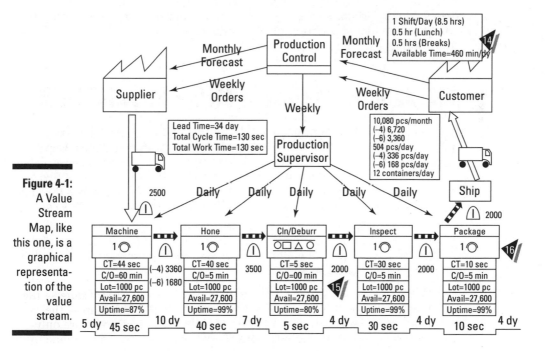

Figure 4-1: A Value Stream Map, like this one, is a graphical representation of the value stream.

The purpose of a Value Stream Map

Why is a Value Stream Map so useful? What does a VSM provide that other process diagrams or activity descriptions don't? Here's the rundown:

- ✔ The VSM always has the customer's perspective and is focused on delivering to the customer's expectations, wants, and needs.

- ✔ The VSM, in a single view, provides a complete, fact-based, time-series representation of the stream of activities — from beginning to end — required to deliver a product or service to the customer.

- ✔ The VSM provides a common language and common view to analyze the value stream.

- ✔ The VSM shows how the information flows to trigger and support those activities.

- ✔ The VSM shows you where your activities add value and where they don't, enabling you to see what ultimate impedes your ability to supply and satisfy your customer.

After you construct the Value Stream Map, not only do you see the process from the customer's point of view, but you also see what is required and how long it takes to deliver the product or service to the customer. The VSM shows you the primary activities, as well as the ancillary processes. And the VSM is not limited to the traditional functional perspective — it shows all the contributing activities and processes.

The people who use a Value Stream Map

Who uses a VSM? The users are many, because it helps everyone involved. Here are some examples of how people in your organization may use the VSM:

- ✔ **Process owners:** These are the people who own the cost of the process and the value it creates. In a VSM, process owners can quickly identify the opportunities for improvement throughout the whole value stream.

- ✔ **Process designers:** These are the people who design and help implement changes to improve processes. They use a VSM to focus on internal process steps and minimize non-value-added activities within and among those process steps.

- ✔ **Process workers:** These are the people who work within processes and must understand the context of the process and process changes. They see in a VSM where their own process activities are located, and they can quickly identify ways to improve their process.

- **Supply-chain managers:** Supply-chain managers must optimize the interfaces with suppliers. They use a VSM to look for opportunities to establish delivery windows, consolidated delivery routes (known in Lean as *milk runs*), and level schedules, as well as other opportunities to improve the logistics of the value stream.

- **Procurement managers:** These are the people who must negotiate relationships with suppliers. In a VSM, procurement managers find opportunities to work with suppliers to receive incoming products and services in a manner that supports the Lean initiatives in the facility. This sometimes includes bringing Lean principles into the supplier community.

- **Information technology (IT):** These are the people who have to manage the supporting information flow. They see in a VSM where they need to develop systems to support Lean efforts and properly link upstream and downstream systems of the value stream.

The elements of a Value Stream Map

The VSM is a snapshot of the value stream at a specific point in its evolution. It's a graphical representation of all the steps occurring in a process. In addition, a VSM contains essential, descriptive process information. Generally, a VSM contains the following:

- **Process Steps:** The VSM depicts each of the process steps in the value stream, including both value-added (VA) and non-value-added (NVA). The VSM reveals process statistics like cycle time, NVA time, changeover time, number of operators, number of pieces, amount of inventory, and percent defective.

- **Inventory:** The VSM highlights storage, as well as the amount and movement of inventory within the process.

- **Information flow:** All supporting information required by the process is depicted on the VSM. This can include orders, schedules, specifications, *kanban signals* (a *kanban* is a signal to replenish inventory in a pull system), shipping information, and more.

- **Box score:** A VSM includes a summary of the key operational metrics of the process. At a minimum, this includes a summary of the total lead time of a process with the value-added and non-value-added times identified. The summary may also include such information as distance traveled, parts per shift, scrap, pieces produced per labor hour, changeover time, inventory turns, uptime, downtime, and more — it's whatever matters to your business.

✔ **Lead time:** Along the bottom of the VSM is the current lead time performance of the value stream. *Lead time* is the amount of time that one piece takes to flow completely through the process. The time is divided into value-added and non-value-added portions. At a glance, you can see where the major portions of non-value-added time occurs.

✔ **Takt time:** A box in the upper-right-hand corner of the VSM shows the customer demand rate or *takt time*. This rate is determined by the customer demand and production time available. Ideally, all steps in the value stream should then produce to this rate. The takt time is like a metronome setting the pace for music.

TIP

Teams often find it unwieldy to try to map the whole value stream at a detailed level all at one time. Start with your immediate customer and map the stream back to the point where you receive inputs from a supplier. Just don't lose sight of where in the overall value stream your process fits.

TECHNICAL STUFF

Pick one *product family* (a series of products or services that pass through the same processing steps) to map. If the product family is processed at more than one location, for instance a eastern service center and a western service center, then focus on one location, but include representatives from the other location on the improvement team.

Row, Row, Row Your Boat: Getting Started

A Value Stream Map isn't difficult to make. In the following sections, we guide you through the process of creating your very own VSM.

Identifying the natural owner

Every value stream has a natural owner, who acts as the hub to make it easier to manage the improvement activities. The natural owner is like the captain of the ship — someone who by her very position or role in the organization manages the value stream. The natural owner is normally *not* a functional boss.

TIP

If you can't readily identify the natural owner, find someone who can be assigned the ownership role to drive the Lean improvement initiative.

Gathering the crew

Begin constructing a Value Stream Map by gathering the cross-functional team that represents all the disciplines involved in the process. Bring them together into a workshop setting. Having all these areas represented in the Value Stream Map improves the quality of the VSM and facilitates conversation between the team members about the "real" process. The workshop setting creates a focused environment where people are away from the distractions of their day-to-day jobs.

Outside Lean experts are also a vital part of the initial crew. They help ensure that the efforts are launched effectively. Lean experts train the organization in Lean tools and techniques, guide the development of initial Value Stream Mapping and facilitate the initial improvement efforts. They also help mentor people in how to think and act in a Lean way.

The ideal core team size has five to seven members. Larger teams are unwieldy, and smaller ones are too narrowly focused. You can bring in support experts when you're analyzing specific value-stream tributaries. Eventually, you'll expand the team to include customers and suppliers as you expand your Lean implementation.

Have someone who is not part of the team act as a facilitator to record the value stream. This helps the team to focus on the content, while the facilitator focuses on capturing the value stream.

Using mapping tools

Mapping the value stream can be as simple or as complex as you choose to make it. Whatever method or combination of methods you choose to use, it's important, in a group setting, that all participants can clearly see the Value Stream Map being created. Your options for mapping include the following:

- **No tech:** Paper stuck to the wall, and markers
- **Low tech:** Templates or preprinted formats
- **High tech:** Software programs like those available from EVSM (www.evsm.com) or iGrafx (www.igrafx.com).

When you draw a Value Stream Map, be sure to follow the conventions for drawing each icon that represents an activity, element, or event. VSM software tools supply these icons automatically. The basic, standard icons used in a VSM are shown in Table 4-1. The book *Learning to See,* by Mike Rother and John Shook, is a good VSM reference manual, including instructions and a complete listing of VSM icons.

Table 4-1	Value Stream Mapping Icons	
Icon	*Icon Name*	*Description*
	Process box	Describes an activity in the value stream. Includes a title and description of the process, as well as data, like process time, setup time, and so on.
	Outside source	Indicates and identifies both customers and suppliers.
	Truck	Indicates an outside delivery — either to a customer or from a supplier.
	Information	Describes information transmitted along the value stream.
	Electronic information transmission	Indicates that the information is transmitted electronically.
	Manual information transmission	Indicates that the information is transmitted manually.
	Inventory	Identifies stored inventory — either raw materials, in process, or finished goods.
	Finished goods movement	Indicates when materials in a finished state are moved along the value stream. This can be a supplier moving its product to a company or a company moving its product to its customer.
	Material push	Indicates material being pushed through the process. The push is usually a production plan or schedule.
	Supermarket	Indicates in-process inventory stored in a controlled environment called a supermarket.
	Material pull	Indicates material movement via a pull signal (kanban)

Icon	Icon Name	Description
	Operator	Indicates that one or more operators are present at a process step.
	Kaizen burst	Indicates the need for and description of a *Kaizen* activity within the value stream.

Gathering supporting information

Capture information about all the process steps at a detailed level. The more detail that is available, the easier it is to uncover the waste — the *muda* (see Chapters 2 and 3). Each team member brings with them supporting information to enable the Value Stream Mapping process. The more information you have readily available during the construction of the VSM, the better the resulting Value Stream Map.

Supporting information needed to build a VSM may include the following:

✔ The end consumer's requirements and expectations

✔ A macro-level view of the entire value stream from the consumer all the way back through to raw materials and information

✔ Customer schedules and demand information

✔ Process-time studies, including

  • Cycle time (C/T)

  • Lead times

  • Number of operators

  • Changeover time (C/O)

  • Working time, less breaks

  • Photos and video of the operations in their current state

✔ Standard work instructions

✔ Quality information

✔ Equipment uptime and availability

✔ Product and process variations

✔ Inventory and work-in-process (WIP)

 ✔ Batch sizes

 ✔ Pack quantities and other shipping information

 ✔ Cost data

 ✔ Any other information that will help you characterize the process

The best way to understand a process is to go to it and watch it yourself for a significant length of time. If you can, videotape the operations. The video will give you an objective perspective — you'll notice things you don't normally see when you concentrate on a specific part of the process over many cycles. People can watch themselves to see what they *really* do, instead of what they *think* they do.

A VSM example: Pre-made gourmet salads

Imagine that you're on your lunch break or heading home after working out at the gym. You're hungry and you want something quick to eat. You don't feel like cooking and you don't have time for a restaurant. So you pop in to your local grocery and grab a pre-made, gourmet salad from the deli case.

You expect the salad to be fresh and flavorful. Because you're paying a premium, you expect a gourmet offering of high-quality ingredients, uniquely combined and pleasingly presented. You want a variety to choose from. And you may be delighted if you tried a salad that then became your new favorite.

Have you ever stopped to think about all the things that have to happen in order to bring that fresh, flavorful salad to you? It seems simple enough — not much more than lettuce, toppings, and a bowl. That doesn't sound too difficult, right? But when you look at it closely, there's much more to it than what you see on the surface.

What's happening behind the scenes? What are all the pieces, who are all the people, and how is it all coming together just right? How much of all the effort, activity, time, materials, and cost involved actually adds value to you, the customer? How consistent is it? Businesses who take the time to map and improve their processes can execute a process like this consistently and effectively thousands of times a day to satisfy discerning customers like you.

The first look at the value stream is always from the consumer's point of view. In this example, the consumer is the hungry person. Her requirements are indicated in Figure 4-2 via a Kano model.

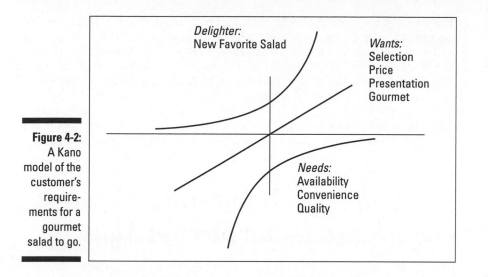

Figure 4-2:
A Kano
model of the
customer's
require-
ments for a
gourmet
salad to go.

After the consumer's requirements and expectations are understood, the next step is to map out the high-level flow of all the process steps that must occur across the entire value stream in order to meet those requirements and expectations. This high-level view is called the *macro-level value stream,* and it's used to set the context within which the provider understands how it must operate.

Macro-level value stream diagrams begin with the consumer and flow upstream through all the various processes that must support the consumer's demands. Unlike a process-flow diagram, a macro-level value-stream diagram moves from right to left, emphasizing the pivotal role of the customer at each step.

The macro-level value stream for the salad production process is shown in Chapter 3. It starts with the consumer and flows all the way upstream to where nature produces wild salmon. This simple chart encompasses a global supply stream — so global that, when taken from its first tributary, raw materials, all the way through to the consumer, it takes years to complete. All for a salad!

Contained within each box in Figure 3-4 are multiple individual processes and different companies that support the overall value stream. By first depicting the value stream at this high level, you can see where the salad company fits into the picture.

Understanding how your part fits into the overall value stream and how you contribute to the consumer's demands is important. Start by creating a macro-level value-stream diagram that shows your contribution to the overall value stream.

Going forward, you aren't going to construct a detailed VSM for the entire value stream. Such an exercise could take years. A full Value Stream Map would nearly evolve into a map of the planet's ecosystem. You don't need to map everything! Start at the level of your contribution, and refine the detail or expand the scope as you dive into the value stream. The waste-devil is in those details — that's where you'll uncover *muda*.

We refer back to this salad company example though the following sections, as we show you how to develop and validate the Current-State Value Stream Map.

Sorting Through the Tributaries: Creating the Current-State Value Stream Map

After you've identified the captain, assembled the crew, and gathered the critical data about your processes, you're ready to chart the course and create your Current-State Value Stream Map. Begin by capturing how your process works now — before any improvement efforts have started. From this initial VSM, you'll begin to understand where the waste is in the process. Before you start to construct the VSM, it's a good idea to *go to gemba* (go to where the action is, and review the process in situ). This will give everyone a common starting point of reference.

Start at the end closest to the customer and record the process from the end, working your way upstream to the beginning. You'll see what your value stream is doing the farther away from the customer you travel.

Identifying the activities

Begin by titling the Current-State VSM, dating it and identifying the major process steps.

Most teams start with the part of the value stream that they own. After you've identified the major process steps, you can use your supporting information to more precisely characterize each step.

In the salad example (see "A VSM example: Pre-made gourmet salads," earlier in this chapter), the salad company owns the part of the value stream where the salads are made and delivered to the grocer. With the participation of the cross-functional team, this process can be further divided into its major process activities. This team includes the owner, the lead chef, the sous chef, the driver, the kitchen hand, and an outside observer. The activities are represented in the Value Stream Map.

The salad company recognizes that it conducts five major process activities. For each salad, these activities are

✔ Preparing ingredients

✔ Assembling the salad

✔ Labeling the container

✔ Packing the container

✔ Shipping to the grocer

On the right-hand side of the map is the customer. You may choose to show the immediate customer as well as the consumer. For any outside player — including the consumer, customer, supplier, or any other source — use the outside source icon.

Along the bottom, from left to right, in sequential order, are the steps in the process of your part of the value stream. The first step on the left side is the first process. The last step on the right side is the final step before the product or service is given to the customer. In the case of the salad company, Figure 4-3 shows that the operation on the left-hand side of its value stream is "Prep Ingredients" and the final process, on the right-hand side, is "Shipping."

After you lay out the process steps, connect them with the appropriate connector. Dashed arrows indicate material pushed through the system. Open arrows are for material movement to or from external sources. Indicate where inventory is stored in the process — beginning, work in process, or end. Unique icons exist for regular inventory, buffer stock, supermarkets, safety stock, and queues. Clearly identify what type of inventory is in process, in addition to the amount of inventory at each location.

Take your first pass through the VSM at a relatively high level. After you characterize the value stream at this level, you can choose an area of focus, and map that at a greater level of detail. The process for creating any map, though, is the same.

Beware of the dangers of mapping paralysis. Don't get caught up in making the VSM so complete and perfect that you don't proceed to the improvement stage. Make your initial best cut and move on. You'll have plenty of opportunities to come back and improve your VSM later.

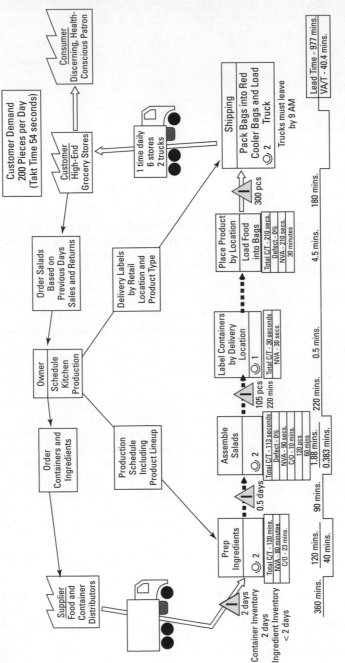

Figure 4-3:
The Value
Stream Map
for the salad
company's
contribution
to the
overall
value
stream.

Qualifying and quantifying

After you've captured the Current-State VSM, it's time to quantify the process and qualify the value-added (VA) and non-value-added (NVA) activities. Cycle time, changeover time, inventory levels, and the number of operators are all types of information you'll use to understand and analyze the process.

Characterizing the process time

When considering process time, there are a number of angles. For each step in the value stream, evaluate the step by asking the following types of questions:

- ✔ What is the actual time required to perform the task identified in the process step?
- ✔ What is the waiting time before each step?
- ✔ If inventory is involved, how long does it take to deplete it?
- ✔ What is the transport or conveyance time?
- ✔ What is the inventory between the last operation and the consumer?
- ✔ How many operators are active at each process step?
- ✔ How long does it take to change over a process when changing product types?

The VSM is a snapshot in time. Use the best data you have available to get the job done. If you have to estimate some of the times, go ahead. You'll be able to validate the estimates later with actual data.

After your team has answered these questions, you can assign a time value for each process step. From these observations, determine the value-added time. (In the next section, we help you decide what is VA and NVA and record a portion of NVA time on the map.) After the entire process has been characterized, sum the individual times to arrive at an overall process time for the Value Stream Map. If you're using a software package, the overall calculation will be done for you based on the information you enter about each process step.

Deciding what is value-added and what is non-value-added

Now it's time to decide which process steps are value-added (VA) and which ones are the dreaded non-value-added (NVA) steps in the process.

To be value-added, an activity must meet the three VA criteria:

- ✔ The customer must be willing to pay for it.
- ✔ It must transform the product or service in some way.
- ✔ It must be done correctly the first time.

Anything that doesn't meet these three criteria is NVA and is, therefore, a waste of some type.

Identify each process step and activity as either VA or NVA. At this early stage, you're not trying to weed out non-value-added activity. The process statistics will show the VA and NVA data for later examination. As you develop the map to a finer level of detail going forward, you'll see exactly which steps add value and which don't.

Don't get hung up on dissecting VA versus NVA classification at this stage. Pick one, assign it, and move on. In the end, you'll improve the entire process. The designation of VA and NVA are guidelines for when you start the improvement activities.

In the salad example, only those steps that directly contribute to the finished salad are value-added. For example, cutting the lettuce, baking the chicken, slicing the chicken, putting the ingredients in the container — these are all VA. These steps, however, are buried in the macro process steps "Prep Ingredients" and "Assemble Salads."

There are two types of non-value-added steps (defined in Chapter 3):

- ✔ **Type-1 *muda:*** Non-value-added but necessary.
- ✔ **Type-2 *muda:*** Non-value-added and not necessary.

In the salad company example, placing labels on the top and bottom of the container is considered type-1 *muda.* The labels do not directly contribute to the customer receiving her salad, but they are required for the scanning and payment processes at the grocery store. Another example of type-1 *muda* is the weighing of the ingredients during the assembly process. The weight adds nothing to the transformation of the salad, but it does ensure the quality and consistency of the product. Examples of type-2 *muda* are trips back and forth to the cooler for forgotten items or disposing ingredients that are still good.

Review the process and designate each step as VA or NVA. For the NVA, note the type: T1 or T2. This information will be handy when you start to identify improvement opportunities.

When the process owner maps the process along with an outside observer, her perception of the process is typically idealized. But when an outside observer goes to *gemba* herself to observe the process, the findings are often eye opening for all involved. ("Holy cow! Do we really do that?")

Quantifying overall lead time

Lead time is the amount of time it takes one piece to flow though the process from start to finish, including process time, inventory time, waiting time, and so on. In the case of the salad example, it's the time from when the shipment of produce arrives until it's transformed into a shipped salad. In the case of a service, obtaining a duplicate driver's license for example, it's the time from when you walk in the door of the DMV until you have your new license in hand. Within the lead time are value-added and non-value-added activities. A detailed time-study analysis will help you to identify these activities — so bring your stopwatch to *gemba*.

On the VSM, you draw a line along the bottom of the map to represent the overall lead time for the product or service. The line is segmented according to the lead time of each major step in the process. Where value-added work is being done, you can record it below the overall lead time line, to visually see the difference between the lead time and value-added time. (See Figure 4-3 for an example.) You may be shocked at what you find — lots of NVA and little bitty amounts of VA. If you use a software package, like iGrafx, it automatically generates the line for you based on the data you provide.

Determining the information flow

Every process transforms a product or service for a customer. In addition to the material (product or service) being transformed, the process requires certain other information — information *about* the transformation. This information flow might include any instructions, orders, or messages that occur through the course of the process. Information flow may also include schedules, orders, shipping transmittals, approvals, and more — whatever is needed to support the process.

One unique feature of the Value Stream Map is the representation of information flow as well as the direct flow of materials and services. What is the information flow, and why is it so important? Information flow is critical to the timely and effective execution of the process, so it's represented directly on the Value Stream Map.

Initially, consider the location, quantity, and frequency of the information flow, using penetrating questions like these:

- What information is being transmitted?
- When is information being sent?
- Who receives the information and are they the right people to receive the information?

✔ Where in the value stream does the information transmittal occur?

✔ How is the information being sent — manually or electronically?

Start with the information that is vital for the value stream to function. You can always add additional information flows to the VSM later. Place the vital information flow on the VSM at the proper location. Indicate information flow using the rectangular information box. Remember that there are two information arrows. Manual transmissions use a straight arrow, and electronic transmissions use a jagged arrow that resembles a lightning bolt. (See Figure 4-3 for an example.)

In the salad example, information flow includes such items as the daily customer order, the production schedule, the order to the suppliers, and the order list for each customer location. Other examples of information flow along the entire value stream include:

✔ The grocery sends orders to the salad company.

✔ Production sheets schedule the kitchen assembly process.

✔ The salad company sends orders to distributors for the ingredients needed and delivery times required.

✔ The salad company sends orders to container suppliers.

✔ Distributors send orders to the growers.

✔ Customs brokers file papers to import produce from other countries.

✔ Suppliers send delivery receipts with produce orders.

✔ The grocery fills out product return sheets and sends these sheets back to the salad company with products that did not sell before the expiration date.

Summing Up the Process

After you develop the initial Current-State Value Stream Map, you summarize the key descriptive process statistics and place them in a summary chart directly on the map.

The graphic for this is called a *box score*. Think of a box score in sports, like baseball — it contains important statistics on players, the score, hits, errors, runs, and so on. The concept of the box score in Lean is similar.

The box score

The box score is a summary of the critical statistics of a process. At the very least, the box score usually includes the total lead time and the value-added and non-value-added time. If the process includes the physical movement of an object, then travel distance is also normally included. Physical movement refers to any object that is transformed as it literally moves through the process. Typically, transformation is thought of as a manufacturing process; however, transformation also happens in transactional processes. An example of a transformation in an office setting includes the completion of paperwork through several departments of a process.

Box-score contents

The box score contains the summary chart of the key process metrics. You often want to contrast the measured scores against an ideal state, where all process steps are only value-added. (More about the ideal state in Chapter 5.)

In the salad company example, its initial box score includes its portion of the value stream — from receipt of ingredients to shipment of the finished salads. The box score is shown in Table 4-2.

Table 4-2	The Salad Company's Box Score	
Metric	*Current State*	*Ideal State*
Total average VA time	40.4 minutes	40.4 minutes
Total average NVA time	746.6 minutes	0 minutes
Total average lead time	787 minutes	40.4 minutes
Changeover time, between types	10 minutes	1 minute
Actual cycle time	113 seconds	54 seconds
Takt time, seconds	54 seconds	54 seconds

In the future, the salad company may need to track other metrics to address other types of waste in its value stream. Some of these metrics may include inventory turns, the value of lost ingredients due to waste or expiration, the number of unsold salads versus shipped salads, or salads as shipped versus salad as priced. As the company dives deeper into the value stream, it will select the measurements that will best gauge improvement efforts.

Additional metrics for a box score

The following are some of the other common metrics that companies may include in their box score:

- ✔ **Parts per shift:** Parts produced during a standard work shift

- ✔ **Scrap:** The percentage of defective parts produced

- ✔ **Pieces per labor hour:** The total number of pieces produced divided by the amount of labor hours expended

- ✔ **Changeover time:** The amount of time required to convert a manufacturing line from the last good part of the previous product to the first good part of the new product

- ✔ **Inventory turns:** The number of times a company's inventory cycles in a year (Inventory Turns = Average Annual Cost of Goods Sold ÷ Average Annual Inventory)

- ✔ **Uptime:** The amount of time the equipment is actually producing versus the planned production time

- ✔ **Cost breakdown:** An evaluation of the cost components at each step of the process

Takt time

Takt is the German word for *beat*. In Lean, it is the pace of production tied to customer consumption. The takt time may be shown in the box score or in a note on the VSM. The formula is Takt Time = Available Production Time ÷ Customer Demand.

The salad company uses its kitchen to support other value streams. For the premade salads distributed to local groceries, the available production time is 3 hours (or 10,800 seconds [$3 \times 60 \times 60$]), and the customer demand is 200 salads per day (on average). So the takt time is 10,800 ÷ 200, or 54 seconds per salad.

Check the Chart: Validating the Value Stream Map

Have you ever driven the same route to work or home but not really seen what you were driving past? Then, one day, you notice a restaurant or business that has been there for years. You've passed it hundreds of times, but for whatever reason, on that day you noticed it for the first time.

The same thing can happen to members of a team with respect to the value stream where they work. You can walk by a process or an office but not really "see" what's happening. When the team is capturing the first VSM, it's important that there be a common starting point — that all the members "see" the same thing.

Although perfection is not a requirement, you do want the baseline starting point to be as accurate as possible. Real improvements happen from a common leaping point. Maybe the team thinks that standardized work is in place, when it's really not. Or maybe the team assumes one step is in a different place than it really occurs. Information that one team member believes is important to be distributed may not be getting to the "right" people, or it may not be so important after all. In any case, you have to validate your VSM before you proceed to the improvement phase of the game.

Although the team members might think they know what's going on in the value stream, the only way to truly know is to go to *gemba* (go to where the action is happening). It's one thing to walk by the process — it's a totally different thing to observe with intention. When you stand and observe the process over a repeated number of cycles, your eyes are opened to what is really occurring.

One powerful tool is videotaping the process, and then reviewing the video with the team. The video will create a common foundation from which the improvements can occur.

The key things that you're validating are

- ✔ Whether the process depicted on the Value Stream Map is, in fact, the process
- ✔ Whether the process time is correct (particularly if you use estimates)
- ✔ Whether the inventory amounts are accurate
- ✔ Whether the number of operators is correct
- ✔ Whether the process is being performed according to a standard instruction
- ✔ Whether the key process statistics are correct
- ✔ Whether all operators are performing the activities in the same manner
- ✔ The number of process changeovers that are performed and how long they take
- ✔ The accuracy of the quality data, and the identification of where the defects are occurring in the process

Sometimes not every person involved in the process is involved in constructing the Current-State VSM. Involving experts to assist you with a portion of the VSM can be a great idea. Not every person is going to know every nuance of every process. Seek out experts who truly know what's going on.

After you've identified the discrepancies, the team can update and correct the Current-State VSM. The team may also decide that it needs to further refine an activity and map it.

Detail is very important. You may start with a higher-level view of the value stream. As the improvement efforts progress, you may take one of those steps and create a more detailed Value Stream Map. The more detail that is available, the easier it is to uncover the waste (the *muda*).

Chapter 5

Charting the Course: Using Value Stream Maps

· ·

In This Chapter

▶ Analyzing the Current-State Value Stream Map

▶ Creating a vision of the future

▶ Planning your Lean implementation within the organization

· ·

*T*o make a change, you need a catalyst. In Lean, the catalyst for change is the recognition that the current state is not where you want to be. Lean is applicable whether you need to fix something that's broken or prepare for new opportunities to come. This perspective comes from the Current-State Value Stream Map (VSM), combined with supporting information like quality data, customer complaints, or financial reports. So like that "fat picture" that sends you to the gym and juice bar to get healthy, the Current-State VSM and supporting information provides that objective reflection that nudges an organization to modify its processes and practices and make the business healthy and vital.

When you decide to make a change, not only do you plan where you're going to go, but you also consider where you *could* go. You ask what's possible. For example, when you decide to get healthy, does *healthy* just mean weighing less? It may also mean better cardio performance, improved flexibility, lower cholesterol, or a smaller clothing size. In a perfect world, what would a perfectly healthy you look like? The thought process is the same when you decide to make changes in your business. In Lean, the *Ideal* VSM is used to define that perfect world — what your business would look like if anything were possible. You then use the *Future-State* VSM to paint the picture of where you want to go next.

In this chapter, we show you how to analyze your Current-State VSM to get a real picture of the process. You discover how to develop the Ideal-State and Future-State Value Stream Maps. Along the way, we answer common questions and respond to common objections about Value Stream Mapping. Finally, you determine how your future plans fit with other organizational initiatives.

Investigating the Value Stream for Clues

In Chapter 4, we show you how to create a Value Stream Map (VSM) for the current state of the business. After this initial Current-State VSM is complete, your next mission is to dive into it and understand where the waste is occurring. You first start looking for waste when you qualify the value of the steps in the stream (see Chapter 4). At *this* point in the process, you look for where the flow is less than ideal.

If the process is in a state of ideal flow, you make one as the consumer takes one (no matter what that "one" product or service is). The process is in perfect balance. All steps take the same amount of time. There is no inventory in process. The process contains only value-added activities. All process steps produce perfectly. You have the exact capacity needed for the consumption rate, with the exactly correct staff.

The Current-State VSM, combined with the use of the supporting data, provide the clues telling you where to start looking for improvement opportunities. In Lean, you strive for the entire value stream flowing unencumbered at a rate equal to the customer's demand in the most effective manner (that is, with the highest quality, the shortest lead time, and the lowest cost). You can quantify this customer demand by looking at the demand rate, or *takt time*. By using this metric, you can start to analyze the current state to evaluate where blockages to the flow are occurring. The blockages can be traced directly to *muda*. You improve performance by resolving and removing the root cause of these blockages.

The Lean process is one of seeking understanding. You seek to understand the customer and the consumer. You seek to understand the nature of your processes and the origins of waste and loss. The most fundamental Lean tool you use in your search is the question. You ask questions — many questions — to discover truth and understanding. Because this process of investigation is one of asking questions, the analysis is *framed* by questions.

Rounding up the usual suspects

As you begin your analysis of the Current-State VSM, start by considering the most common causes. What does your customer say about you? The answer to this question will provide immediate insight. Even if the customer voices issues that aren't at the root of the problem, the customer may give you clues as to what the issue truly is. If you aren't getting any indications from the customer, start looking for evidence of the three Ms: *muda, mura,* and *muri*.

While conducting the analysis of the current state, mark up a copy of the Current-State VSM. If you're using the low-tech, pencil-and-paper method, use a different color to indicate where in the value stream the opportunities for improvement exist.

Putting your ear to the street

When analyzing the Current-State VSM, start with the customer — *always* start with the customer. What are your customers saying about you? Listen closely and carefully — and objectively — to what your customers say. As you hear the feedback, examine the issues and identify where they occur in the value stream. For example, are your customers complaining about not getting your product when they want it? Look at the critical path to delivery. Are they complaining about not getting the right mix of product? Examine the material flow and information flow. Are they concerned about the quality of your product? Study the design and manufacturing processes. If you're lucky and your customers are all singing your praises, you may need to make room for new business.

An effective tool for analyzing potential causes of customer issues is the *Ishikawa Diagram,* also know as the *Cause-and-Effect* or *Fishbone Diagram.* With this tool, you can identify where in the value stream the issues originate. Figure 5-1 shows an example of an Ishikawa Diagram illustrating a case in which the customers complain that the product is late.

Examine the many possible causes for the delays. Use your supporting information to help you identify the most likely root causes of the delays, and to quantify how late "late" really is. Is the complaint a recent development or has there been a chronic problem? Look in the value stream to find the operations that are sources for the major issues. Ask these types of questions to identify issues in the value stream that are directly affecting the customers:

- Are the operations running slower than takt time?
- Are there deviations to the work standards?
- Is the product not available for shipment?
- Have there been material supply issues?
- Are the drivers leaving late from the facility?
- Have there been any personnel changes?

Focus on fixing the process, not assigning blame to people. Lean is all about respecting people. Most of the time, you will find a process problem (like a lack of defined standards) preventing people from performing at their best.

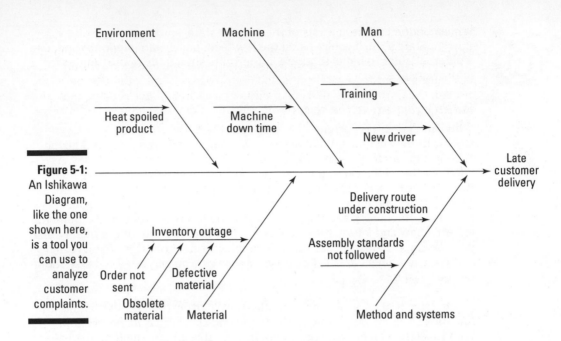

Figure 5-1:
An Ishikawa
Diagram,
like the one
shown here,
is a tool you
can use to
analyze
customer
complaints.

If you answer "yes" to these types of questions, you have the opportunity to use what's called the *5 Whys*. The aim of the 5 Whys is to find the root cause of a problem. When using 5-Why questioning, you ask "Why?" until you've exhausted answers and found the root cause of the problem. Practicing 5 Whys is like becoming a curious three-year-old again, when the question "But why?" was the first thing out of your mouth. Here's what this technique looks like in action:

Are the drivers leaving late from the facility?

Yes. But why?

Because the product isn't ready. Why?

Because the production line was behind. Why?

Because the supplier was behind. Why?

Because the order was issued late. Why?

You get the idea. In this example, these *why*s would lead you to look at the ordering process.

Start your Current-State VSM analysis by finding the sources of your customers' irritations. After you've identified those sources, the next step is to look for *muda* (see the following section).

Searching for muda

You've seen your business through the eyes of your customer and examined the direct causes of customer dissatisfaction. Now you must look within, and find causes of waste occurring inside your business. During the first pass through the Current-State VSM, you initially designate process steps as value-added (VA) or non-value-added (NVA). Now it's time to examine these designations more closely.

Refer to Chapter 2 for the precise definitions of value-added and waste.

Lean strives to eliminate *all* wasteful forms. To find waste, ask the following types of questions:

- Is excess inventory or work-in-process accumulating along the value stream?

- Does the step create value? If not, why does the step exist in the process and can it be eliminated?

- Does the step create scrap or rejects? If so, it's a candidate for improvement and, at the very least, further study.

- Is the step capable? If not, the step should be improved using statistical tools, like those found in the Six Sigma methodology. (For more information on Six Sigma, see *Six Sigma For Dummies,* by Craig Gygi, Neil DeCarlo, and Bruce Williams [published by Wiley])

- Does the step perform as designed?

- Is the equipment needed to perform the step functioning?

- Are the materials required available, at the right quality level, and in the right quantity?

- What is the capacity of the process step? How does it compare to the takt time?

- Is the step flexible?

- When changing from one product or service to the next, how long is the process step not producing? (This question is aimed at understanding changeover time.)

- Does the process step flow or is the step a bottleneck in the process?

- How does the process time of the step compare to the customer demand?

After designating each process step, the team can calculate the value-added portion of the process and compare it to the non-value-added portion.

Anytime you use *re–* in front of a word, it is a candidate for waste elimination, because, by its very definition, it means you aren't doing it right the first time.

Get a physical layout of the work areas, and create a two-dimensional flow diagram that reflects the physical movement of material or people through the process. This technique is especially useful in manufacturing processes, lab processes, restaurant kitchens, and other places where physical material moves through processes and places. These layouts are commonly known as *Spaghetti Diagrams* (see Chapter 7), because after all the movements are drawn out, it tends to look like a plate of spaghetti!

Analyzing from different perspectives

Different players in the value stream bring a different set of eyes and information to the evaluation of the Current-State VSM. Whether you're improving an unhealthy business practice or enabling the pursuit of a new opportunity, take the time to examine the value stream through different perspectives. As you strive to find the *muda*, these different views can be invaluable sources of insight.

The VSM team will involve people working in the process who have a daily operational perspective. This will include process owners, including the value-stream owner, and perhaps even the business owner. In addition to these participants, others have a keenly valuable perspective.

Lean principles: The Lean sensei's view

The *Lean sensei* is the master and teacher of the Lean principles and knowledge. (For more information about the Lean *sensei* see Chapter 12.) The Lean *sensei* guides and teaches the organization to learn, implement, and embody the Lean philosophy. The lens through which the *sensei* evaluates the Current-State VSM highlights the short-term and long-term opportunities to institutionalize Lean in the organization. The Lean view poses these types of questions:

- How closely is the process producing to takt time?
- How can the process be more visual?
- How can workers be more empowered to stop the line when quality issues arise?
- How is the material flowing through the process?
- Where best can continuous flow be implemented?
- Where do supermarkets need to be implemented?

✔ Are standardized work instructions available, being followed, and visible?

✔ How can the workload be leveled?

✔ Where can operations be combined to improve flow?

✔ What exists in the value stream preventing the implementation of Lean at this time? How can it be addressed?

Quality

The quality practitioners — whether they're from a formal quality function, or, trained Six Sigma experts — examine value-added from the perspective of correctness: Does the transformation happen correctly? Is it done right the first time? Is the process capable of producing defect-free results regularly?

Think of debris dumped into a river and what it does to the flow of the current. When quality losses occur in the value stream, it is like debris dumped into stream — impeding its flow. The quality practitioners evaluate the process to identify where it isn't capable of creating good product or service, and where suppliers or downstream contributors create poor quality for the consumer. Analyzing the value stream from a quality perspective will lead you to ask the following types of questions:

✔ Where is poor quality reaching the customer? What are the defects?

✔ How are quality issues reported from the customer, transmitted into the organization, and resolved?

✔ What is the fall-off rate at each step?

✔ Where are the losses the greatest?

✔ What is the most common cause of scrap?

✔ What is the root cause of the scrap (design, equipment, training, and so on)?

✔ How are suspect items handled?

✔ How are reworked items returned to the normal flow?

✔ How can the process, design, or equipment be designed to prevent errors?

✔ What is the capability of each step?

✔ Which suppliers are the providers of the poorest quality?

✔ How frequently have quality spills occurred and in what location?

✔ What steps have been taken to quarantine defective product?

Supply

Most processes have inventory — either by accident or by design. Inventory can collect at the beginning, somewhere in middle, or at the end of the process. Inventory acts like a dam to the flow of the value stream. Where there is inventory, there is no flow. Likewise, where there are outages, there is no flow. Balance comes in orchestrating the flow of material supply and processing precisely to customer demand — in other words, matching the cycle time to the takt time.

Strategically design the location of the inventory, the size of the inventory, and the information flow throughout the value stream. Examine the Current-State VSM for how well it consumes supply and moves material through the process. You can do so by asking the following questions:

- ✔ What is the inventory turn level?
- ✔ What is the size of the storage?
- ✔ Where is the storage? In a warehouse? In process?
- ✔ How low can it go? Can you maintain an inventory of one?
- ✔ How is the inventory managed?
- ✔ Do you practice first in first out (FIFO)?
- ✔ What signals the withdrawals from the inventory?
- ✔ What are the reorder signals in the process?
- ✔ Where is material pushed through the system?
- ✔ Where is the material pulled through the system? Where else can pull signals be used in the process?
- ✔ How are the raw material quantities balanced with the shipping quantities?
- ✔ How far does material travel in the value stream?
- ✔ How are the incoming material shipments coordinated?
- ✔ How is first in first out managed?
- ✔ When a quality issue arises, how is the inventory handled/quarantined?
- ✔ What is the dollar value of the inventory?
- ✔ What is the cost of floor space to handle the inventory?

Engineering

Evaluate the Current-State Value Stream from the perspective of the engineering disciplines: design, production, and maintenance. The engineering perspective will also help you examine the interfaces of the people, equipment, and processes.

Think about the Army Corps of Engineers. They engineer the flow of the U.S. waterways. They examine the current state and look for where modifications need to be made. They dredge to create movement. They dam to manage downstream flows. They design how and if flow happens. In a Lean organization, the designers engineer how flow happens inside the value stream.

At this juncture, you're evaluating the current state of production processes and practices. Be aware that the designers are meanwhile developing future designs of new products and services. Because the majority of cost is established during the design phase, you want to involve the design engineers during the Current-State VSM analysis. You also want to include the production engineers to ensure continuity.

Analyzing the value stream from a production-manufacturing engineering perspective, will lead you to ask the following types of questions:

- Is the process designed for flow?
- Can processes be combined? Can alternative processes be used?
- How can operations be laid out to maximize the effectiveness of operators?
- How far away is the material or inventory being stored? How far does it travel between operations?
- How is material presented into the process?
- How are the raw material quantities balanced with the shipping quantities?
- How can changeovers occur more quickly? How can concepts like the "Indy pit crew" be applied during changeovers?
- What modifications can be done to equipment to prevent errors, facilitate the operation, eliminate workload from operators, combine operations, or facilitate flow?
- Is standardized work being followed? How can it be modified to improve quality and eliminate unnecessary processing or movement?
- How can cycle times be balanced with takt time?

Analyzing the value stream from a design engineering perspective, will lead you to ask the following types of questions:

- What type of product defects occur during the process? Where do they occur?
- How can features be built into the design so it cannot be made incorrectly?

- What issues in the current design might be in the future designs?

- Can the design be simplified to facilitate production without compromising customer requirements?

- Are certain design specifications unnecessary for the customer requirements? Where can specifications be eliminated or changed without impacting customer requirements?

- Are the design tolerances properly specified to ensure the product can be made right the first time, every time?

Analyzing the value stream from a maintenance/equipment engineering perspective, will lead you to ask the following types of questions:

- What is the uptime of the equipment?

- What is the current maintenance schedule? Is it reactive or planned? If planned, is it preventive or predictive?

- What modifications can be made to the equipment to prevent defects from being produced?

- What pieces of equipment have the greatest maintenance issues?

- Are there different brands of equipment performing the same function/operation? Is there a difference in performance level?

- What modifications can be made to the equipment, tooling, and process to facilitate quick changeovers? (See Chapter 8.)

- What is the process to notify maintenance? How can it be improved?

- When there is an issue, what is the response time for maintenance to respond? What is the time to resolve the issue?

- What simple maintenance activities can be transferred to the operators to perform?

- What modifications, features, or controls can be added to the equipment to enable operators to run multiple pieces of equipment?

- What controls can be added to the equipment to automatically stop when defects are produced or equipment problems arise?

Although the questions in this section relate to the production of a product, they also apply to a service environment. In a transactional environment, like the hospital admissions process, the quality perspective is customer-service and data-integrity related. The material perspective is patient flow and data related. The process engineering perspective may be from a software engineering perspective. The wording of the questions may be slightly altered, but the nature of the questions or analysis is similar to the example questions in this section.

Information

The VSM depicts the flow of information that supports the product and material flow. Your analysis of the current state should include a focused examination of the information component. The purpose of this analysis is to find opportunities to eliminate waste or make improvements based on information.

Answering the following questions will help you when determining where waste, or *muda,* exists in the information flow:

- ✔ Does the information flow to the customer, without delays?

- ✔ Does the information flow from the customer, without delays?

- ✔ Does the information flow through the organization smoothly?

- ✔ Is the information flow accurate? Is the right information going to the right people in the right place? Complete? Contradictory?

- ✔ Does the information arrive at the right time? Is it too early or late? Is there too much or too little?

- ✔ Are the right people in the information flow and receiving the right information?

- ✔ Is the information being transmitted in the most efficient way?

- ✔ Is the information being acted upon?

- ✔ Are prompt and proper approval chains in place?

Evaluating the evidence: An analyzed example

A salad company supplies local, high-end grocery stores with gourmet salads on a daily basis. It operates on one shift: The morning is assembly, and the afternoon is ingredient preparation for the next day. The drivers are scheduled to leave the facility by 9 a.m. so that their deliveries will be complete by 11 a.m., in time for the lunch crowd. They conscientiously adhere to health and safety standards for food preparation.

The salad company's direct customers (the grocery retailers) have one major complaint: The deliveries tend to run late. When the salad company reviews its shipping data, it realizes that its drivers are leaving late from its commissary — about 45 minutes late, almost every day.

After reviewing the video from production one morning, the team realizes that several things were causing the product to be late in the morning. However, the main place they need to start is with the salad assembly process. In order to better understand where the waste is occurring, the team makes a detailed assessment of that process. The full analysis would be much longer, but an excerpt is shown in Table 5-1.

Table 5-1		Analysis of the Salad Assembly Process			
Step	**Operation**	**VA or NVA?**	**Type-1 or Type-2 Muda?**	**Time**	**Type of Waste**
88	Walk to office end of work area and place dressing in salad.	NVA and VA	Type-2	8 seconds	Transportation
89	Grab large dressing container.	NVA	Type-1	2 seconds	Motion
90	Walk to cooler with large dressing container.	NVA	Type-1	30 seconds	Transportation
91	Walk around kitchen looking for balsamic chicken.	NVA	Type-2	315 seconds	Transportation
92	Bring balsamic chicken to far end of work surface (wet area end).	NVA	Type-1	25 seconds	Transportation
93	Walk to wet area end of kitchen to get clean, green cutting board.	NVA	Type-2	15 seconds	Transportation
94	Bring green cutting board back to work area.	NVA	Type-1	15 seconds	Transportation
95	Get clean knife.	VA	N/A	4 seconds	N/A

Step	Operation	VA or NVA?	Type-1 or Type-2 Muda?	Time	Type of Waste
96	Put on gloves.	NVA	Type-1	11 seconds	Motion
97	Slice four chicken breasts; throw away top slice.	VA and NVA	Type-2	27 seconds	Excess processing
98	Place sliced chicken in hand, as much as can carry.	NVA	Type-2	4 seconds	Motion
99	Walk to office end of work area	NVA	Type-2	6 seconds	Transportation
100	Place approximately three-fourths of a breast on salad, fanned out.	VA	N/A	24 seconds	N/A
101	Walk back to chicken and cutting board.	NVA	Type-2	6 seconds	Transportation

The team observes that the following issues directly contribute to lateness:

- In general, the process was disorganized.
- The work standards were not well defined.
- Considerable time was lost wandering around looking for things.
- The ingredient preparation work was not completed the afternoon before.
- Ingredients had not been ordered on time, causing them to send one of the workers to purchase them at a premium from a retail store.
- Untrained workers were called in to help get the product out the door.
- The finished product was stacked at the end farthest from the door, causing the drivers to have to "swim upstream" to get the finished product, as well as have to carry it farther. Drivers are working in and among the people assembling the final product.

In addition, they notice other wastes occurring in the process:

- ✔ There was an unnecessary loss of ingredients as a result of the current process. Good product was thrown away. Containers were overfilled, causing ingredients to fall to the work surface.

- ✔ Ingredients were not being measured, which could affect the quality and consistency of the product, not to mention contribute to inventory losses.

- ✔ The workload was unbalanced. Some operators appeared overloaded and others were waiting on product to process. Drivers were waiting on product to label.

- ✔ The number of labels did not match the production sheet causing them to question which was correct.

- ✔ The order of production caused extra dishes to be dirtied unnecessarily.

This Current-State Value Stream analysis not only identifies numerous contributors to the lateness problem, but also many other sources of waste. The foundation has now been set for considering improvement options. The first step is to ponder the ideal state — what would be possible if all constraints could be cast aside. Then define the future state and set the plan to achieve the first increment of improvement.

Painting a Picture of the Future

The Current-State VSM is a snapshot in time — it's where you are now. That's an important view, but it's only part of the story. After you've characterized the current state, it's important to set your sights on the view of where you're going. In this section, you take the opportunities for improvement that you've identified in your Current-State Value Stream analysis and turn them into a design of the future.

In Lean, you consider two future views.

- ✔ **The view of the utopian or ideal state:** In a perfect world, with only value-added steps, how could you best meet the customer's requirements?

- ✔ **The more-grounded future state that you can implement relatively quickly with a focused plan:** In the future state, you make incremental improvements to the current state, eliminating waste and reducing the non-value-added steps.

Creating the Ideal-State Value Stream Map: Where all is perfect in the world

If your process is in a state of ideal flow, you make one as the consumer takes one. The process is in perfect balance. All activities are value-added. All process steps take the same amount of time. There is no inventory in process. All process steps produce perfectly, without defects. You have the exact capacity needed for the consumption rate, with the precisely correct number of staff, trained perfectly for the tasks.

Ponder this for a moment: the process where everything is exactly right. Don't ruin the thought with the realities of imperfection — that's for the next section. For now, picture utopia. See it all working perfectly.

Why define an Ideal-State VSM? Why spend legitimate business time and effort considering something that you probably can't have? The reason is simple: Because you *can* have it. When you allow people to imagine cutting the ties of the past and letting go of the constraints of the current environment, you raise the collective consciousness and enable teams to engage in radical thinking that often identifies breakthrough opportunities. You simply can't soar when your feet are nailed to the floor.

Frequently, the Ideal-State Value Stream Mapping exercise results in dramatic gains. The power of imagination is unbounded. When unbridled, ideas flow freely and great things emerge. The Ideal-State VSM produces the options for the next step: the future state.

Stepping closer to perfection: The Future-State Value Stream Map

Now it's time to take all the mapping efforts, the analyses, and the ideal-state visions and marry them to define the future state. The improvements that you select now become the foundation for your planning activities. The Future-State Value Stream Map is your next increment of performance improvement.

Pacemakers, supermarkets, and heijunka, oh my!

Before you can envision the Future-State VSM, you need to understand several Lean principles and concepts. Chapter 2 addresses the principles of Lean. Chapter 3 addresses the concepts of value added, non-value added, flow, and the 3M's (*muda, mura* and *muri*). Here is where you put those principles and concepts into action, as well as some of the following new ones:

- ✔ **Pacemaker operation:** The pacemaker operation sets the pace for the rest of the value stream. It's the one and only operation that receives the production schedule. The pacemaker produces to the takt time and sets the pace for the upstream operations to produce only enough to replenish what the pacemaker operation has consumed. Downstream of the pacemaker operation, the process must produce in a continuous flow (unless a storage area, known as a supermarket — see later in this chapter — is required for finished goods). Multiples of pacemaker production fit the quantity shipped to the customer. For example, if the shipping quantity to the customer is 60 per container, then you may release 20 at a time to the pacemaker operation.

- ✔ **Bottleneck process:** The *bottleneck process* is the process with the longest cycle time.

- ✔ **Work modules:** *Work modules* are aggregated operations fit into a compact area, in order to facilitate continuous flow, and single-piece production. Work modules are capable of performing all, or most, of the operations required for the value stream to deliver its product or service. This is wholly different from a traditional departmental organization.

- ✔ **Supermarkets:** *Supermarkets* are stores of in-process inventory used where the process cannot produce a continuous flow. Examples of supermarkets include when one operation services many value streams, when suppliers are too far away, or when processes are unstable, have long lead times, or have out-of-balance cycle times. The supplying operation controls the supermarket and its inventory. Supermarket inventory is tightly controlled.

- ✔ **Standardized work:** *Standardized work* is the description of the work being performed, and it includes the takt time, specific sequence or activities and defined work-in-process inventory. It's the standard to which the actual process is compared, and it represents the foundation on which to improve.

- ✔ **Kanban:** *Kanban* are the signals to move and produce. In a *pull system,* where material or work is "pulled through" a process by demand, kanban is instruction that declares that a withdrawal has been made, so you can produce more. The signal can come in many forms: an empty container, a card, a ball — it takes whatever form best tells the supplying operation to produce. Kanban identifies a standard production quantity.

- ✔ **Heijunka:** *Heijunka,* also known as *workload leveling* or *production smoothing,* is the practice of smoothing out the volume and mix of the schedule for what's to be produced. The goal of *heijunka* is to level work schedules to the point where there is little variation on a daily basis. *Heijunka* makes continuous flow, pull signals, and inventory minimization possible.

✔ **Pitch:** *Pitch* is the amount of time required to make a standard container of finished product. If the standard container is 60 pieces and the takt time is 45 seconds, the pitch is 45 minutes.

Marking up the Current-State VSM

The Future-State VSM begins as a markup of the Current-State VSM. Don't start with a clean sheet of paper; make changes directly on the Current-State Map. Identify where and what type of improvements you intend to make. Based on the team's evaluations and observations, indicate what changes will address the issues. The markup technique is to indicate the changes in a sunburst icon called a *Kaizen burst*.

Marking all of the areas you want to change doesn't imply that you'll necessarily make all the changes at the same time, but it defines an endpoint to this particular improvement phase. With this picture, you can predict the type and extent of improvement you anticipate from the implementation. By identifying such things as how much NVA time will be reduced, and how much key process times are reduced, you can quantify the improvement goals.

In the salad company example, the team marks up their Current-State VSM with numerous ideas for improvement as a result of their observations and ideal-state brainstorming. Figure 5-2 shows the areas where the team would like to improve. They start with a 5S activity to clean up and organize the work area. In particular, they identify standard containers and scoops for the ingredients, and improved visual controls in the area. Because they observed that not all team members understood the work standard for the salad line, they review the process and establish formal, written standards. Because the salad-preparation work was not complete, they evaluate ways to eliminate NVA time and implement pull signals between assembly and preparation.

Eventually, the team also wants to improve the inventory management in the value stream. In addition, they want to involve their suppliers in identifying ways to receive more-frequent deliveries and better stock rotation.

Gazing into the crystal ball: Seeing the Future-State Value Stream Map

As soon as you've identified the candidate changes, create a new picture: your Future-State VSM draft — the picture of what the value stream will look like after implementing the improvements. Begin with the Current-State VSM and implement the proposed changes. Leave the *Kaizen* bursts in place for reference.

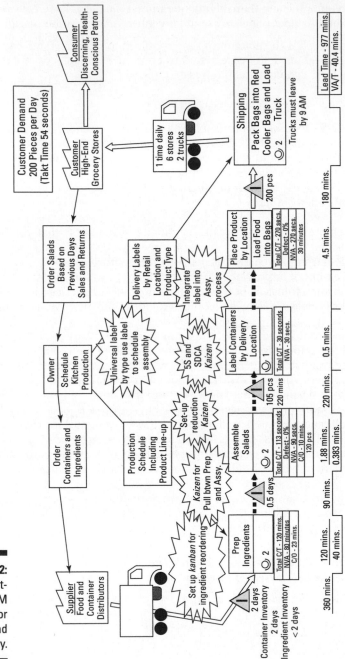

Figure 5-2:
The Current-State VSM markup for the salad company.

Also ask yourself a set of qualifying questions. (See the "Pacemakers, super-markets, and heijunka, oh my!" section, earlier in this chapter to clarify any of these questions.) Indicate the answers on the future-state VSM draft, either directly or through the selection of the correct icons for *kanban*.

✔ What is the takt time (confirming it hasn't changed from the current state)?

✔ Where is the bottleneck operation?

✔ Where can continuous flow happen?

✔ Where can work cells be implemented?

✔ Which is the pacemaker operation?

✔ What process will be scheduled ?

✔ Where will you use *kanban* signals ?

✔ Where do supermarkets need to be located?

✔ What is the right lot size between processes?

✔ What is the standard shipping quantity for the customer?

✔ What is the pitch?

✔ What are the current setup times?

✔ How can schedules be smoothed at the pacemaker operation?

✔ How much time, of the available hours, is being used for production and how much is left over for changeovers?

After you've answered these questions and indicated the changes on the Future-State VSM draft, you can analyze the map and predict what the future-state process should look like. If you're using a software program, the lead time along the bottom will update as you change the information for the step in the value stream.

Figure 5-3 shows the Future-State VSM draft for the salad company. Note the changes. The company will first establish standards and improve the sched-uling for the preparation operations by implementing a supermarket and preparing for replenishment. By establishing standards and eliminating the push inventory, the company sees significant reductions in lead time. They move the labeling operation into the assembly process. They use universal UPC codes to eliminate the label-by-store sorting.

As with the Current-State VSM analysis, don't get stuck analyzing the poten-tial changes for your Future-State VSM. Lean is an iterative process. Identify what you want to improve, then improve it, and repeat the cycle. The Future-State VSM is a snapshot of where you want to go. Make the picture and move to *Kaizen* (Chapter 6).

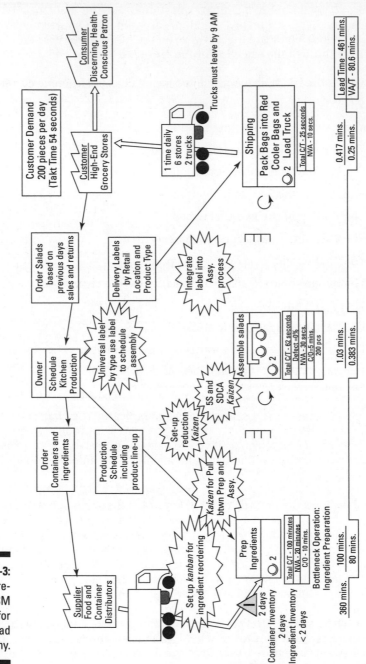

Figure 5-3:
The Future-State VSM draft for the salad company.

Answering real questions about Value Stream Maps

Value Stream Mapping is uniquely related to Lean. You typically don't encounter VSMs outside of Lean practice. If you're new to Lean, you'll naturally have questions. In the following list, we answer some frequently asked questions:

✔ **What makes a VSM so useful, as opposed to standard process-flow diagrams?** A process-flow diagram is a valuable tool for identifying resources and interfaces, but that's only part of the picture. A Value Stream Map is a more complete process flow — and it's customer-centric. The Value Stream Map, in one place, shows not only how material flows through the value stream, but also the information flow, takt time, bottleneck operations, operator location, size and type of inventories, modes of transportation, as well as the relationship of customers and suppliers along the whole value stream. The value stream is much more comprehensive than a process flow diagram.

✔ **Why create an Ideal-State Value Stream Map?** Creating an Ideal-State VSM encourages you to think outside the box, looking at the value stream with an objective viewpoint to identify breakthrough ideas. It opens up your mind to the possibility of dramatic innovation, sometimes referred to as *Kaikaku*. Although the main focus of Lean is in making regular, small, incremental improvements, if you never take the time to contemplate or dream of a radically different state, you'll be missing an opportunity for truly innovative improvement.

✔ **Where is the best place to start with Value Stream Mapping?** As always, start with your customer. If your customer is not the end consumer, you still start with your customer — but keep in mind how your processes are affected by the consumer. After you've identified the customer's requirements, work your way upstream.

✔ **What is the "right" level of detail?** There is no single "right" level of detail — it depends on your context and condition. The right level of detail is a balance between defining enough detail to find and eliminate meaningful amounts of waste and not having so much detail that you bog down and never move to the improvement phase. Value Stream Mapping is an iterative process, so with each pass through, you can add more detail as necessary.

✔ **What is the difference between the macro (or high-level) view of the value stream and the Value Stream Map?** The macro-level view is a diagram that shows you where your process fits in the overall value stream relative to the consumer and the first supplier of the rawest of raw materials. If you were to try to construct a VSM on a detailed level of the entire VSM, it would be unwieldy and you would never get to the improvement phase. With the simple macro diagram, you gain perspective.

✔ **Which is better: creating a manual VSM or using a software package to create the VSM?** Some experts would say that manual drawings are preferred, because they're simple, quick, and more visual for a team of people constructing the map. The tech-savvy people point to the transportability, versioning, attributing, and consistency of a software package. Although it takes some time to learn the software tools, they're easy to use and far better in the long run.

(continued)

(continued)

> *Warning:* Creating a Value Stream Map from behind the computer does carry with it one risk: You tend to map from the office and miss the opportunity to get out and walk the flow, observe the work first-hand, and interface with the people involved in the value stream. The most important thing is not the tool you use to create the map, it's the map! The only way to make an accurate map is to walk the streets.
>
> ✔ **How do I VSM the same product made in different places?** Start at one location and
>
> carry the knowledge to other facilities. As you form the team, include members from the other locations. When you *go to gemba* (where work physically is done.), include the other facilities to observe what variation exists in the process. Both of these steps will prevent the "not invented here" syndrome when you spread the knowledge across the organization. You're also more likely to create a blend of best-practice ideas to implement.

Creating the Mosaic of Continuous Improvement: Setting the Stage for Kaizen

Value Stream Mapping is part of a cycle and philosophy of continuous improvement. It may sound like it's a big effort — creating a Current-State Map, then an Ideal-State Map, then a Future-State Map draft, and finally a Future-State Map that you can actually implement. You may feel like you need to command significant resources to bring a team together, analyze all the data, brainstorm all the ideas, and involve all the different perspectives. You may be thinking you're developing a new career in cartography with all these maps! But the role and purpose of Value Stream Mapping is not about conducting huge efforts, big projects, and long implementation programs. Value Stream Mapping is a concise effort, performed in a short time-span of just a few days.

Looking toward the annual horizon

Take the improvements that you identified on the future-state VSM, and establish implementation priorities and a plan. The plan should be concise — just a few pages, no frills — a brief look at the year ahead. Scope individual improvement activities to days, weeks, or months, depending on the complexity of the activity. The plan should be a list of the projects that you will complete, with timing and responsibilities clearly defined.

To maintain the proper scope and focus of your future-state plans:

✔ Address a minimum number of key metrics for improvement. Don't try to solve all the problems at once.

✔ Prioritize changes that are most meaningful to the customer.

✔ Make the project just large enough to be meaningful and measurable.

✔ Remember that you're going to be doing it again!

How often should you revisit the Future-State Value Stream Map? Revisit your Future-State Value Stream Map at least every six months, and revisit your Ideal-State Value Stream Map annually. You don't have to go through the entire Current-State–Ideal-State–Future-State Map exercise each time you make a change to the current state. The emphasis is on the improvement, not the mapping exercise. If you have completed all your planned improvements before six months, then create a new future state VSM.

Some organizations have multiple continuous-improvement initiatives, such as Lean and Six Sigma, occurring at the same time. Include your Lean activities in your annual plan under a continuous-improvement banner.

Future-State implementations

After you have the maps and the plan, you're ready to implement. In Chapter 6, we show you how to implement Lean projects. At this juncture, you may be wondering, "What happens to the maps as I make improvements?"

✔ **Update the Current-State VSM to reflect the new state as you make improvements.** Not everyone does this, but it's good configuration-management practice. It's like updating the current state to a new standard. It also gives you a record of where you are on the way to your goal. Keep a copy of your first Current-State VSM. Two or three years from now, you won't believe how much change you've made. The old maps are also good to have on hand so you can remind people just how far you've come.

✔ **Compare the new current state to the predictions on the Future-State VSM.** If you aren't on track, you may need to adjust your plan.

✔ **After all the ideas have been exhausted or you're at the end of a planning period, start the mapping process again.** Use the latest Current-State VSM, and move through the exercise of creating a new Ideal-State VSM and building the Future-State VSM.

As you execute the improvement plan, align the right tools with the improvements you intend to make. The Lean toolbox has many tools (see Part III). However, some of your improvements may be better suited using Six Sigma or other methodologies. Pick the right tool for the job.

Chapter 6

Flowing in the Right Direction: Lean Projects and *Kaizen*

Recognize that a Value Stream Map (VSM) is just that: a map. A VSM of the *current state* reveals what needs to be improved; a VSM of the *ideal state* shows you what paradise looks like. But a VSM does not tell you *how* to improve. If you were to take a trip, you would pack your map, but the map alone won't get you out of your driveway. You need to know the *how*s of the journey: modes of transportation, routes, timing, number of travelers, available resources, and so on. *Kaizen* is the how. *Kaizen* is the way you improve the value stream; it's practiced through a continuing series of workshops and projects.

Have you ever traveled so much that you're just as comfortable on the road as you are being at home? Experienced travelers reach a point where taking a trip is no big deal. They don't have to think about what they're going to pack, which bag they're going to take, how to make travel arrangements, or any other details. Traveling becomes second nature to them. As you travel down the road of Lean, a similar thing happens: The change is no longer a special event, but rather the very way you conduct yourself and your business. You begin to address problems continuously and to act in a Lean manner. You begin to behave in a Lean way. *Kaizen* is this way of life.

In this chapter, we tell you what *Kaizen* is, how to practice *Kaizen* in your own organization, and how to conduct *Kaizen* workshops and projects.

Kaizen: A Way of Life

Kaizen comes from two Japanese characters: *kai,* meaning "change," and *zen,* meaning "to see, or to gain wisdom from doing." Combined, these two characters mean "change for the better or continuous improvement."

The goal of *Kaizen* is to eliminate waste in the value stream. You accomplish that through performing just-in-time delivery, leveling production, achieving standardized work, pacing (takt time) of moving lines, right-sizing of equipment, reducing inventory and work-in-process, and more. The reason you do *Kaizen* is to improve quality and safety and to reduce cost.

Although *Kaizen* has typically been practiced in the West more simply as an improvement workshop or event, true *Kaizen* is a way of life. It governs everyday thinking and business. *Kaizen* is a regular, daily activity that considers the process as well as the results. It examines the big picture and takes in the whole of the environment, as well as the immediate issue at hand.

Kaizen respects people first. Equipment, facilities, processes, and technology are tools — and they're subordinate to people. *Kaizen* focuses on humanizing the workplace and eliminating hard — both mental and physical — work. It never blames or judges people for the mistakes of the past, because blaming is wasteful.

Kaizen involves everyone, at all levels, and is not relegated to an isolated function or specialty. Although the framework for *Kaizen* is usually structured at the individual or group level, everyone — from the CEO to the last office worker or factory worker — practices *Kaizen*.

Kaizen: The philosophy

Kaizen is a philosophy of improvement that encourages continuous, incremental changes in life across all aspects — personal, social, work, home, play. *Kaizen* means not letting a day pass without some form of improvement. Western philosophy might be summarized as "If it ain't broke, don't fix it." By contrast, *Kaizen* says that even if it isn't broken, it can — and must be — improved. Do it better and make it better. The alternative is stagnation and decline.

As a work philosophy, *Kaizen* is continual, incremental change in all areas — large and small, internal and external — that improves the whole organization. Business *Kaizen* considers the entire system of the business; improvement activities at all levels are conducted with a systems view. The business philosophy of *Kaizen* also calls for an unending effort for improvement that involves everyone in the organization — managers and workers alike.

The philosophy of *Kaizen* in business concentrates on the processes that influence the outcomes — cause and effect. The *Kaizen* philosophy also sees the business through two lenses: setting new standards and maintaining existing standards. More specifically:

- ✔ ***Kaizen* maintenance** establishes the policies and rules that help maintain the performance levels set by the present managerial and operating standards.

- ✔ ***Kaizen* improvement** focuses efforts on the continuous improvement of existing standards and processes or the innovation of new ones.

Kaizen has been attributed as the basis for the many successes of the Japanese in global automotive, electronics, and other business and consumer markets. In Japan, *Kaizen* is the overarching strategy for business. Everyone is encouraged to make regular suggestions for improvements. In companies like Toyota and Canon, 100 suggestions *per employee per year* are defined, written, shared, and implemented. That's two per person per week! And these suggestions aren't limited to anyone's specific work area. *Kaizen* is based on making changes anywhere that they might lead to business improvement.

Kaizen in action

Kaizen requires involvement of everyone — from the CEO to the last office or factory worker. But everyone's role is not the same. At each level of management, the roles and responsibilities of *Kaizen* are different:

- ✔ **Senior management is responsible for defining the *Kaizen* organization, setting goals, and creating the culture in which *Kaizen* can thrive.** Wherever *Kaizen* requires investment and innovation, senior management's role is to provide the resources required for implementation.

- ✔ **Middle management is required to ensure that the employees have the skills, materials, and tools to perform *Kaizen*.** They ensure that *Kaizen* is occurring across functions in the organization and achieving the goals. They also implement *Kaizen.*

- ✔ **Supervisors make sure that *Kaizen* is occurring on both an individual and a workgroup level.** Supervisors also ensure that the standard operating procedures and practices are being followed. Supervisors train employees and foster morale. They provide their own *Kaizen* suggestions.

In addition, all members of management must practice *Kaizen* themselves. They show leadership by doing.

In the following sections, we present the Lean definition of waste, introduce the Plan-Do-Check-Act cycle used in *Kaizen,* and review the foundations of *Kaizen* implementation.

Eliminating waste

Kaizen focuses you on eliminating waste in the value stream. When you examine the value stream in small increments, you see waste that you may not have seen before. Through the lens of *Kaizen* glasses, you suddenly see the extra movement, the work that can be done more efficiently, or the effort that doesn't truly transform the product or service.

This waste may be the result of people and systems that are not performing to the established standards and practices, or you may need to define improved standards and practices. In either case, when you eliminate this waste, you improve not only the value stream, but also the conditions for the people who work in it.

Examine your value stream for waste, or *muda,* created in these seven areas:

- ✔ **Transportation:** Is there unnecessary (non-value-added) movement of parts, materials, or information between processes?

- ✔ **Waiting:** Are people, parts, systems, or facilities idly waiting for a work cycle to be completed?

- ✔ **Overproduction:** Are you producing sooner, faster, or in greater quantities than the customer is demanding?

- ✔ **Defects:** Does the process result in anything that the customer would deem unacceptable?

- ✔ **Inventory:** Do you have any raw materials, Work-In-Process (WIP), or finished goods that are not having value added to them?

- ✔ **Movement:** How much do you move materials, people, equipment, and goods within a processing step?

- ✔ **Extra Processing:** How much extra work is performed beyond the standard required by the customer?

In addition to these seven "classic" areas of waste, Lean Master Shigeo Shingo defined an eighth form of waste: the underutilization of people. While waiting is part of the underutilization, the eighth waste is more about not allowing your people to contribute fully their talents, ideas and energy to their work environment. When you don't capitalize on your human capital, you are missing out on a lot of opportunities for improvement. How can you better engage your people in continuous improvement?

Examine each of these forms of *muda* from the basis of existing operating standards and practices. Are the standards defined? Are they followed? If not, *Kaizen* compels you to implement training and support in order to perform to established standards. If waste is occurring in these areas, despite performance to standards, *Kaizen* requires you to define and implement improvements.

Using the Plan-Do-Check-Act cycle

The Plan-Do-Check-Act (PDCA) cycle is the Lean operating framework — the methodology for implementing *Kaizen*.

The PDCA cycle was first developed in the 1930s by Walter Shewhart, the Bell Telephone physicist often call the father of statistical quality control. PDCA was brought to Japan in the 1950s by W. Edwards Deming; in Japan, it's known as the Deming cycle. Alternatively, it is referred to as Plan-Do-*Study*-Act (PDSA).

Here's what the four parts of the PDCA (or PDSA) acronym mean:

- **Plan:** Create a plan for change, identifying specifically what you want to change. Define the steps you need to make the change, and predict the results of the change.

- **Do:** Carry out the plan in a trial or test environment, on a small scale, under controlled conditions.

- **Check or study:** Examine the results of your trial. Verify that you've improved the process. If you have, consider implementing it on a broader scale; if you haven't, go back and try again.

- **Act:** Implement the changes you've verified on a broader scale. Update the standard operating procedures.

Standardizing work

Kaizen requires you to have standards — standard specifications, standard processes, standard systems, standard procedures, standard work instructions, and so on. All work should be measured and performed to standards. After you implement any improvement, you must standardize to perform consistently to this improved state.

But what if you don't have standards in place to begin with? Because *Kaizen* requires standards, where do you start? The answer is Standardize-Do-Check-Act (SDCA). A variation on the PDCA cycle (see the preceding section) is SDCA, where the *S* stands for *standardize*.

Use the SDCA cycle whenever you need to establish initial standards and stability within a process. After you've reached the first threshold of standardization, you can apply the PDCA cycle. Standardization occurs in all aspects of the process — man, machine, methods, systems, materials, measurement, and environment.

Innovating with Kaikaku

Kaizen is generally considered to be steady, incremental change. But what if there is a need for fundamental change, dramatic improvements, or a new system? When more radical change or innovation is required, *Kaizen* takes a different form, called *Kaikaku,* or "radical change." (*Kaikaku* is also sometimes known as *breakthrough Kaizen, flow Kaizen,* or *system Kaizen*).

Kaikaku innovation still uses the PDCA/SDCA methodology, but to solve bigger problems. Other, more sophisticated or new methods are also appropriate. Seek inspiration from other applications, environments, or industries, and use new technologies or apply the results of new discoveries.

Here's an example: *Milk runs* for inbound product pickup are commonplace today; the materials are picked up on a regular schedule and routed from multiple suppliers by a single truck. When milk runs were first introduced, though, they were a radical departure from the commonplace method of receiving product shipments. The inspiration for milk runs came from the food industry; the innovation was developed by the manufacturing industry. The change was not implemented overnight; small-scale implementations were expanded to form a new business standard.

Improving the Value Stream with Kaizen

Kaizen improves the value stream by applying the Plan-Do-Check-Act (PDCA) cycle in the form of Lean projects. You'll find improvement opportunities across the entire value stream, but you prioritize and select projects based on their impact to customer value. The goal is to make regular, steady, incremental improvements, as opposed to large, breakthrough changes.

A common problem in *Kaizen* is oversized projects. Either you've selected too large a project, or you've allowed the project scope to creep up to an unmanageable size. To avoid oversized projects, focus on eliminating a single form of waste at a time, rather than multiple forms or all seven forms (see "Eliminating waste," earlier in this chapter) at the same time. Don't try to fix the entire value stream in a few projects.

Selecting projects

Kaizen projects can be performed at three different levels: the individual level, the team level, and the management level. You can perform a Lean project as part of routine daily business, as part of an improvement initiative, or as part of a formal workshop. The overall scope of the project depends on the size and type of waste you're targeting for reduction.

Select your projects based on a combination of several factors. Begin by analyzing the VSM and selecting the biggest contributing problem areas. Then, employ both qualitative and quantitative measures to seek out the data that highlights the key issues, particularly through direct customer feedback.

Finally, use your experience to target the waste areas for improvement. Initial projects should be ones that will be highly visible to the customer and will make a significant impact on the business; these characteristics will create momentum for a Lean transformation.

Many Lean companies also have a suggestion program for identifying projects. In Japanese companies, these can be prolific sources of project ideas. The ideas can come from anywhere, but usually they begin from within local areas or workgroups.

Lean projects are mostly focused on eliminating one or more of the seven forms of waste (TWO DIME), or *muda, mura,* and *muri* (see "Eliminating waste," earlier in this chapter).

Take before and after photos of the physical aspects of the problem you're addressing. These photos will give you an objective visual record of the improvement and help you to realize how far you've come.

Project methodology

Lean projects follow the simple but specific framework of the PDCA cycle. The level of depth, as well as measurements, analyses, and controls may vary, but the foundational methodology is the same. After you've defined the project scope, begin the project cycle.

Within the *Kaizen* methodology, one critical rule is that you must go to *gemba* — the Japanese word that means "where all activities are taking place." According to *Kaizen* Master Masaaki Imai, *gemba* is where customer value is added in the value stream. *Gemba* is the most important place for management. Imai urges all managers to go to *gemba*.

The Plan Phase

During the Plan Phase, you objectively describe the change you want to make in order to address the problem identified by the selection process. Include the following:

- An identification of what processes you intend to change
- The steps needed to make the change in both the prototype/test and production operation environments
- A prediction of the results of the change

Use the same quality data and analysis tools to support the plan development.

What to expect: The project individual or group evaluates the situation using the data, as well as personal — and sometimes, physical — evaluations. They determine the changes that they intend to make, the steps needed to make those changes, and the measurements they'll take to confirm the proper effects of the change. They predict performance targets and create an action plan that includes the definition of who makes the change, what is to be done, and when it will occur. They identify the required resources. Normally, the individual or project group will make the changes themselves, but sometimes outside resources are required. If a physical layout or a work area will be changed, then before and after layouts are constructed during the Plan Phase.

The Do Phase

The Do Phase is simply an implementation of the plan in a trial or prototype environment — on a small scale and under controlled conditions.

What to expect: Select a proper test or prototype environment. It should be small enough that you can conduct the test quickly, but large enough that the outcomes are statistically significant and representative. Be sure to identify the differences between the test and target environments so that you can properly extrapolate the results.

The Check or Study Phase

In this phase, you're examining the results of your trial or prototype. Quantify the degree to which the changes you made improved the trial process, and predict the extrapolation of these results to the greater process.

What to expect: The project individual or group reviews the trial data and determines whether the change is a valid improvement — using statistical methods if possible. If the trial objectives were met, then the project proceeds to the Act Phase. However, if the improvement was not sufficient, you may determine that the trial must be rerun, or may need to return to the Plan Phase. Because *Kaizen* calls for small, incremental improvements, you often decide to proceed, and afterwards enter the cycle again. If the trial failed outright, the project returns to the beginning for failure analysis and new planning.

The Act Phase

In this last phase, you implement the changes on the full scale of the process. Update the standards and specifications, and verify performance. Report the results.

What to expect: The project individual or group implements changes to all affected process people, systems, and technologies. They update all standard documents and procedures, including work instructions and visual controls, to reflect the change. Monitor the changes to ensure that the expected outcome is real and as expected. Finally, conclude with a final report or presentation to affected stakeholders and management.

Individual projects

Kaizen philosophy empowers every employee to improve her work area, as well as suggest improvements in any other work area. With such grand empowerment comes the rightful expectation that every employee will also participate in the improvement of those work areas. In a *Kaizen* environment, employees implement the ideas.

Kaizen calls for small, incremental improvements to the value stream. *Kaizen* at the individual level is often related to improvements in an individual's work area, or in how the individual performs her work. These changes are normally very low-investment ones that the individual implements herself on a regular basis.

Think *MacGyver*. He was that character on a U.S. TV program by the same name in the 1980s. With a piece of dental floss, a chunk of wood and a wad of gum, he could always create something to escape from the tight spot he managed to find himself in on every episode. At the individual level, *Kaizen* is done the same way.

Even at the individual level, the project follows the same PDCA cycle, using the same measurement and analysis tools. Individual projects are usually focused on the direct work area and responsibilities of the individual. The duration of individual projects is shorter than the duration of group projects; individual projects are often completed in a matter of days. If the job being studied does not occur on a daily basis or is highly complex, then the duration may be longer.

Although Lean is a disciplined system, it's also a creative system. *Kaizen* sets the stage for creativity to shine through. *Kaizen* enhancements can be as simple as creating a fixture from a piece of wood to perform an operation, outlining the shape of your tools on a tool board so you can see that all of the tools are present, or adding a guide to more quickly align and staple a stack of papers.

Group projects

Kaizen projects performed at the self-directed group level are also known by the Japanese term *jishuken*. They follow the PDCA cycle, but the scope is typically much larger than the scope of projects performed at the individual level. Group projects may last weeks or even months. Observing the process, collecting the data, identifying the form of waste, defining and implementing the improvements, measuring the results, and standardizing the new work — it all takes time.

Management projects

Management projects usually address strategic issues, administrative processes, cross-functional problems, or support systems. They tend to be technical and complex in nature. Their aims are to:

- ✔ Reduce bureaucracy within the organization and its systems.
- ✔ Ensure that the measurement and business systems support a Lean enterprise.
- ✔ Ensure that requisite facility improvements are in place.

Management projects are commonly conducted by task forces and cross-functional teams. They usually require a higher technical or engineering expertise. These projects follow the PDCA cycle but may use more advanced statistical methods and simulations.

Work team projects

A work team that dedicates part of its normal working time to *Kaizen* can tackle a Lean project. A work team project involves and affects the whole team, not just an individual. Work team projects are usually self-directed, with the manager or supervisor advising team, instead of leading the project.

Work-team project meetings follow the principle of standardized work:

- ✔ They have a timed agenda.
- ✔ The team uses tracking documents.
- ✔ Before and after pictures and charts track the team's progress.
- ✔ The team meets in an assigned area near the work space, *not* in a conference room!
- ✔ In the assigned meeting area, the team displays key data that it uses for its problem-solving and improvement efforts.

Although the work-team projects are usually larger and more involved, they still follow the small, incremental, low-investment model that the individual projects follow.

One of the challenges to work-team projects is that they can lose momentum and the team can become demotivated over time. The supervisor's job is to set goals for improvement, keep the team on track, and celebrate the wins. Management's role is to keep the supervisors on track.

Kaizen: The Workshop

One of the ways to quickly improve the value stream is through the use of the *Kaizen* workshop. Also known as a *Kaizen event* or a *Kaizen blitz,* the *Kaizen workshop* is a fast and furious run through the PDCA cycle, typically in five days or less. During the *Kaizen* workshop, the project team directly targets a specific area to find the *muda,* and remove the waste from the value stream. The source may be anything — quality, communications, changeover time, organization, and so on — but the workshop process you follow and your end goals are the same.

In order to focus properly on the workshop, the project team halts its normal work completely and does not produce its normal product or service. Advanced planning is required to ensure that your customers, as well as other areas of the business, are not adversely affected while the improvements are being discovered and implemented. *Kaizen*-workshop solutions are famous for requiring minimal investment and yielding great benefits to the value stream.

Most people think of a production or manufacturing area when they think of a *Kaizen* workshop, but remember that *Kaizen* is for everyone in every area of the business. The Wiremold Company, which has long been held as a pinnacle of Lean success, understood that every area benefits from *Kaizen*. They even held a *Kaizen* event on the trunks of their salespeople's cars!

Planning the Kaizen workshop

A successful *Kaizen* workshop requires the right project scope, with the right team, working full-time together for three to five days. To pull this off requires planning. In this section we will tell you how to scope a *Kaizen* project, select the right team and follow the workshop agenda.

Kaizen workshops interrupt operations for a few days. With proper planning this doesn't have to be a problem. Depending on the current situation, inventory may exist to cover the days that the area will not be producing. If the inventory does not exist, coordination within the organization must occur to protect the customer deliveries.

Workshop scope

In most cases the team starts with the Current-State VSM already completed. The successful workshop has a clear focus and baseline metrics established before it begins. These, along with customer satisfaction, quality, and operational data, help decide where to focus the *Kaizen* efforts. If the area has never experienced a *Kaizen* workshop, focus first on *5S* (see Chapter 8).

The initial *Kaizen* workshops ought to be conducted where the work occurs and be scoped to have a significant impact. The best *Kaizen* workshops are those that solve a nagging issue (especially one directly related to the customer) or otherwise accomplish something believed to be impossible (such as reducing machine setup time from days to minutes).

Make sure you take several before photos of the area being improved, even office areas. Those photos are a great way to show how far the *Kaizen* journey takes you — like vacation photos!

Workshop project team

The *Kaizen*-workshop project team is cross-functional, consisting of members of senior management, the value-stream owner, people who work in the area, representatives from support functions, and usually even a few people from elsewhere in the company who are unrelated to the area.

You may wonder why a *Kaizen* workgroup contains people from unrelated areas. Isn't it a waste of their time? The answer is a resounding "no!" The role of the unrelated team member is to ask the innocent and objective questions that make the team think in new ways. The outsider provides valuable experience and perspective to those who might wonder what's happening elsewhere in the business.

Companies that have been very successful implementing Lean have had members of the leadership team, if not the CEOs themselves, conduct the initial *Kaizen* workshops. Leadership must take a very active role in the *Kaizen* process, demonstrating the support and commitment for the transformation, as well as creating relationships with employees whom they might not otherwise meet. At the same time, it's critical for leadership to "authorize" change — not dictate change. Leadership does not have all the answers; their role is to "lead." The people who make the product or provide the service are those closest to knowing what has to be done to eliminate waste. Leadership's job is to empower the employees and support change.

Including people on the *Kaizen*-workshop team from unrelated support functions will give the team a set of fresh eyes. It also gives the team a greater understanding of the business and how their contribution affects other areas.

The *Kaizen* workshop usually lasts from three to five days, depending on the experience level of the team and the number of hours per day that the workshop lasts. If there are multiple shifts, the *Kaizen* should not only include representation from all shifts, but also occur during part of each shift. Although standards are in place, depending on how disciplined the organization is, you usually find that different shifts do different things.

A typical agenda

The agenda for the *Kaizen* workshop is prescriptive and deliberate. Table 6-1 shows a sample agenda, indicating the major activities that occur during the workshop.

Table 6-1	The *Kaizen* Workshop: A Typical Agenda	
Day	*Theme of the Day*	*Topics and Activities Addressed during the Day*
1	Training	Train on Lean concepts and principles.
		Create team connection and interaction. (team building)
		Train on the seven wastes
		Review the Value Stream Map.
		Train on data-gathering tools and continuous-improvement tools
		Complete pre-*Kaizen* metrics.
		Plan for Day 2.
2	Current-state analysis	Analyze current process.
		Brainstorm improvements.
		Design new work methods.
		Plan for Day 3.
3	Process implementation	Implement 5S.
		Establish one-piece flow.
		Implement process changes — participants do the hands-on work.
		Instruction of changes
		Identify additional improvements.
		Pilot changes in work area.
		Play for Day 4.

(continued)

Table 6-1 *(continued)*

Day	Theme of the Day	Topics and Activities Addressed during the Day
4	Observe and refine	Validate Day 3 improvements.
		Verify full-rate production.
		Refine improvements.
		Establish standard work.
		Plan for Day 5.
5	Sustain and celebrate	Establish visual controls.
		Complete all changes to standards.
		Establish follow-up plan.
		Complete post-*Kaizen* metrics.
		Present the results and celebrate.

Conducting the Kaizen workshop

After you have your plan in place, it's time to rock and roll. The team members work hard during the workshop, doing work that is not normally in their job descriptions and making a lot of improvements to the value stream in a short amount of time. In this section we tell you what to activities to expect and remind you to celebrate your successes.

Workshop activities

Have you ever watched one of those home-improvement makeover shows, where the homeowners, with the help of a design team, remodel a room in a house over a weekend? Or an organization show, where they take a few junk-laden rooms in a house and make the owners get rid of 90 percent of the contents? Whether they realize it or not, these shows are doing *Kaizen* events in these people's homes. They're implementing 5S (sort, straighten, scrub, systematize, and standardize). They work long hours in a short time and, at the end of the show, there is a complete and amazing transformation.

Usually, the designer or show host asks the homeowner, "What is not working with this space?" Then they create a plan to address these issues. In this case, the homeowner is the customer. In the case of a work scenario, you have customer data that answers the "What's not working in this space?" question. It could be related to poor performance or, better yet, it could be related to new business. No matter what the focus, you as a team member will roll up your sleeves, get your hands dirty, work long hours, and do work that is dramatically different from your daily activities!

If the aim of the workshop is to free up floor space, then you'll be cleaning out the unnecessary items, like inventory, tools, boxes, and things that just don't have a real home in the area. The team creates a new process flow and rearranges the equipment as needed. Then the floor space is cordoned off to protect it.

Oftentimes multiple *Kaizen* workshops will create pockets of space, but not necessarily *usable* space. You need an overall plan for the facility to coordinate floor-space-clearing *Kaizen* workshops.

An automotive facility received new work into an already full plant. Through the implementation of multiple, coordinated workshops, it was able to create usable space. Over a six-week period, the customer was not impacted at all, yet 39 work areas were transformed over six weeks to create 60,000 square feet of usable space. All the teams participating in the *Kaizen* knew that free space needed to be created and why it needed to occur. The coordination among the teams working toward a common goal was the key to the success.

If the workshop is related to equipment downtime, then the team will usually clean the equipment. If it's appropriate, the team may paint the equipment a light color. If, for example, the team is working on a stamping press; the new paint provides a clean surface for all to see leaks or other issues. They use maintenance data and history to investigate the issues. They may examine spare parts availability and inventory. They establish a new preventive-maintenance standard. By the end of the workshop, a transformation will occur.

Celebrate the win!

By the end of the workshop, the area will be transformed and the team will be highly motivated. During the span of a few days, many changes will be incorporated, although there are usually a few items that remain open. The follow-up plan will enable the team to ensure that all the items are closed. All open items should be closed within 30 days of the workshop.

If the *Kaizen* is part of a coordinated effort, like in the automotive example, then not only celebrate the success of each step taken, but also celebrate with everyone when the collective goal has been achieved.

Sustaining the Kaizen-workshop gains

After the workshop is complete, one of the most important steps must occur: changing the standards to include the changes. Frequently, teams omit this vital step, causing the gains to be short lived and many of the benefits to be lost. The supervisor is responsible for ensuring that the standards are being followed. The employee is responsible for executing to the new standards. This concept of shared responsibility should be built during the workshop.

If the workshop was aimed at clearing out floor space, then one technique to consider is constructing a barrier around the new space. Put a sign in the area communicating why the space was cleared out. Monitor the area to make sure that "mysterious" items don't suddenly appear to fill the space again. If you aren't diligent, the space will fill up again.

 Establish weekly and monthly (7-day, 30-day, 60-day, and 90-day) verification points to ensure that the changes are functioning in a regular daily environment as designed. Schedule reviews with management, particularly if you need them to provide resources. When all of the items are complete, conduct a final review session of what was accomplished and what results were achieved. Did you achieve the goals and objectives laid out at the start of the *Kaizen*? This communication is vital to securing management support for sustaining the improvements, and garnering their commitment to do more *Kaizen* workshops.

Part III
The Lean Toolbox

"We're using just-in-time inventory and just-in-time material flows, which have saved us from implementing our just-in-time bankruptcy plan."

In this part . . .

You develop the Lean lifestyle for your business with tools that facilitate customer understanding, value, flow, pull, perfection, and leadership. In this part, we tell you about the tools in the Lean toolbox and how best to apply them on your Lean journey.

Chapter 7

Customer and Value-Stream Tools

· ·

In This Chapter

▶ Looking at customer focused tools

▶ Using value-stream tools

▶ Working with basic process tools

· ·

*N*o matter where you work or play, having the right tools for the job is important. Imagine trying to play a round of golf with only a driver, or scaling a mountain in flip-flops. You wouldn't. To maximize your performance and results, you would get the right "tools" for the job, whether that job is a round of golf, a mountain trek, or a Lean transformation.

In this chapter, we introduce you to the tools that you can use to capture the customer's wants and needs, to evaluate the value stream, and to work with basic data. Along with the flow and pull tools described in Chapter 8, the perfection tools in Chapter 9, and the management tools in Chapter 10, these tools make up the overall Lean toolbox. You need all these tools to support Lean practices.

Communing with the Customer

In any business, really understanding who your customer is and what your customer is all about is vital — but this is particularly true for anyone embarking on a Lean journey. The tools in this section help you capture the voice of the customer, understand the customer's wants versus needs, and evaluate the competitive marketplace.

Capturing the voice of the customer

Not only do you need to know what the customer wants, but you have to translate that information into language that the various parts of the organization can understand — and use. The *house of quality,* also commonly referred to as Quality Function Deployment (QFD), is a key tool to make the translation. This tool is a sophisticated product-planning matrix.

The house of quality is really more like a *neighborhood* of quality by the time you're finished with it! Each matrix defines the relationship between what you're trying to accomplish and how you'll accomplish it. Figure 7-1 shows the interrelationship of the houses of quality, outlined here:

- ✔ The first house translates the voice of the customer (VOC) into functional requirements.

- ✔ The second house translates the functional requirements into product-design requirements.

- ✔ The third house translates product-design requirements into process-design requirements.

- ✔ The fourth house translates the process-design requirements into process-control requirements.

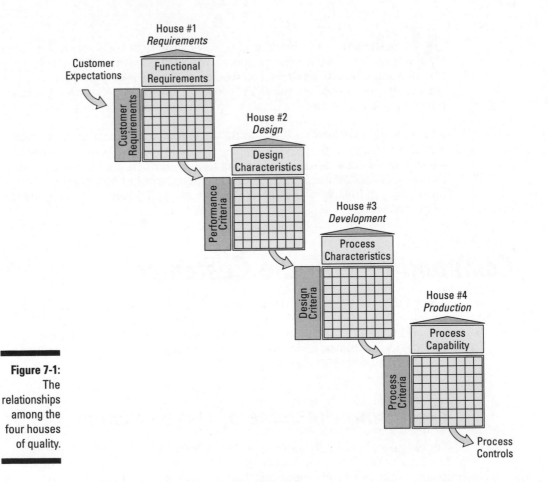

Figure 7-1:
The relationships among the four houses of quality.

You gather the VOC through various means, including customer surveys, focus groups, personal interviews, product clinics, warranty data, or third-party industry reports. Multifunctional teams work together to construct the various houses. Having marketing involved in the fourth house is just as important as having manufacturing involved in the first house — they keep each other honest. It's marketing's job to make sure the customer's voice doesn't get incorrectly translated into tech-speak, but it's everyone's job to understand the customer and how everyone impacts customer satisfaction.

Inside the interior of the house are a series of matrices. Figure 7-2 shows the interior floor plan of the house of quality. You construct from left to right. The filled circle indicates the strongest relationship; the open circle, a moderate relationship; and the triangle, a weak relationship.

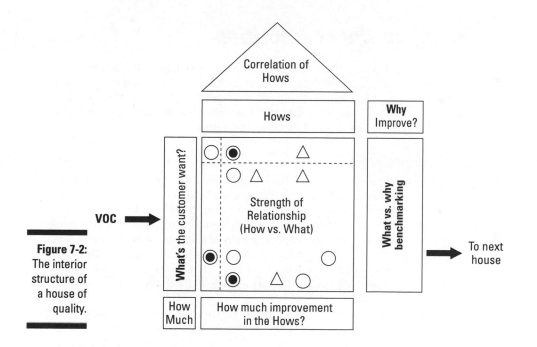

Figure 7-2: The interior structure of a house of quality.

Understanding customer satisfaction

Kano modeling is a way to differentiate the customer's needs, wants, and delighters. When you're capturing the VOC, the customer may not explicitly state all of their requirements. Kano modeling provides you with another way of understanding your customer (see Chapter 3 for much more on Kano modeling). Table 7-1 shows you an example of data for a Kano model.

Table 7-1	An Example of Kano Modeling		
Item	*Needs (expected requirements)*	*Wants (one-dimensional requirements)*	*Delighters (unexpected requirements)*
Hotel room	Bed	Nonsmoking	Free in-room WiFi
	Television	King-size bed	Free full breakfast
	Cleanliness	Fresh linens daily	Bottled water
	Safety	Specific room location	Coffeemaker

Sizing up the competition

Benchmarking is the process you use to compare your products, processes, or services usually against your direct competition. You can also compare against the best in the world in a given segment or activity. You may not be a retail store, but you can compare your customer service against the highly touted Nordstrom department store — and you should!

Benchmarking steps

The first step in benchmarking is to identify what you're evaluating (that is, the key characteristics of the activity, product, or service). Then you make your comparisons against your direct competition and the best in the world for that particular characteristic. Based on those comparisons, you evaluate how you perform, identify the gap, and then brainstorm ways to close that gap. You might try to directly copy and incorporate your findings into your process. You could create new ways to adapt their ideas to your system. Or your team could innovate to try to surpass the market standard.

Benchmarking is not a one-time process. The market is always changing and the competition is always on a quest to unseat the market leader.

Benchmarking in action

Nowhere is benchmarking more apparent than in the World Cup. Once every four years, the world stops to watch the top countries vie for the title of best of the best. Traditionally, Brazil has always been the one to beat; this soccer behemoth has dominated the game for decades. Although they may not always win, Brazil is always at the top of the list of the ones to watch.

In the two years prior to the finals, qualifying matches are played to narrow the field. During that time, all the coaches — from small Caribbean islands to the traditional powerhouses of Brazil, England, Germany, and Italy — are benchmarking their play and adjusting their strategies in hopes of qualifying their country's team for the finals. Table 7-2 shows average key metrics, from a sampling of five matches that they use to evaluate their team's performance.

Table 7-2	An Example Benchmarking Analysis					
Metric	*Benchmark*					*Your Team*
	Brazil	*France*	*Argentina*	*England*	*Italy*	*Team Dummies*
Average time of possession (in minutes)	49.00	42.00	47.34	47.16	44.61	38.00
Average goals per game	2.00	1.29	2.20	1.00	1.71	0.85
Average goals made by opponents per game	0.40	0.43	0.60	0.40	0.29	0.73
Average corner kicks per game	6.20	5.86	5.60	6.00	6.29	3.00
Average fouls committed per game	15.00	17.86	20.20	15.00	21.71	23.00
Total yellow cards over five games	11	16	12	9	11	21
Total red cards over five games	0	1	1	1	2	1

The benchmarking process does not end here. The coach and his staff must do something with the data to create change, improve skills, and modify strategy. These are the general steps they would follow and repeat continuously:

1. **Establish target performance goals for their team.**

2. **Study the competition (match films, player positioning, or training regimes).**

3. **Brainstorm ideas for improvement.**

4. **Create and implement a game plan.**

5. **Evaluate performance over a set period of time.**

Their overall strategy would address the fundamentals of running and kicking, how and where the bodies are positioned on the field, the array of players used, and which players occupy which positions. Their detailed game plan might include drills to improve free kicks, training sessions at higher altitudes or humidity levels to build up resistance for real game conditions, or experimenting with different players in different roles. The benchmarking process provides a foundation and direction for improvement.

When benchmarking the competition, you evaluate not only overall performance, but also the performance of the parts. The automotive industry for years has used *teardown rooms*. Within the room are a collection of the manufacturers' vehicles alongside vehicles from the competition. Typically, an entire vehicle is parked in front of tables full of disassembled components of the same model. Representatives from various functional areas spend hours evaluating the parts and the parts in context of the overall vehicle, in order to plan their next iteration of product or gain ideas to solve ongoing product issues. Teardown rooms are an effective strategy if your company is product based.

Working with the Value Stream

The customer-related tools help you understand what your customer wants. The value stream is how you provide goods and services to meet those needs. Chapters 4 and 5 cover the key tool for analyzing the value stream — Value Stream Mapping. The tools presented here are supplementary to the Value Stream Map.

Quantifying the value stream

When you're quantifying the value stream, three tools are beneficial. We cover each in the following sections.

Takt time

Takt time sets the pace for the value stream based on the customer demand. Takt time is the total net daily operating time divided by the total daily customer demand. (You can find out more about takt time in Chapter 4.)

Box scores

Lean box scores — like the box scores of professional baseball — summarize and track performance to key metrics. Table 7-3 is an example of a box score. (We discuss box scores in greater detail in Chapter 4.)

Table 7-3	An Example of a Box Score	
Metric	*Current State*	*Ideal State*
Total average value-added time	40.4 minutes	40.4 minutes
Total average non-value-added time	746.6 minutes	0 minutes
Total average lead time	787 minutes	40.4 minutes
Changeover time, between types	10 minutes	1 minutes
Actual cycle time	113 seconds	54 seconds
Takt time, seconds	54 seconds	54 seconds

Lead time

Lead time is the elapsed time for one item to make it through the system from the initial step to customer shipment (in manufacturing, from receipt of an order to the shipment of the product). Understanding the lead time and percentage of value-added time of a process is critical in Lean. Although this information is displayed on the Value Stream Map, teams have used a more simplistic tool to consider just the lead time.

The lead-time reduction chart is a simple ladder diagram. The chart is constructed top to bottom on a sheet of paper. The beginning of the process starts at the top of the page. The steps are listed in sequence, with non-value-added activities on the left-hand side and value-added activities on the right-hand side. The boxes are drawn in proportion to time, visually depicting the percentage of value-added and non-value-added time. Figure 7-3 shows an example lead-time reduction chart.

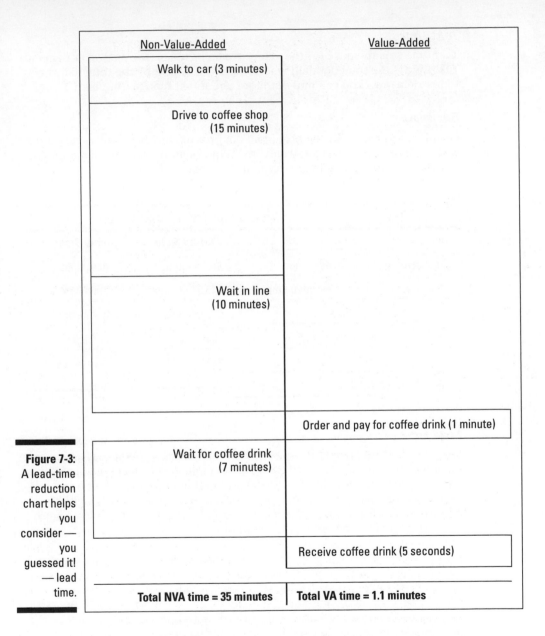

Non-Value-Added	Value-Added
Walk to car (3 minutes)	
Drive to coffee shop (15 minutes)	
Wait in line (10 minutes)	
	Order and pay for coffee drink (1 minute)
Wait for coffee drink (7 minutes)	
	Receive coffee drink (5 seconds)
Total NVA time = 35 minutes	**Total VA time = 1.1 minutes**

Figure 7-3:
A lead-time
reduction
chart helps
you
consider —
you
guessed it!
— lead
time.

After you make the lead-time reduction chart, you work to eliminate the non-value-added activities and minimize the time required for the value-added ones.

Making Woodward and Bernstein proud: Investigating your value stream like a reporter

Journalists learn early on the importance of asking the right questions. You start by covering all the basics, and then dive deeper to uncover the truth. When you analyze your value stream, be the ace reporter. In the following sections, we show you how.

The 5 Ws and 1 H

What, when, why, where, who, and how. Sounds simple enough. Yet time after time, teams don't have the patience to dig up the true answers to these questions when analyzing the value stream. Half of the equation is asking these key questions; the other half is really listening to the answer. After you've listened, ask clarifying questions to ensure that you truly understand what's happening in the value stream.

This tool is useful in many scenarios within Lean, whether you're proactively improving a situation or reactively solving issues.

Lean is a people-focused methodology. "Who?" is one of the questions, but it is not the first question asked nor is it the only question asked. Point and blame is *not* the name of the Lean game.

Spaghetti diagrams

Spaghetti Diagrams, also known as *layout diagrams,* are really helpful when you're analyzing the flow of traffic or movement. Think about the last time you misplaced something in your house. If you created a Spaghetti Diagram of that mad search to find that important paper or set of keys, it would look something like Figure 7-4.

This example may seem far-fetched, but most Spaghetti Diagrams look worse. People don't realize how much travel or movement is waste. Every day, people look for tools, information, and parts — particularly at the beginning of Lean, before standards are implemented and enforced. In the beginning, just mapping the movement is enough to show you where to start. As you progress, you can add more details, like the distance traveled.

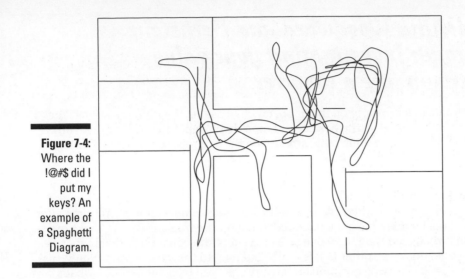

Figure 7-4:
Where the
!@#$ did I
put my
keys? An
example of
a Spaghetti
Diagram.

Spaghetti Diagrams are simple to make and very eye-opening. Here's how to make and use one:

1. **Get a layout or blueprint of the area.**

2. **Pick the subject to follow.**

   This subject can be materials or people.

3. **Record every movement of the target until it's finished.**

4. **When the diagram is finished, brainstorm ways to eliminate the excessive travel.**

5. **Improve the process or job design to eliminate the excess movement.**

   You may want to do this in a *Kaizen* event.

Using color can give your Spaghetti Diagram additional flavor. If you're tracking components and assemblies, you can use certain colors for components and others for assemblies. If you're mapping a work team, you can use one color for each team member or job function. You can see things like where how parts can end up in the wrong place or where people are crashing into or tripping over each other. This additional information will enable you to create better solutions.

Using Qualitative Tools

The Japanese Union of Scientists and Engineers (JUSE) was influential in defining a set of basic tools that could be used for improving processes. These came to be known as the *seven tools of quality control* (see Chapter 9).

After establishing the seven tools of quality control, which were formal, statistical tools, JUSE established the *new seven tools* — a set of qualitative tools. The new seven tools are just as important as the original seven tools. The new seven tools are

- Relations Diagram
- Affinity Diagram
- Tree Diagram
- Matrix Diagram
- Matrix Data Analysis Chart
- Process Decision Program Chart
- Activity Network (Arrow Diagram)

These tools are especially good for qualitative data analysis. Although the names may sound complicated, most of these tools are easy to use. We cover them all in the following sections. If you want to know more about these tools, refer to Chapter 18. In particular, to see more examples, go to www. syque.com/quality_tools/toolbook/toolbook.htm.

Relations Diagrams: Relating to each other

You use a relations diagram when the interrelationships of a situation are complex. Through a network of boxes and arrows, you can analyze the complexities and interactions to arrive at solutions. Figure 7-5 shows the structure of a relationship diagram.

Like most tools in Lean, relations diagrams are best developed with multi-functional teams. In a group setting, sticky notes or index cards are great materials to use to construct the diagram. Here are the steps to creating a relations diagram:

1. **Describe the central issue.**

2. **Identify all the causes (one per box).**

3. **Group similar causes together.**

4. **Arrange according to cause-and-effect relationships.**

5. **Refine the causes (add, delete, reword, modify).**

6. **Indicate with arrows all the interrelationships.**

7. **Highlight the ones with strong or principal causal relationships.**

One type of relations diagrams is a *mind map*. Mind maps use minimal words and images to capture key information about a subject. Because of their visual impact, they're a highly effective method for depicting complex situations. The human brain records pictures and can more easily retain the information.

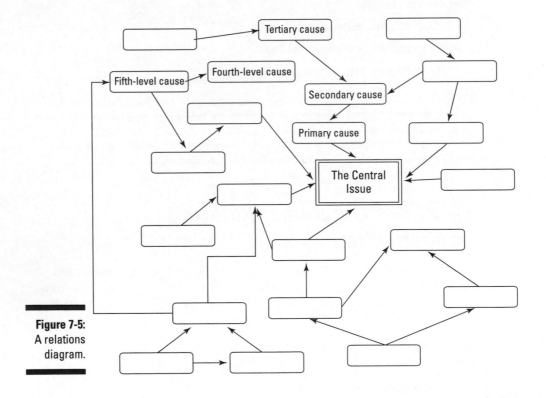

Figure 7-5:
A relations
diagram.

Affinity Diagrams: Like meets like

Affinity Diagrams are used to synthesize large amounts of verbal information, particularly in conjunction with brainstorming sessions. Using Affinity Diagrams, teams grasp the overall situation, classify the assumptions behind it, and better understand the unique perspectives of the team members.

After identifying a central theme for a problem, the individual ideas are written on cards or sticky notes, one idea per card. Place the cards on a wall and organize them into themes. Write an *affinity card* — a title or label for the theme. Then arrange the ideas within a theme into similar subcategories. Create an affinity card for each subcategory. After all the ideas have been assimilated into a theme or discarded, the diagram is finished. Figure 7-6 shows the structure of an Affinity Diagram.

Tree Diagrams: From trunk to leaves

A *tree diagram,* also known as a *work breakdown structure,* is a tool used to break down something into progressively smaller parts, making it easier to understand and act upon. Whether you're designing software, constructing a house, or planning a gala, this tool will help you eat the elephant one bite at a time.

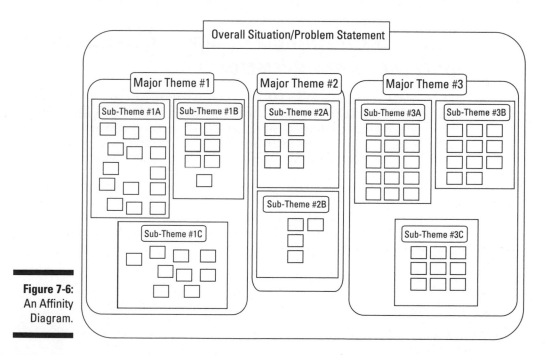

Figure 7-6:
An Affinity
Diagram.

At the top of the diagram, you place the overall issue — such as "build the house." In the next level down, you identify the major components that make up the overall issue — excavation, foundation, framing, drywall, electrical, plumbing, and so on. Then, under each of these, you identify the key components over and over again until you've identified the lowest-level activity or element.

In Chapter 3, the high-level view of the premade salad value stream shown in Figure 3-4 is one example of a tree diagram.

Matrix Diagrams: Where information meets

The matrix diagram allows you to take two lists of information and depict the relationships of each individual element. The most commonly used form of a matrix diagram is the *L* shape. One list is displayed in a column on the left; in a row across the top, the other list is displayed. At the intersection of the column and row, the corresponding information is displayed. Two common examples of how a matrix diagram looks are multiplication tables or city-to-city distances on a map. In Lean, the central part of the interior house of quality (shown in Figure 7-2) is a matrix diagram showing the connection between *what*s and *how*s.

Matrix Data Analysis Charts: Comparing multiple characteristics

The Matrix Data Analysis Chart (MDAC) is used to compare multiple items to multiple characteristics. It's one of the most difficult of the seven new tools to use and it's frequently replaced with a prioritization matrix. Examples where MDAC could be beneficial are increased sales and increased customer satisfaction for a store or improved material performance while reducing costs.

Evaluate multiple items against the two chosen factors, like customer satisfaction and cost. Then plot each item on an *x–y* chart. When the plot is finished, you'll see clusters of items in each quadrant. Focus on the items in the quadrant corresponding to performance you desire (in this case, higher satisfaction and lower cost).

Process Decision Program Charts: Understanding and mitigating risk

The Process Decision Program Chart (PDPC) is used to understand risk and mitigate it through the implementation of countermeasures for any situation. The structure of the PDPC is a tree diagram on its side, flowing from left to right. So for each activity of the tree diagram, you identify possible risks and for each risk you identify one or more countermeasures. Ideally, these countermeasures prevent the problem from happening.

The PDPC is a great tool for new situations like new products, facilities, or lines of business. In one chart, you can see your entire risk picture. It's useful for the development of Failure Mode Effects Analysis, a perfection tool (see Chapter 9).

Activity Networks or Arrow Diagrams: Networking activities

Activity networks, also known as arrow diagrams or PERT charts, are used to map a series of activities, including timing, critical path, and dependency information. You can very clearly see the critical operations that need to be monitored within the operation.

Most people who are building a house expect the contractors to take months. The different skilled trades need to be scheduled in a particular order to complete their tasks, and each task has a specific duration. This process is full of waiting and waste. Now it may happen through the magic of television, but one television show (ABC's *Extreme Makeover: Home Edition*) has managed to take a process normally lasting months — demolition and construction of a house — and accomplish it in one week. You can only imagine the activity network required to manage all the volunteers and tradespeople needed to build a house in a week!

Working with Software Tools

Lean practitioners regularly debate the best way to gather data and create initial charts in a team environment — manual versus computer-generated. Most teams find it easier to maintain their data and analysis with software tools. Several programs exist to aid in the creation of Value Stream Maps, houses of quality, and data analysis charts.

Lean practitioners use both specialized and general-use programs. Programs like Visio enable you to quickly create Spaghetti, Arrow, and Affinity diagrams. Programs like iGrafx and Lean View have Value Stream Mapping capability. QFD/Capture is one of the better known house-of-quality construction packages. On the Internet, you can also find templates that function in Excel for everything from house of quality to Spaghetti diagrams. (See Chapter 18 for other places to go for assistance.)

Chapter 8

Flow and Pull Tools

- -

In This Chapter

▶ Preventing interruptions to flow

▶ Organizing the process for flow

▶ Orchestrating the material flow

- -

In Lean, the concepts of flow in the value stream, and pull from each customer through the value stream, are fundamental. Specific Lean tools help you implement the flow and pull techniques. These two toolsets are the subject of this chapter; use these tools to set the pace of your system and eliminate blockages to flow. Start with the flow tools. Applying the flow tools first clears out the obstructions and gives you a solid foundation upon which to create a *kanban*-based pull system using the pull tools.

Along with the customer and value-stream tools in Chapter 7, the perfection tools in Chapter 9, and the management tools in Chapter 10, these tools make up the overall Lean toolbox. You need all these tools to support Lean practices. To maintain balance in your overall system, you must use the full complement of tools in the Lean toolbox.

Attempts to implement Lean can fail because the organization tries to implement a tool in isolation and at the wrong time. This has been particularly true with pull signal tools. You can't use only one Lean tool like *kanban* and expect to be wildly successful. You have to look at your system as a whole. For example, a system plagued with defects or equipment outages will never be able to produce to a pull signal at a given takt. For this reason, success requires you to use all the tools, follow the principles, and apply the philosophies of Lean. No cherry-picking!

Flow

You can see the power of flow all around you. Traffic flows, unless it is rush hour, where the demand is exceeds the capacity of the road system, or someone has made a mistake and caused an accident. Music flows, as the musicians play together to a defined tempo; if one musician were to get out ahead or fall behind, the flow would be disrupted, and that disruption is the difference between beauty and cacophony. Skateboarders in a skate park flow for an awesome ride, as long as they stay in balance and there are no obstructions or defects in their path. In our bodies, blood flows as a life force, although we know that obstructions can be debilitating or even fatal.

In each of these examples, you can see how perfect flow achieves the goal, but also what happens when flow is interrupted. In Lean, eliminating waste is eliminating obstructions to flow — of people, products, services, information, or materials. In the examples in the preceding paragraph, you can see that flow is dependent upon all the elements of a system working in concert. When one part of the system is not functioning properly, you won't have flow. When all parts are working together, flow happens.

Establishing order through 5S

To establish orderly flow, start with the *5S technique* — eliminating waste by organizing the workplace. 5S is simple and practical, and is implemented in two phases. Phase 1: Get rid of all the junk! Stop working around it. Phase 2: Create a system so there is a place for everything and everything stays in its place.

Unless you have a very small facility, don't try to address the entire facility at once. You'll overwhelm everyone, and you risk not really eliminating items, but just shuffling them around. Before you start the 5S process, determine the bounds of the area you're addressing.

The five steps of the 5S process are:

1. **Sort.**

   Divide all the items in the workplace into three R categories:

   - **Retain:** Retain items that are essential to the functioning of the work area. These items fall into two main groups: regular use and occasional use.

   - **Return:** Return any items that belong to another department, location, supplier, or customer.

- **Rid:** Rid the area of all other items. Physically move them straight to the recycle bin or dumpster for disposal, or a staging area for immediate disposition. Note that any item located in the staging area must be tagged with clear information about its disposition.

  Isolate the *rid* items from the others. Red tags are particularly useful for items that the team wants to throw out, but that need some type of authorization for disposal. The tag should include the date it was moved to the area, the contact person and her contact information, the desired disposition, and the functions that need to sign off on the disposal. As a general rule, no item marked for disposal should remain in the staging area more than 48 hours.

2. **Straighten.**

   Find a place for everything and put everything in its place. Move the items that are always needed to where they're needed. Establish and delineate the standard location for every item. Label everything. Make it visual. Better yet, make it sensory. Move those items that are not needed on a frequent basis to a standard place, near the area — but not a place that could disrupt flow.

3. **Scrub.**

   Clean the entire area. Whether you're in an office, a kitchen, or a factory, this means deep-clean *everything!* If the area or equipment needs a fresh coat of paint, get out the brushes and the rollers. Cleaning is everyone's job — not just the janitor's or painter's. This step is important for several reasons:

   - People working in a clean area tend to have a more positive attitude and be more productive.

   - Clean equipment helps you to more quickly detect leaks and problems with equipment.

   - Clean and clear areas make safer work environments.

4. **Systematize.**

   Now that you've gone to the work of cleaning the area once, establish the schedules and systems to maintain the area regularly, just the way it is on the first day after you've cleaned it.

5. **Standardize.**

   Turn a one-time event into the way you conduct business. This step is the most difficult one, because you're creating new habits and levels of performance expectations. Forming new habits requires constant reinforcement and time, before the new habits become the standard.

Note: Some people have added a sixth *S — Safety*. Whether you call it out as a separate *S* or not, creating a safe work environment is basic to respecting people.

Housekeeping tours are a good way for management to accomplish several goals:

- ✔ Stress the importance of the orderly environment.
- ✔ Practice a form of standardized work.
- ✔ Connect with the organization.

Management tours should cover the entire facility, inside and out. Tours should not be ad hoc — they should follow a set process, with an established checklist of items to review, including an agenda and facility route, restroom visits, and safety equipment. Non-conformances should be recorded and addressed. On the next tour, these items should be followed up on. Refer to Chapter 12 for more information on *gemba* walks.

You'll encounter resistance to the long-term maintenance of the 5S results. Engineers who need to work with parts or highly creative types who need a little chaos to feed their creativity are some of the biggest resisters. You have to establish the standards for your organization. Some organizations require that desks are cleaned off every night; others have deemed this cleaning up at the end of the day as non-value-added. Both sides have merit. Determine what's right for your organization.

Take one, make one

The ideal state of Lean is continuous flow production, calibrated perfectly to the customer demand. When you can organize your work area and perfectly balance the operational times so that your document or widget is always in a state of value-added transformation, you've reached Lean nirvana. You may never actually get to this point, but you should never stop trying to get there. To do so, you have to think constantly about how you organize the value stream. The tools in the following sections will help you to move closer to the zenith of continuous flow.

Don't get hung up on the language of *continuous-flow production* or *single-piece flow*. The terms may have originated in a manufacturing environment, but they apply whether you're making products or providing services. You "flow people and information through a service process" just as you "flow material and information through a manufacturing process." In both cases, the goal is to things moving effectively — no stops for queues or inventory and no unnecessary movement or transport.

Finding common ground through group technology

Group technology is the process of identifying commonality in process through the analysis of all the products. Your aim is to identify product families. This information is used to reorganize how you do business.

The term *product* is used here generically, to refer to physical products as well as nonphysical items like software, transactions, and service processes (such as hospitality and healthcare). Refer to Chapter 15 for more on how services are like products.

To perform a group technology (GT) analysis, review all your products and the operational steps they require. A product family contains the same or highly similar operational steps. Table 8-1 shows a group technology analysis example. The shaded parts represent a product family because they pass through the majority of the same types of operations.

Table 8-1	All in the Family: A Group Technology Analysis						
Process Operation Types							
	Type 1	Type 2	Type 3	Type 4	Type 5	Type 6	Type 7
Part Number 16958439			X	X		X	X
Part Number 16980437	X		X	X		X	X
Part Number 17389433		X	X				X
Part Number 14967210		X	X		X	X	
Part Number 997325	X			X		X	
Part Number 26390548		X		X	X		X
Part Number 340955	X		X	X		X	X
Part Number 7304-4659-32	X		X	X		X	X

After you've identified all your product families, you can start to organize the areas that produce them by family rather than by operation function.

Organizations that have a low-volume, high-mix custom environment often struggle to see how group technology applies to them. Even if your product details are unique every time, recognize that at a macro level, your products pass through similar processing steps. You can use a sampling of past products to identify generic product families. Then when you spec out a new product, you can slate its production for a specific area.

Creating work modules or work cells

Traditional organizations are set-up by functional department, whether in the office or on a manufacturing facility. When you use in the results of your group technology analysis and reorganize your facility accordingly, you naturally reduce inventory, improve quality and communication, and save space. Similar benefits apply when moving office workers into modules. Each work module (or work cell) should contain all the functions required to make the product or complete the service.

Managing the monuments

A Lean work module contains all the operations that can be moved together into a continuous-flow arrangement. Sometimes you have fixed *monuments* (equipment or processes that cannot be moved or large-capacity equipment that services multiple product families). When this undesirable situation occurs, the flow is stopped.

Some options for managing the monuments include the following:

- ✔ Arrange affected work modules around the monument.

- ✔ Establish supermarkets (an in-process, controlled storage area) to create controlled storage and flow to the monument operation.

- ✔ Create continuous-flow work modules before and after the monument.

- ✔ Consider purchasing smaller, more flexible technology to achieve the same function, and then incorporate it into work modules.

Challenge your belief that there is nothing you can do about a monument. Ask yourself, "How can we do this operation differently?" For instance, one company thought its paint facility was a monument. After persistent questioning, it found a way to incorporate a lower-technology miniature paint booth into its work module. Through persistence and a new perspective, it lowered inventory, eliminated a paint line that required lots of maintenance and frequently broke, and improved quality defects related to inventory and in-facility transit.

Balancing the operations

The capacity of the cell is based on the collective demand of the customer for the product family as well as the capability of the team members. From the example of Figure 8-1, assume that the takt time is 60 seconds. Figure 8-1 shows a graph of operation times compared to takt time for this product family. In this case, independent of the part being made, operation times fall below takt time of 60 seconds. If operations exceeded takt time, you would consider additional capacity for the cell.

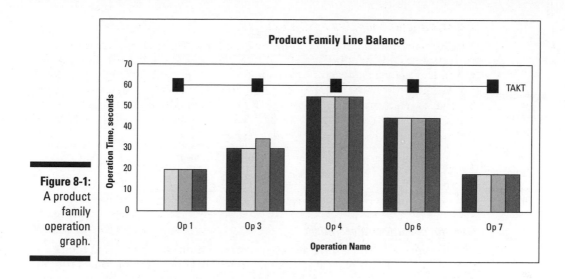

Figure 8-1:
A product
family
operation
graph.

Take the part number with the longest operation time and evaluate it for line balancing. You can then seek to combine operations 1 with 3 and 6 with 7, and still meet the takt time. Figure 8-2 shows the results. As you can see, the combination of operations 6 and 7 cause the cycle time to exceed the takt time. Figure 8-3 shows the final line balance. The work cell requires four operators to run five operations. Going forward, the team would then seek to reduce the time required to complete operations 6 and 7, by at least 3 seconds — the time to balance to the takt time — and enable the cell to run with three operators.

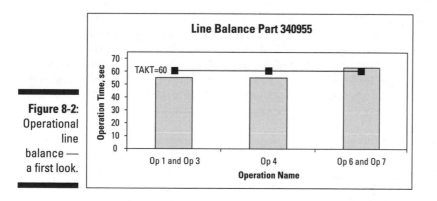

Figure 8-2:
Operational
line
balance —
a first look.

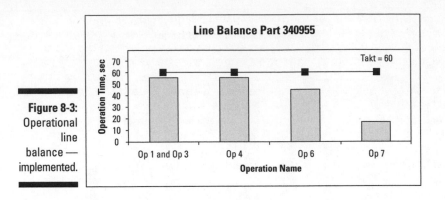

Figure 8-3:
Operational
line
balance —
implemented.

Identifying bottleneck operations

Within every cell, you'll have a bottleneck operation — the one that limits throughput and runs closest to the takt time. This operation becomes the critical operation to flow because there is no slack time or no option to add more people, if there is a machine issue. To identify the bottleneck, create a graph like the one in Figure 8-2 for all the operations in the value stream.

Storing at the point of use

Point of use storage (POUS) means you store what you need, in the quantity you need it, at or near where you use it. This storage should be incorporated into the 5S standards. You have to identify the bill of materials, quantity used, and size of each component in order to establish where you'll store each item, what type of container you'll use for storage, and where best to locate the items.

When establishing POUS storage and work module arrangement, remember to evaluate the ergonomic impact of the operators. Considerations like shelf heights, reach distances, standup versus seated operations, and maximum heights are among some of the critical characteristics to evaluate. Investigate current industry standards and governmental regulations for more information. (See Chapter 18 for resources.)

Understand bottlenecks, output, work balance, staffing, and storage requirements before you arrange the furniture. This information can be quickly gathered, analyzed, and understood. Failure to understand these foundational elements of your work cell will lead to ineffective modules — full of *muda!*

Arranging the work module

The recommended shape for a work module is a *U* shape, flowing counterclockwise. *U* shapes don't work in every application, but they're a good place to start. (The reasons for counterclockwise flow are numerous, but fundamentally, the right hemisphere of our brains process spatial relationships, so humans flow better to the left.) Specifically, the U shape provides a safer environment where maintenance and material replenishment occurs on the outside of the *U*. The people making the products are the only ones inside the *U*.

Create a layout before you start moving, to ensure everything fits in the space allotted. Depending on how difficult it is to move the equipment, you can use a layout tool like Visio or AutoCAD, scaled "paper-doll" cutouts of the equipment, or even full-size mockups of the module to establish the plan. If you've never created a work cell or work module before, and you have large pieces of equipment, like presses or molding machines, you'll want to use full-scale, three-dimensional replicas. This enables the team to ensure that the plan will work.

When you understand the foundational requirements of your work module, you're ready to set up the module. Figure 8-4 is an example of a work module layout.

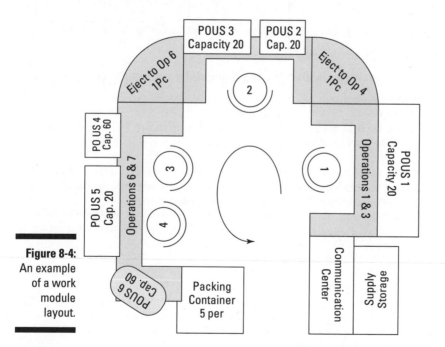

Figure 8-4:
An example
of a work
module
layout.

If this is your first module, start with a pilot or test module. This will help you learn, work out the bugs, and introduce the organization to the concept before you physically tear up the entire facility.

The use of *autonomation* (automation with a human mind), or *jidoka,* in a workstation has two benefits:

✔ Automatically unloading equipment enables an operator to do other tasks, instead of having to stand around until the machine has finished.

✔ Automation that stops equipment when defects or nonstandard conditions are detected prevents bad product from progressing through the value stream.

People in the process

Work modules are run by teams, sometimes referred to as *employee involvement teams.* These teams are usually autonomous, self-directed work teams. Often a team leader emerges or is named based on experience. The team leader is responsible for the execution and performance of the cell:

✔ Production output, quality, delivery, and controllable cost performance

✔ Line balancing

✔ Cross training and team behavior

✔ Performing *Kaizen* (regular improvements)

✔ Maintaining the work area (cleaning and daily equipment maintenance)

✔ Problem solving

Supervisors take on an advisory role and have more work teams reporting to them. The daily task load is shifted to the team.

When moving to a Lean work cell environment, the teams and the supervisors will need training in new skills — particularly the interpersonal skills of conflict resolution, teaming, coaching, and communication.

Orchestrating the operations

When evaluating each work station or work area within a work module, apply industrial engineering techniques like left-hand/right-hand analysis or Therblig analysis. Evaluating and standardizing the movements at a micro level will increase flow, eliminate waste, and improve the effectiveness of the operations. Improvement at a micro level will enable the team to shave off the four seconds needed to eliminate that fourth operator in the earlier example (see the "Balancing the operations" section).

Preventing blockages to flow

After you've created your work modules, you have to make sure that they continually run as designed. In other words, you have to eliminate any and all causes that prevent flow from happening — flow of quality, material, or equipment.

Ensuring quality at the source

In addition to the use of autonomation, you can establish quality at the source by using source inspection, progressive inspection, and *poka-yoke* (error-proofing).

Source inspection

Source inspection means you review your work before you pass it on to the next station. What you review, how you review it, and how much time it should take to review the work is identified as part of the standardized work for the operation. The benefit to source inspection is to identify, correct, and contain a problem before it enters into the value stream via the next processing operation.

Progressive inspection

Progressive inspection means that the operator reviews key characteristics of the product from the previous step before beginning a new transformational step. Once again, these inspection steps should be designed into the standardized work plan. Investing in critical inspection before any further work is performed protects the customer and minimizes the risk to the value chain.

Poka-yoke

Because inspection is a form of *muda,* a more certain and proactive type of quality at the source is error-proofing, known as *poka-yoke* or *mistake-proofing.* A *poka-yoke* is something in a product, process, or procedure that physically or procedurally prevents you from doing something incorrectly.

Examples of *poka-yoke* are everywhere. Whenever you fill up your car at a gas pump with both diesel and regular gas, you're using a *poka-yoke* device. The size of the diesel spout is larger than the gasoline spout, so the diesel spout can't fit in the regular gas tank opening — which prevents you from doing serious damage to your engine! Other examples include: electronic devices that only allow you to plug in a specific way; CDs that have writing on one side to visually cue you how to load them in the machine; and online surveys that have logic to check that you've answered all the questions before you can proceed to the next page.

In performing *poka-yoke,* begin by evaluating each operational step for common quality problems. Identify guides, gauges, or fixtures that will ensure the operation is done correctly every time. Follow the Plan-Do-Check-Act (PDCA) methodology to evaluate their effectiveness. Installing things on equipment or incorporating checklists into standardized work will help the situation, but the best way to error-proof is through the design of features in the product.

Design for Assembly and Manufacturability (DFA/DFM) is a methodology to identify ways to design in error-proofing and improve the ease of assembly. Performing Failure Mode Effects Analysis (FMEA) on the design and process (DFMEA/PFMEA) will help you to identify the risk and frequency of potential failures. With this information, you can prioritize your error-proofing efforts to mitigate risk.

Part of the foundation of Lean is respect for people. Don't use the term *idiot-proofing!* The proper terms are *poka-yoke, mistake-proofing,* or *error-proofing.*

Although error-proofing may seem like detailed, picky analysis, it could mean the difference between life and death. Consider, for example, two medications: They have similar names, and they're placed in almost identical packaging. If the manufacturer changed the container shape, size, or color so that the two medications were obviously different, the people in the hospital would be less likely to make fatal mistakes, by giving the wrong medicine to the wrong patient.

Figure 8-5 shows an error-proofing worksheet.

Devising flexible and reliable equipment

When you no longer can hide behind inventory and waste, the role of your equipment becomes more important. It must be ready and functioning properly when you need it. You'll also change how you design and purchase equipment for modular manufacturing: You want to find the smallest, simplest, most flexible equipment you can for the job. In order to make the full compliment of product mix every day, your equipment has to be able to be changed over very quickly.

Maintaining the equipment

Total Productive Maintenance (TPM) is divided into three areas:

- ✔ **Autonomous maintenance:** *Autonomous maintenance* means that the operations within the work module perform their own routine maintenance tasks. This frees up the more skilled maintenance trades to focus on the more specialized planned and predictive maintenance activities. Standardized work descriptions for the maintenance tasks including frequency are used by the operators to perform regular maintenance.

✔ **Planned maintenance:** Planned maintenance is vital in a Lean environment. You proactively schedule equipment to be taken out of service in order to replace major, high-risk, or high-wear components. As components are replaced, data is collected to develop predictive failure scenarios. You can use the data tools in Chapter 9 to understand the performance of the components from a statistical perspective. You then can use this information to create predictive maintenance routines.

✔ **Predictive maintenance:** When the maintenance organization arrives at a place where it can anticipate failures, it can better control costs and perform its maintenance activities at the right time, not just the scheduled time. Additionally, it can identify which parts and what quantity to keep in inventory for routine maintenance, planned maintenance, and emergency response.

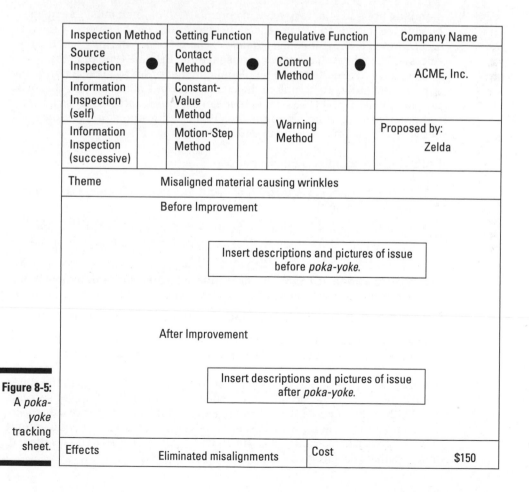

Figure 8-5:
A *poka-yoke* tracking sheet.

The aim of TPM is to maximize the Overall Equipment Efficiency (OEE) and minimize production losses due to equipment failure or malfunction. OEE is a performance metric tracked on the Balanced Scorecard, especially for manufacturing organizations. It is calculated like this:

$$OEE\% = \text{Availability} \times \text{Performance Rate} \times \text{Quality}$$

Even with the best TPM plan in the world, unexpected downtime will still happen. Create emergency response teams who respond at the flash of an *andon* light. These teams should have standardized work descriptions and diagnostic checklists to follow.

Mastering the quick change

What does an actor between entrances, a NASCAR team in the pits, and a stamping press in a factory have in common? All of them must use quick-change techniques to be successful. In Lean, quick changeover is known as *SMED,* which is short for *single-minute exchange of die.* In this case, the *die* refers to a machine that cuts or forms material in some type of press or a forging device. The die has to be reconfigured in order to make a new product, and the goal is to complete the changeover in 1 minute. From this original use, the term SMED has come to mean any quick setup process or other reduction of setup time. The aim is to minimize downtime or lost time between the end of one activity and the beginning of the next.

Here's how to organize a quick change:

1. **List all the steps, required tools, and materials to change from one thing to the next.**

2. **Identify which activities can be done before or after the change (offline, or external, activities) and which have to be done in the moment (online, or internal, activities).**

3. **Create standardized work for offline activities. Organize tools and material offline to support the online ones.**

4. **Refine and standardize the online activities to minimize lost time.**

5. **Constantly evaluate the performance of the overall changeover process to improve the performance time and eliminate waste.**

For the NASCAR pit crew, fractions of seconds in the pit can mean the difference between victory and defeat. For the theater actor, fractions of seconds can be the difference between a missed entry and a stellar performance. For the factory, implementing quick setup enables production of the full complement of products every day — ultimately the difference between a satisfied and dissatisfied customer.

Pull

We tell you about flow tools and pull tools in the same chapter because they work in harmony with one other to keep the entire value stream moving toward the customer at the rate the customer consumes. You can't have flow linked to customer demand without pull and vice versa. All the tools in this section make the system work better, with minimal waste.

Smoothing out the bumps

In order to provide the customer with what they want, when they want it, while keeping the value stream flowing at a steady pace, you need to smooth out the production schedules. This concept is known as *heijunka,* which means "production smoothing, leveling, or level scheduling." The concept is this: Instead of making large batches of one product, and then storing them in a warehouse until you hope the customer orders them, you make a certain amount of all the products, every day.

The faster the changeover times (SMED — see "Mastering the quick change," earlier in this chapter), the easier it will be to smooth out production.

Figure 8-6 contrasts traditional lot production with level production. Notice that, throughout the sequence, the various products are interspersed.

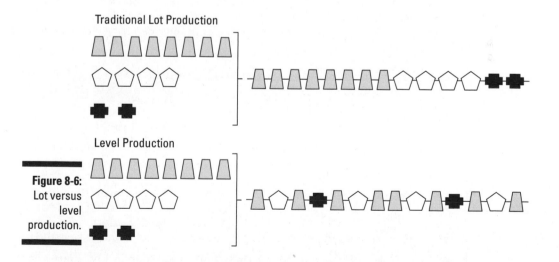

Figure 8-6:
Lot versus level production.

The calculation of the optimal sequence is a complex algorithm. It is based on cycle times, available work hours, setup times, and demand. You can purchase software programs to help you determine your optimal mix.

Production smoothing protects the suppliers in the value stream from the bull-whip effect, where the effects of small fluctuations on the customer end translate into radical volume swings upstream.

Signaling replenishment

In a Lean environment, you don't use forecasted demand schedules — these represent *pushing* production, and they usually don't correlate well with real customer demand. In Lean, the value stream is signaled to action through a demand indicator known as a *kanban*.

Creating kanban

A *kanban* signal can come in many forms — a card, an empty container, numbered ping-pong balls, or an empty space that needs filling. You determine the most effective *kanban* for the specific application. In a work module that is relatively balanced, the empty space may be the best solution. With the supply base, the electronic *kanban* card may be the most effective method. Whatever method you use, the *kanban* must signal how much, and of what part, needs to be delivered to what location.

Using the philosophy of "take one, make one," as inventory is consumed, the signal *(kanban)* is sent upstream to call for replenishment activities. One common way to think about *kanban* is the two-bin system: It's like batters in baseball — one at the plate and one on deck.

The number of *kanbans* you need is a function of the average demand per unit of time — usually daily — total time and container capacity. The calculation is as follows:

Number of *Kanbans* = ([Average Demand$_{(Time)}$] × [OC + PT + TT] × [1 + BT]) ÷ CC

where:

- ✔ OC = Order Cycle
- ✔ PT = Processing Time
- ✔ TT = Transit Time
- ✔ BT = Buffer Time (not over 10 percent)
- ✔ CC = Container Capacity (not more than 10 percent of Average Demand)
- ✔ Average Demand is a function of Time (daily, weekly, monthly, quarterly, and so on)

A *heijunka* box is designed to house the *kanban* cards related to the production sequence. Slots that represent a specific part number and increment of time during the day contain the *kanban* for the parts to be made during that time.

Controlling inventory with supermarkets

Sometimes, because of monuments or other process constraints, you cannot have a continuous-flow system. When this happens, you create what's called a *supermarket*. A supermarket is like your corner grocery, in that every item has a designated location and amount. The inventory is tightly controlled and *kanban* signals are used when a "customer" makes a "purchase" from the store. The supplying operation is the owner of the supermarket. The *kanban* signals the replenishment upstream.

Supermarkets should be located to minimize the "Transportation" waste of excess travel. It's better if you don't have to use them, but sometimes you can't avoid it. If you implement supermarkets, you must control them; if not, you may find you've given away the store!

Planning for every part

Plan for Every Part (PFEP) is a master planning document (usually in the form of a database or spreadsheet) used to plan where raw material, supplies, parts, and/or product are to be stored within the facility. The planning information includes the stock number, part name, inventory levels (minimum and maximum), and the storage locations (supermarket, central warehouse, point of use, and so on).

Connecting MRP and kanban

Kanban and MRP/ERP planning systems both have their appropriate functions. When you use *kanban* internally, you don't need the demand forecast portion of the system. However, you'll want to maintain accurate business records. One technique to relieve inventory is called *backflushing*. Not all experts agree that backflushing is the best way to maintain the inventory records. You have to decide the best method of data management for your organization. Whatever method you use, approach it with the mindset of eliminating waste to find the most effective solution for the organization.

Moving to pull scheduling will require changes to your current scheduling processes — remember that you're working to eliminate waste, and some of what you have historically viewed as value added scheduling was really type-1 *muda* (see Chapter 3).

Changing logistics

When you're operating in a Lean system, you have to rethink the way you approach logistics. Traditionally, a supplier would send a truckload of stuff "whenever." Instead, set up your organization for success by implementing creative logistical solutions, aimed at supplying you with what you need, when you need it, in the quantity you need it.

Collecting from multiple suppliers: The milk run

Sending a truck on a fixed route at fixed times to collect product from a several suppliers is known as a *milk run*. Instead of having to deal with many partially loaded trucks at your facility, you can attend to fewer shipments, which contain a predictable load and arrival time.

Shipping Less than Truckload (LTL)

LTL shipments, if done correctly, can be cheaper than waiting to cube out full trucks. (*Cube out* is the process of maximizing shipping density of a load in a semi-trailer.) LTL shipments are used when the suppliers are not located in a place that you can feasibly construct milk runs.

Delivery windows

Delivery windows enhance the both the predictability and stability of your incoming materials. To establish a delivery window, you schedule suppliers to deliver a specified amount of product, to a specified location or dock, within a specific window of time. In many industries, failure to comply with the delivery windows may result in hefty fines to the supplier or loss of business.

Delivery routes

Delivery routes are schedules that dictate the timing, location and amount of material moved within the value stream. Delivery routes help to regulate the pace of the material flow. Think of a city bus route — it's like a delivery route. People are moved through a city by a bus that picks up and drops off passengers at set locations according to an established time schedule as signaled by passengers at the bus stop (a *kanban*). In a product manufacturing environment, material is moved by a specific type of equipment, according to a set schedule, to established locations as signaled by *kanban*.

Using the Plan for Every Part (PFEP) tool and a facility layout will help you to establish your delivery routes.

Chapter 9

Perfection Tools

*I*n a Lean environment, you compare everything to a standard, and then work to improve it. You don't change anything indiscriminately — twiddle, or hack, or "just do it" to improve performance. You use information, data analysis and visual tools to help you deliberately identify where waste and defects are cropping up. Along with the customer and value-stream tools in Chapter 7, flow and pull tools described in Chapter 8, and the management tools in Chapter 10, the perfection tools in this chapter make up the overall Lean toolbox. You need all of these tools to support Lean practices.

In this chapter, you discover how to create standardized work — the foundation upon which activities and processes are built, and the basis upon which improvements are made. We show you how to organize *Kaizen* events for continuous improvement. By using visual-management tools, you'll understand how to create a world where it's possible to "manage by eye." Finally, you find out about the everyday statistical tools that help monitor and analyze the performance of the system. This is the part of the toolkit that enables you to strive for perfection.

Beginning with Standardized Work

Your pursuit of perfection begins with standards. Standardization is essential to effective work. The standardization of your activities, processes, and procedures directly enables the Lean goals of higher quality, lower costs, greater efficiency, effective communications, and the highest respect for people.

Standardized work, sometimes referred to as *standard work* or *standard operations,* applies at all levels and in all areas of your business:

- ✔ *Specification standards* include descriptions and quality, methods and tools, communications and terminology.

- ✔ *Subject standards* include company rules and policies, business management, regulatory and compliance.

- ✔ *Technical standards* include materials, components, products, and services.

Begin with the routine work tasks that most directly affect your ability to deliver to customer demand. Characterize this work in such a way that you can measure both the variability and waste in its operation, as well as apply methods and tools to continually improve performance over time. Repeat this process until you have standardized work for all activities.

Standardized work sets the foundation for improvement. To apply analysis and improvement tools, you must first characterize what you're doing now — the current processes. You have to standardize processes to have a basis for measurement. You must establish a culture and mindset around standardized work.

Failing to define and perform to standardized work is a slippery slope. Without standardized work, you have no firm basis for truly understanding today's problems and challenges. You also can't accurately value planned improvements. Plus, you have no way of implementing new processes and procedures and working to them with any regularity. You also have no accurate basis of measuring and understanding what you've changed. But worst of all, you breed an ad hoc, free-for-all work culture.

Guiding rules for standardized work

Five rules govern your approach to implementing standardized work. Follow these rules as you develop your standardized work practices:

- ✔ **Adjust to human ease and effectiveness, not machine efficiency.** The goal of standardized work is to help people be more safe and effective at what they do. Define work processes and procedures to optimize people — not machines. Machines are tools that assist people, not the other way around. Machine capabilities and limitations should not control your implementation of standardized work.

✔ **Standardize all repetitive work.** Standardize any and all work that's performed repeatedly. Certain work may be easier to standardize, and you may be tempted to just do the easy stuff. Don't avoid standardizing the more difficult processes as well, because you'll receive the benefits from standardizing all processes.

The more you can repeat a process, the better you can standardize it and reap the benefits. Strive to look for elements of what you do that are repetitive so that you can standardize them.

✔ **Keep the equipment and systems in condition.** Materials, computers, machines, and other systems support your work processes. Keep these in the standard conditions necessary to ensure you're producing both a high quality of output and an even flow of work. Breakdowns and lack of quality materials will disrupt your flow and impact product and service quality. Substandard systems should be repaired or upgraded independent of the work being performed.

✔ **Make standardized worksheets visible and accessible.** People can easily stray from performing to work standards. Everyone needs constant references and reminders. In addition, capturing key metrics — particularly deviations — isn't always easy. Keep standardized worksheets visible and readily accessible. Be certain that you're making it easy to know when variations occur.

✔ **Revise regularly.** Update and improve standardized work whenever you can. Jump on every chance to reduce variation, minimize inventory, improve workflow, and keep individual cycle times balanced with the overall takt time. Change the standard as often as necessary.

People will routinely find better ways than the standard. Don't treat standardized work as an end in itself. Standardized work is the routine, but when you have an improvement to standard, make the adjustments regularly through *Kaizen*.

Implementing standardized work

Standardized work — in the form of tasks, activities, processes, and procedures — is work that's conducted in a standard manner: it's specific, documented, measurable, and repeatable. Standardized work can apply to a person working by himself, or a group of people working collaboratively. It can include equipment and systems as well as human-to-machine interfaces. This standardization of work occurs not only in production or operations areas, but across the enterprise — in all functions and throughout all value streams.

To implement standardized work, follow this six-step process:

Step 1: Check equipment

Analyze all facilities, systems, and equipment to ensure that they're in proper and sufficient condition to meet the needs of the process activities. Adjust and tune systems to maximize ease of use and effectiveness.

Step 2: Check time

Determine the initial cycle time for the work — how long it takes you or your team to complete a unit of work. Then, compare that cycle time to the takt time requirement — how long you should be taking, as pulled by customer demand.

When you have these two values, determine the difference. Are you high or low? Chances are that the work time is longer than the takt time. You must make adjustments to equalize them. Usually, this means adjusting the time that it takes to complete a unit of work, rather than attempting to adjust the takt time. To reconcile work time–takt time discrepancies, perform the following analysis and improvement efforts:

- ✔ Analyze the workflow, sequencing, and organization of your internal process, and identify where speed and efficiencies can be gained.

- ✔ Restructure your internal process as necessary so that your cycle time is in concert with the takt time.

- ✔ Institutionalize the new production times as part of the standardized work instructions.

Step 3: Check Work-In-Process (WIP)

Your next step is to minimize Work-In-Process (inventory *muda*). Examine your work module or area for ways to reduce the amount of inventory or Work-In-Process required. You want to define standardized work for all processes in such a way as to require minimal amounts of WIP. Be sure to establish the acceptable range for inventory levels.

Step 4: Post it

Now that you've initially verified your support systems, balanced your productivity rate with the takt time, and established the inventory range, it's time to baseline your process and issue standard instructions. Standardized work instructions can take nearly any form — as long as they're precise, understandable, and measurable — and as long as they can be followed by the individuals performing the work.

Standard instructions can be printed on paper, read on a computer screen, printed on signs, or transmitted by any manner of communication — as long as it works. Examples of standard instructions include the following:

- **Instruction sheets:** These describe the procedure, including the organization, flow, and timing of the activities; the WIP range to maintain; and supporting equipment and environmental conditions, where applicable. Instruction sheets should be brief, easy to read, visible, and referenced.

- **Operating manuals:** These describe equipment, facilities, software programs, and other systems in terms of how they're used in the process activity. Operating manuals should be developed as training and reference documents that are kept handy in the workplace.

Poka-yoke (error-proof) your work instructions. Wherever possible, implement methods that help ensure not only that people will follow the instructions properly, but also that they will be prevented from not following them.

Step 5: Monitor, measure, and manage

Congratulations — you've crossed the starting line! You have implemented a unit of standardized work and can begin to observe it in action. Now you must actively monitor the activities and continuously measure performance of the work module. Regularly compare performance to standards, and strive to maintain performance to standard:

- For any variances you observe, where the work activity is not conforming to the standard instructions, identify the cause and intervene to correct the deviations — and restore the activity to comply with the standard.

- Seek to identify waste, and identify the cause of the nonconformance.

When you observe deviations from the standard, don't try to modify and update the standard on the fly. Everyone's goal is to work to the standard. If you measure consistent deviations from the standard, the analysis will serve to support a formal adjustment. However, until the standard is changed, the old standard still applies — and everyone should always be working to the standard!

Step 6: Adjust and update

Going forward, you'll apply numerous mapping, measurement, and analysis tools to characterize and evaluate the effectiveness of your standardized work processes. You'll support the team with management tools, and you'll conduct *Kaizen* events to determine improvements. (These many Lean tools are the subject of the latter part of this chapter and the other chapters in Part III.) As a result of using these many tools, you'll regularly determine that the standards should be updated.

When a change is warranted, make it — and make it quickly. Making rapid and detailed revisions to standard should be a normal, routine process; make sure you can implement formal changes swiftly and easily, and introduce them into your environment smoothly. The rapid adjustment process is critical to continuous improvement. Your team should be conditioned to absorb regular updates.

Because you want everyone working to standard, the standards must always be right and proper — and this means the update process must be routine and smooth. If your standards are out of date, everyone will quickly conclude that it's no longer necessary to work to standard, and you've lost the battle.

Updating standardized work is an integral part of *Kaizen!* If you're doing *Kaizen,* you'd better be updating standards.

Standardizing operations is one of the most important tools of a Lean enterprise. Standardizing work processes helps you to achieve a consistently high quality of product and services, performed by proud and productive workers, received by satisfied customers, within a safe environment and strong cost performance. Reducing variation in work processes leads to remarkable productivity improvements.

Improving with Kaizen

Kaizen is the act and art of continuous, incremental change and improvement. Kaizen tells you that even if something isn't broken, it can and must be improved: Do it better and make it better. The continual, incremental changes of *Kaizen* occur in all areas and at all levels — large and small, internal and external — in ways that improve the whole organization. Lean *Kaizen* maintains the focus on customer value and the reduction of waste in the value stream. (Refer to Chapter 6 for an in-depth discussion and explanation of *Kaizen.*)

Kaizen sees the enterprise through two lenses — setting new standards and maintaining existing standards. *Kaizen* maintenance is the act of establishing the policies and rules that help maintain the performance levels set by the present managerial and operating work standards. *Kaizen* improvement then focuses on the continuous improvement of existing standards and processes, as well as the innovation of new ones.

In all cases, the *Kaizen* requires the application of the needed training, materials, tools, and supervision to improve and maintain standards on a continual basis.

The *Kaizen event* — also known as a *Kaizen workshop* or *Kaizen blitz* — is a powerful and effective tool for engaging everyone within a work module or process area in a focused improvement activity. A *Kaizen* event is a complete run-through of the Plan-Do-Check-Act (PDCA) cycle, typically lasting five days. During the *Kaizen* event, the project team focuses on a specific area to find waste or other hindrances to value creation, and removes them from the value stream. The stimuli may be from issues in quality, changeover time, communications, organization — almost anything. *Kaizen* events are famous for requiring minimal investment and yielding great benefits.

The *Kaizen* project team will halt its normal work completely and will not produce its regular product or perform its services while it's participating in the *Kaizen* event. Advance planning is required to ensure that the customers, as well as other areas of the business, are not impacted inappropriately while the improvements are discovered and implemented.

Because the *Kaizen* event is conducted within a week's time, you will need to perform follow-up work to complete the change process. Track the completion of change items, and don't hesitate to perform additional changes and updates as required. Follow-up items should be completed within 30 days of the event. (For more about *Kaizen* events, see Chapter 6.)

Seeing Is Knowing: Visual-Management Tools

If a picture is worth a thousand words, an area with lots of visual-management tools in action must be worth a thousand minutes, a thousand dollars, and a thousand steps! When you use visual management, you don't waste time, energy, or effort looking for things, people, or defects. You can easily see what's happening, and whether things are running according to plan or not.

Keep the visual-management tools simple. Institute visual-management standards. Make them sensory — color, lights, sound, visual cues, or space. The more senses you appeal to, the more quickly you can gain status information.

Use cartoon drawings. Whether creating visual aides, writing up an issue, or conveying safety information, simple cartoon drawings bridge any language or literacy gap. Lean companies frequently use simple cartoon drawings throughout documents, meetings, facilities, and operations.

Andon

In ancient Japan, an *andon* was a paper lantern (a handy vertically collapsible paper lampshade with an open top and a candle placed at the central section of the closed bottom). To the ancient Japanese, the *andon* functioned as a flashlight, a signaling device in the distance, or even a commercial sign.

Nowadays, an *andon* is an electronic information or signaling device that may include graphics, colored text, and maybe even audio. *Andons* are used throughout public and private environments to communicate important status and failure messages to employees and customers. *Andon* is focused in particular on informing when a process or product is in jeopardy of failure, or has failed.

In manufacturing environments, an *andon* can be as simple as a three-color signal board that indicates in-spec, near-limits, and out-of-limits conditions for a running process. In service environments, *andon* displays can indicate queues and customer wait times. Transaction *andons* can be computer programs that warn operators of imminent failure conditions in data processing systems or at interface points.

Consumer *andons* have been increasing in popularity. Displays in airports indicate departure and boarding status. Freeway signs indicate accidents and backups. And what about that little light that comes on your dashboard warning you that you're low on gas? That's an *andon*.

Display boards

Display boards communicate vital information about the customer, process performance, standardized work, kaizen improvements, or team status. Display boards serve as effective and useful communication centers.

Display boards are operational nerve centers for the the organization, located where the action is. Often, they're handmade and include data charts, photos of customer contacts or team members, and process data before and after *Kaizen* improvements. Figure 9-1 shows an example display board.

Standardize the format of your display boards throughout the organization. By creating this commonality, no matter where you are you'll quickly be able to absorb the key information for the particular area.

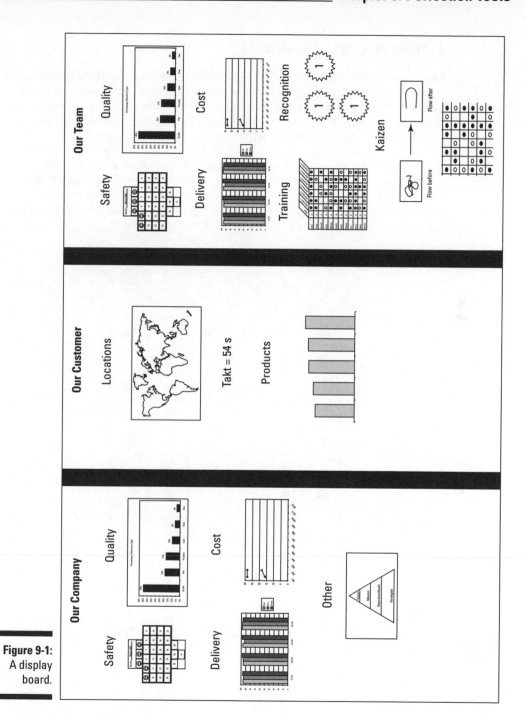

Figure 9-1:
A display
board.

Cross-training charts

Ideally, everyone is trained to do every job according to the standardized work design. Cross-training charts track the team's progress to this objective and identify people and their skills. In a cross-training chart like the one shown in Figure 9-2, all operations within a work module are listed across the top and each of the team members is listed by name along the left side.

When a team member is trained in a standard operation, a circle is placed at the intersection of his name and the operation. When he can competently perform the function according to the standardized work, the circle is filled in. Figure 9-2 is an example of a two-crew operation. On each team, at least one person can perform all the operations to the standard.

Name	Team	Operation 1	Operation 2	Operation 3	Operation 4	Operation 5	Operation 6
Ariel	A	●	●	●	●	●	●
Daisy	A	●	●		○		
Donald	A			○	○		●
Huey	A	○		●		●	
Mickey	A	●	○	○	●	○	●
Ursula	A		●		○	●	
Belle	B	●	●			●	○
Dewey	B		○		○	●	
Eric	B	●	○	●	○		○
Louie	B	●	●	●	●	●	●
Peter	B	○			●		○
Wendy	B	●	○	●	●	○	●

Figure 9-2: A cross-training chart.

Cross-training charts are a powerful visual tool. At a glance you know:

- ✔ Who can fill in when others are absent, without risking performance.
- ✔ Who is the most expert member of the team.
- ✔ When untrained employees are performing operations.
- ✔ Where the team is weak.

Additionally, cross-training charts provide valuable information when creating training and development plans.

Pictograms

Pictograms (or *pictographs*) provide a quick way to see where defects are occurring — in a place, on a part, or in the system. Police use "murder maps" to track where the murders or other crimes happen. Armed with this information, they can properly staff neighborhoods, create relationships with the neighbors and work to solve and prevent crime. This same idea can be used in any situation to visually identify defect patterns so that corrective and preventative actions can be taken.

To create a pictogram, make a visual representation of what you want to study — a city map, a factory layout, a drawing of a part, or any graphical representation you choose. Visually indicate where the defect happens, with pushpins, markings, or colored dots. Detect the patterns and use *Kaizen* to improve the situation. It's amazingly powerful!

Everyday Improvement Tools

The beauty of the Lean everyday improvement tools is in how simple they are to use. They're visual; they show you what you need to see. They don't require advanced math or statistics to use and understand. They can be done by hand, on a calculator, or a computer. These tools can be used by everyone within the philosophy of Kaizen for regular, continuous improvement. They support opinion with facts and data.

The 5 Whys

To seek out the cause of an issue or problem, you ask why it happened. But probing just one layer gets you to just the first cause of the problem. The root cause is usually much deeper. You have to keep probing. Noriaki Kano, creator of the Kano model, likens this to drilling down, "going an inch wide and a mile deep" to gain real understanding, rather than the superficial understanding gained from the converse — a mile wide and an inch deep.

The 5 Whys is a simple probing tool that helps you get to the root cause of a problem. At each level of explanation, keep asking "Why?" until you get to the true underlying reasons. Ask at least five times.

Why five times? The number five is arbitrary. The point is not the number — it's the probing. You may get to the bottom in 2, or it may take 10 or 20 or 50 times, depending on the complexity of your situation.

Never take the first answer as the true reason. Keep asking "Why?" until you're satisfied that you've found the real root cause.

Consider this humorous example: The marble surface of the Washington Monument was disintegrating. That's terrible! Let's ask why:

- Why is the surface of the monument disintegrating?

  Answer: Extensive use of harsh cleaning chemicals have eroded the marble veneer.

- Why are we using such harsh chemicals?

  Answer: An inordinate number of pigeons collect around the monument, and they deposit high levels of pigeon poop on the marble surface.

- Why are there so many pigeons?

  Answer: Pigeons eat spiders, and there are an unusually high numbers of spiders on the monument.

- Why are there so many spiders on the monument?

  Answer: Spiders eat gnats, and there's a high gnat population at the monument.

- Why are there so many gnats?

  Answer: Gnats are most active at dusk and are attracted by bright lights. The National Park Service illuminates the monument at dusk, attracting the gnats, which increases the spider and, therefore, the pigeon population.

The solution? Adjust the timing and characteristics of the lighting.

At each level of this example, you could have stopped asking and begun treating the symptoms, never reaching the bottom and discovering the true cause. This example also illustrates that the fix to the real problem is often simpler and more straightforward than attacking the symptoms!

Probe deeply, but carefully. You'll likely need to go to the next "Who?" in order to find someone with the expertise to answer the next "Why?" Also, examine the problem from different angles, because you may get different answers, depending on whom you ask.

The seven basic tools of quality

The quality toolbox contains many, many tools for analyzing and improving the quality of products and processes. Some of the more involved tools, such as analysis of variance (ANOVA) and process capability analysis, are powerful and important. However, you don't use those advanced tools every day.

The basic everyday quality toolset consist of seven simple tools that anyone can use. These are long-standing tools that have been used in quality circles for decades. If you apply these basic tools regularly, you'll conquer the majority of your quality challenges.

In keeping with the philosophy of visual management, these tools are primarily graphical in nature. Graphical representations communicate more information than raw data and present the data in a form that often enables the problem to be obvious.

Cause and effect: Fishbone Diagrams

As you probe the nature of a problem and ask the 5 Whys, you'll begin to paint a mental picture of which causes are affecting what outcomes. You represent this graphically in what's known as a Cause-and-Effect (C&E) Diagram.

This diagram is also known as an Ishikawa Diagram, named after Kaoru Ishikawa, who first applied them in the shipyards of Kobe, Japan, in the 1940s. A C&E Diagram is also sometimes called a Fishbone Diagram, after its graphical appearance.

The C&E Diagram enables you to represent the influences and connections on a particular outcome. Figure 9-3 is a generalized C&E Diagram that exemplifies the categories and subcategories that can make up the chain of causation.

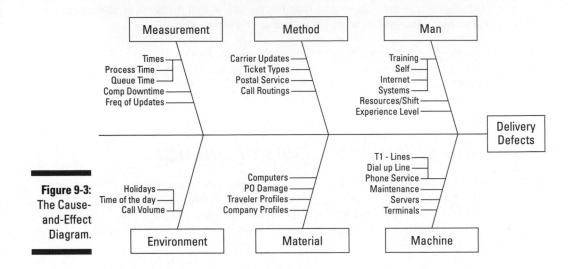

Figure 9-3:
The Cause-and-Effect Diagram.

A C&E Diagram is simple to create and apply. You can draw one on a white-board or the back of a napkin. You simply identify the major categories of influence on an outcome. Within those categories, you indicate the causes and how they connect. The C&E Diagram immediately presents a picture of all the causes and contributions to an outcome, and suggests the next level of probing and analysis.

The C&E Diagram aids the 5 Whys and affinity exercises, because it helps probe cause and also categorizes and aligns the influences.

Pareto Charts: Finding the significant few

A *Pareto Chart* is a special type of bar chart where the values are arranged in descending order, with the largest contribution first. It is named after the Italian economist Vilfredo Pareto, who discovered the "80-20 rule" now also known as the *Pareto Principle* (the principle that 20 percent of the causes are responsible for 80 percent of the outcomes). The Pareto Chart is a fast and effective way to identify the significant influences — and separate them from the insignificant ones.

To make a Pareto Chart, you simply stack up observations with the greatest values on the left, and observations with decreasing values onward to the right. Figure 9-4 is an example that shows categories of cost in an expenditure profile. From this chart, you can easily see the significance of each cost element to the total — and that salaries are the largest contributor, with equipment second, and everything else minor by comparison.

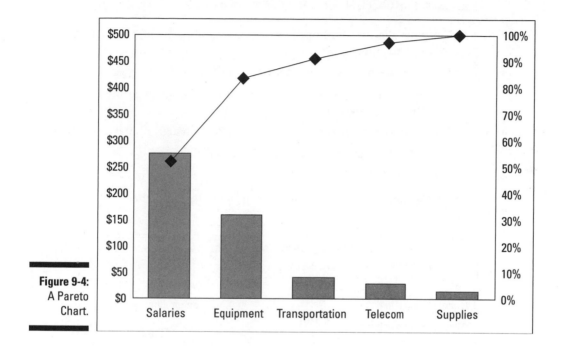

Figure 9-4:
A Pareto
Chart.

As shown in Figure 9-4, a Pareto Chart shows both the absolute number as well as the percentage of contribution. The right vertical axis indicates percentage, and a line is plotted that depicts the cumulative percentage total, up to 100 percent with the last rightmost item. From the figure, you can quickly see that salaries and equipment combine to represent over 80 percent of the cost.

You can use the Pareto Chart to plot just about anything. It can plot data from the C&E matrix, and can quickly show the primary causes of defects, costs, complaints, time, inventory, returns — whatever you can measure!

Check Sheets: Capture and see

A *Check Sheet* is basically any standard way you can gather data and view an activity as it's happening. The name comes from the historical use of a piece of paper or chart on which someone would indicate activity and check it as it was occurring. Figure 9-5 shows an example of a Check Sheet.

You can set up Check Sheets for a variety of uses:

✔ **Tallying:** Simply count up the occurrences of an event, such as runners crossing the finish line.

✔ **Defective items:** Mark the occurrence of defects by category.

✔ **Process distribution:** Indicate the occurrence of an event by value. This will build a Histogram.

✔ **Location plot:** Mark the location of an event on a graphical depiction.

✔ **Defective location plot:** Mark the location of a defect.

✔ **Causation:** Indicate the likely cause of events as they occur.

✔ **Work sampling:** Indicate how time is spent by category.

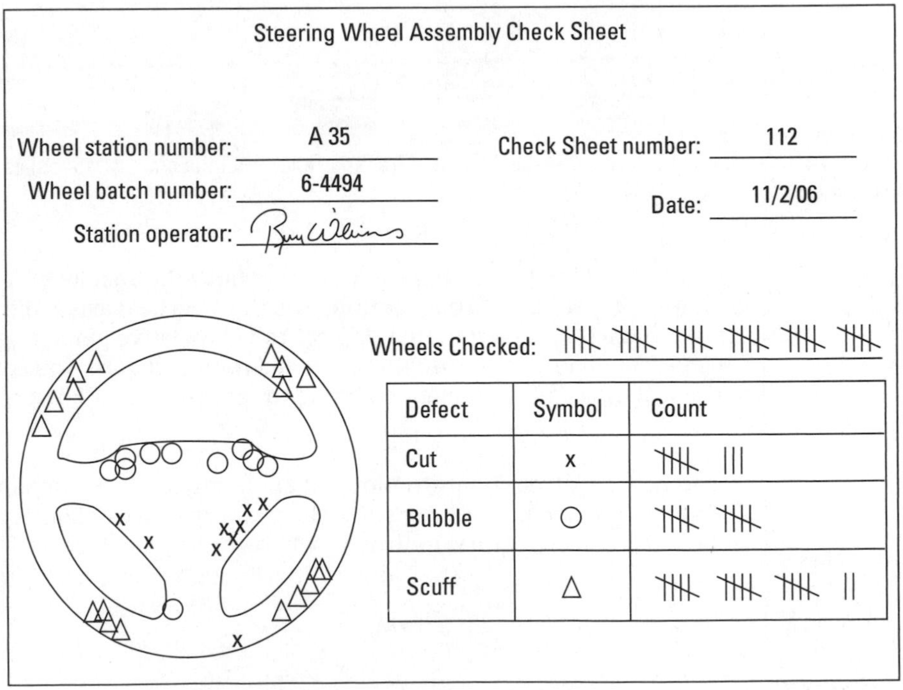

Figure 9-5: A Check Sheet.

Scatter Plots: Relationships at a glance

A Scatter Plot is the simplest of all plots — and yet, it's also sometimes the most revealing. It graphical depicts the relationship between two items or variables (see Figure 9-6).

Making a Scatter Plot is easy. You simply draw and label a couple of axes and plot the data. Then sit back and look at it. What do you see? Is there a trend (known as *correlation*), or is it just random? Based on what you're seeing, you can draw conclusions about what's likely to occur next.

The Scatter Plot shows at a glance whether a relationship exists between the two variables, and what the nature of that relationship might be. The number of dots on the plot indicates how much data you've collected — the more data, the more valid the observations.

In this example, there's an obvious correlation between year and local index. Further analyses would indicate the nature of that correlation.

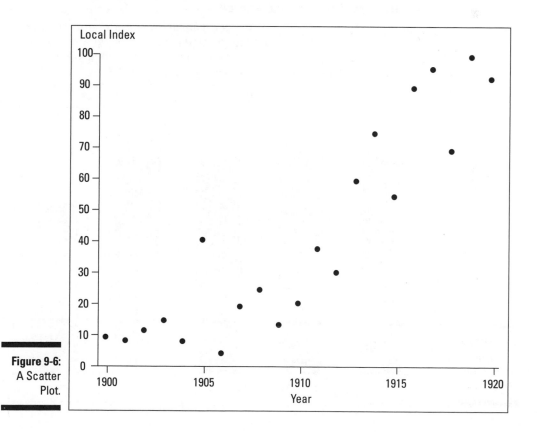

Figure 9-6:
A Scatter
Plot.

Bar Charts: How things stack up

The Bar Chart is a great way to see the differences between items in a small set of related data. Bar Charts are enormously popular, easy to make, and easy to read. Figure 9-7 shows an example of a Bar Chart.

Each entry is a count of the data for that category, and is displayed in a vertical column as a rectangular solid bar that is proportional to its value. A common variation on the Bar Chart is called a *Stacked Bar Chart,* where two or more items that make up the value are displayed independently. Figure 9-8 contains a Stacked Bar Chart.

In a Bar Chart, you look at the tallest and shortest, to understand the range, and get a sense for the mean and the deviations. You look at the bars relative to one another, to get a sense of trends, correlations, or other relationships. From the Bar Chart, you'll have a sense of what to examine or look for next. It turns out that that new surfing movie was released last Friday!

Histograms: Frequency of occurrence

A *Histogram* is a type of Bar Chart that is organized to show counts of how frequently something occurs. In a Histogram, each bar is of equal width and represents a fixed range of measurement. Over a period of time, you can easily see how the data is distributed (see Figure 9-9).

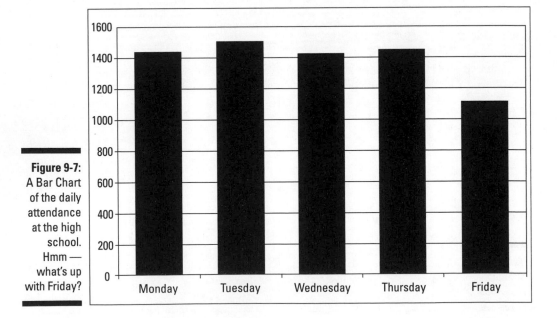

Figure 9-7: A Bar Chart of the daily attendance at the high school. Hmm — what's up with Friday?

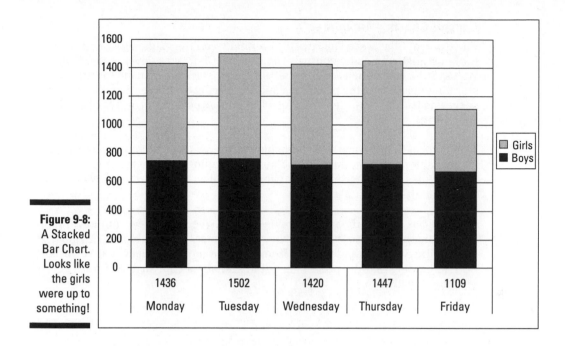

Figure 9-8:
A Stacked
Bar Chart.
Looks like
the girls
were up to
something!

Histograms are enormously powerful ways to see how processes function
and the degree of variation and other factors influencing performance.

Figure 9-9:
The
Histogram
on the left
shows a
"normal"
distribution
of data,
while the
Histogram
on the right
depicts a
non-normal
two-peaked
"bimodal"
distribution.

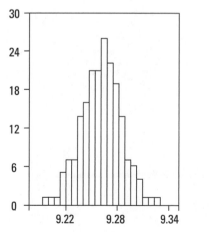 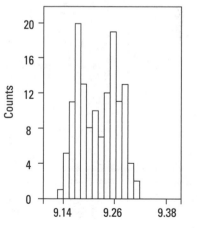

Control Charts: "Make it so"

The Control Chart (see Figure 9-10) is considered the single most important tool of statistical quality control. The Control Chart was developed by Dr. Walter Shewhart of Bell Labs in the 1920s as a statistical means for understanding manufacturing processes and improving their effectiveness. It serves as the basis for determining whether a process is in or out of statistical control.

The Control Chart is a graphical display of the value of some process or quality characteristic over time. It displays the running value of the item, and usually includes the centerline target value as well as the upper and lower control limits.

Typically, as long as the sample values fall between the upper and lower control limits, the process is "in control." However, if the distribution of values is systematic and non-random, this is an indication of a special cause of variation, indicating that the process is not in statistical control and should be examined further.

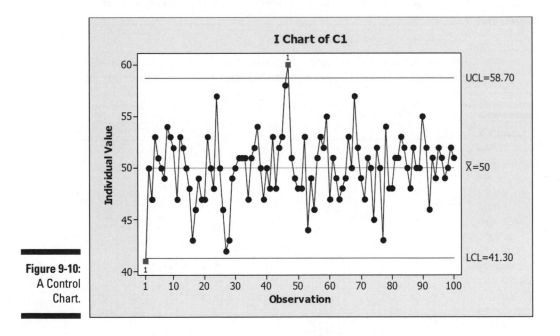

Figure 9-10:
A Control
Chart.

A collection of the sample values in the Control Chart over time will form a Histogram, as well as permit statistical analysis of the variation in the performance of the quality characteristic.

Computer Tools

 Numerous software tools for data analysis have been developed in recent years. Other tools can capture and display information. These tools are increasingly sophisticated and capable. You can use these tools with confidence in supporting your work.

See Chapter 10 for a more detailed discussion of computer tools that support Lean implementation.

Chapter 10

Management Tools

*L*ean is a strategic initiative. You undertake Lean because it makes good business and financial sense as a long-term direction for your organization. Yet, Lean requires not just a strategic vision, but a daily commitment to improvement. You need to have the right measurement system. You need to closely watch the short-term and long-term metrics. You need to learn from your experiences — both the successes and the failures. And you need for everyone to be actively involved on a daily basis.

Without the attention of management and the leadership of executives, the changes developed in a Lean implementation are not sustainable. In this chapter, we introduce you to tools that support the development and tracking of the business strategy, tactical initiatives, and the overall performance of the business.

Like other aspects of Lean, managerial tools are visual. Along with the customer and value-stream tools in Chapter 7, the flow and pull tools described in Chapter 8, and the perfection tools in Chapter 9, these tools make up the overall Lean toolbox. You need all these tools to support Lean practices.

The chapter concludes with a general discussion of software tools that support Lean implementation. Although Lean is about simplicity and the elimination of waste, it is also about the appropriate implementation of technology. Follow a philosophy of: simplify and/or eliminate, then automate and integrate. This will help guide the management team to the appropriate level of technology implementation.

Managing Strategy

A successful management team manages both the long-term strategy of the organization and the tactical, day-to-day activities of the business. It's the same in a successful Lean organization. Creating the master plan and measuring everyday progress to that plan is essential. In keeping with Lean fundamentals, the process of strategy development, deployment, and measurement should be simple and visual.

Strategy and measurement tools are plentiful in the marketplace, and the ones included in this section align with the tenets of Lean. The Plan-Do-Check-Act (PDCA) cycle central to *Kaizen* also provides a great foundation for strategy development and implementation. Collectively, these tools help the management team effectively lead their organization through the Lean transformation.

In all that you do, your mantra should be "Simplify, eliminate, automate, then integrate." Lean is all about simplifying, eliminating waste, applying technology appropriately, and identifying ways to integrate functions or processes. Management teams often fall prey to consultants or IT vendors offering the latest and greatest whiz-bang solutions to all their problems. Automating bad business practices will not fix your problems. Magic wands do not exist. Whether developing strategy, performing *Kaizen* activities, or evaluating technology, don't stray from the essence of Lean: eliminate waste in everything you do.

Hoshin: Balanced planning

The term *hoshin kanri* means "direction setting." The Lean planning system built around it is known as *hoshin* planning or policy deployment. In *hoshin,* the organization makes plans and then conducts a regular standardized self-analysis. The results provide inputs for updating the plan.

Hoshin planning is a two-pronged approach of a) strategic planning and alignment, and b) everyday operations fundamentals. The goal of *hoshin* planning is to ensure that the organization is developing its longer-term (two- to five-year) objectives and strategies, as well as managing short-term everyday business execution. It is also fundamentally based on the principle that you achieve the best results when everyone in the organization fully understands the goals and is involved in the planning processes to achieve them.

Using the new seven tools of quality control (see Chapter 7) helps you to process background information as you create your *hoshin* plans.

Hoshin planning, to be truly effective, must also be cross-functional, promoting cooperation along the value stream, within and between business functions. The different departments of an organization must support each other in order to achieve the remarkable results only possible through synergy and cooperation.

Understanding the hoshin planning process

Hoshin planning systematizes strategic planning. The format of the plans is unified via standards and measured through tables. This standardization provides a structured approach for developing and producing the organization's strategic plan. The structure and standards also enable an efficient way to link the strategic plan through the organization. This ultimately leads to an organization-wide understanding of not just the plan but also the planning process.

Hoshin planning is a seven-step process, in which you perform the following management tasks:

1. **Identify the key business issues facing the organization.**
2. **Establish measurable business objectives that address these issues.**
3. **Define the overall vision and goals.**
4. **Develop supporting strategies for pursuing the goals.**

    In the Lean organization, this strategy includes the use of Lean methods and techniques.
5. **Determine the tactics and objectives that facilitate each strategy.**
6. **Implement performance measures for every business process.**
7. **Measure business fundamentals.**

Be sure you identify the critical business issues confronting the organization and select an objective and goal that will overcome the issues. To develop a complete plan and to guide the organization, you must identify supporting strategies with measures and owners.

Setting the hoshin tables

Plans don't collect dust on a shelf somewhere; you check them regularly against actual performance. The *hoshin* process employs a standardized set of reports, known as *tables,* in the review process. These reports are used by managers and work teams to assess performance. Each table includes

 ✔ A header, showing the author and scope of the plan
 ✔ The situation, to give meaning to the planned items

- ✔ The objective (what is to be achieved)
- ✔ Milestones that will show when the objective is achieved
- ✔ Strategies for how the objectives are achieved
- ✔ Measures to check that the strategies are being achieved

The different *hoshin* tables are

- ✔ *Hoshin* **review table:** During reviews, plans are presented in the form of standardized *hoshin* review tables, each of which shows a single objective and its supporting strategies. A group or individual responsible for several objectives generates several review tables in order to cover all objectives.

- ✔ **Strategy implementation table:** Implementation plans are used to identify the tactics or action plans needed to accomplish each strategy. Implementation plans usually present the following information:

  - The tactics needed to implement the strategy

  - The people involved in each tactic and their exact responsibilities

  - The timeline of each tactic, usually presented as a *Gantt Chart* (a time-phased graphical representation of project activities and tasks).

  - Performance measures

  - How and when the implementation plans will be reviewed

- ✔ **Business fundamentals table (BFT):** Business fundamentals, or the basic elements that define the success of a key business process, are monitored through its corresponding metrics. Examples of business fundamentals are safety, people, quality, responsiveness, or cost. BFT figures must be in control before the long-term strategies are attended to.

- ✔ **Annual planning table (APT):** Record the organization's objectives and strategies in the annual planning table. The APT is then passed down to the next organizational structure. This pass-down process flows throughout the entire organization. Each level develops its plan to support the overall top level organizational plan.

The real change occurs when you're clear about the assignment of responsibility for every item in the implementation plans.

Making the annual plan

Senior leadership is ultimately responsible for establishing the strategies, goals and process performance measures to address the organization's issues for the coming year. Some organizations have been successful at using issue teams or management quality teams. These teams consist of the functional managers and senior leaders most involved with a particular issue.

Together, they formulate objectives and strategies to best address the critical business issues at hand.

The organization's leadership should be convinced that successfully implementing the selected strategies will make it possible to achieve objectives and resolve issues.

Record the organization's objective and strategies in the annual planning table. The APT is then passed down to the next organizational structure. As the plans cascade through the organization, the strategies of one level become the objectives of the next level down in the organization. This provides direction and hierarchical linkage to the plan's highest level. At each succeeding level, strategies are owned, expanded, and turned into implementation plans that contribute to reaching the objective and the overall goal.

As each succeeding level accepts its portion of the plan, it has been involved in the plan's development by adding detail where it can best contribute and add value. This is also how the organization buys into the plan; it now has some ownership of the plan itself. The *hoshin* methodology is a strategic planning process with the built-in ability to empower the organization.

Implementing hoshin

The implementation *do* process includes the execution of the *hoshin* activities, along with the timelines and checkpoints for specific events. Use the implementation plan as an ongoing decision-making tool. Plot or note the actual performance to plan along the planned events and checkpoints. Include how and when the plan will be reviewed.

The implementation plan usually requires coordination both within and between departments and process owners. Implementation plans are not just the responsibility of an individual completing the lowest-level annual plan. Each level in the organization carries detailed responsibilities to ensure support for and successful completion of the organization's plans. This is how the *do* step of PDCA happens.

The annual hoshin review

Because *hoshin* is a cyclic process, the review of the previous year's performance is the basis for the next year's plan.

✔ **For those objectives that were completed successfully,** perform an analysis to determine what went right and to determine if the supporting strategies and performance measures initially established were truly appropriate. Also, note any exceptional results and how they were obtained. This step is critical to capturing knowledge of how to exceed goals, and then transferring that knowledge to the organization.

> ✔ **For each objective that was not attained,** determine the reasons for the deviation. Typically, the analysis consists of the detailed supporting data of all strategies associated with the objective. The strategy owners also should identify what their teams would have changed to have been more successful in the year just completed as well as for the future. This process of both looking back at the past and ahead to the future is the key to improving organizational learning. It can greatly benefit the organization in identifying future opportunities.

These reviews are conducted at all levels of the organization. Starting at the lowest level that has plan ownership, the review is completed and the information passed up the organizational structure (management levels). Each level then uses the review tables from previous structures (management levels) to complete its own review. Discussions between the different structures of the organization are very important and should result in consensus on the review table results.

In addition to listing objectives from the previous year's plan, the review table can call attention to important issues for the coming year. When the review reaches the senior management team, the *hoshin* review tables highlight the areas in which the organization made significant progress and attained the identified goal, and where changes should be made or more work is needed.

The review is completed using information from:

✔ *Hoshin* review tables

✔ Corporate objectives

✔ Business plans

✔ Economic projections

✔ Customer inputs

✔ A quality assessment (if conducted)

The senior management team can determine whether last year's critical business issues and business objectives (which were selected to address the issues) are still appropriate for the coming year. This also is the time to make sure the organization is providing value to its customers as described by the purpose. Finally, consider whether the vision for the organization is still appropriate for business conditions.

Reviewing progress periodically

Although the planning cycle is annual, you don't just make the plan then forget about it until next year. Review business fundamental metrics monthly to ensure that performance is trending in the right direction. Review the annual plan quarterly to ensure that the plan is still the right plan.

If the metrics aren't trending in the right direction, identify countermeasures to get the plan back on track. The actions may comprise as many as three phases:

✔ Alleviating the immediate problem with an emergency countermeasure.

✔ Preventing the problem from recurring with a short-term fix.

✔ Determining and removing the problem's root cause. This is the permanent solution that will prevent the problem from recurring.

The final annual review is essentially a compilation and summary of the *hoshin* review tables accumulated during the year. This final review returns you to the *study* step described earlier. The *study* step plays a crucial role in improving organizational learning ability. When actual performance and results are compared and a deviation-from-plan analysis is completed, those closest to the strategy make visible to the organization's leaders a great deal of information.

Reflection — analyzing what went right or what went wrong in each strategy — is an important aspect of management reviews. Determining objectively which strategies and actions worked and which strategies and actions need improvement because they failed to hit their targets is required in the organization's learning process. This is not a blame session. Focus on the strategies and actions, before you point fingers.

The Balanced Scorecard

Organizations are traditionally measured on their financial performance. Corporations report revenues, costs, and earnings; nonprofits measure fundraising; government organizations track budgets. And though the numbers are very important, everyone knows that numbers are only one of several indicators of the true health and status of the organization. In order to create a more balanced picture, Harvard researcher Dr. Robert Kaplan and his colleague Dr. David Norton developed a concept in the early 1990s called the Balanced Scorecard.

Kaplan and Norton recognized that a retrospective on financial performance alone is a wholly inadequate way to measure and guide organizations in the emerging postindustrial information age. It is both impractical and inappropriate to use financials as the sole basis for evaluating and managing the broad spectrum of customers, employees, suppliers, and distributors, as well as the processes and technologies that enable a modern enterprise. Something more holistic is needed.

As Kaplan and Norton formalized it, the Balanced Scorecard is a framework for both evaluating and managing an organization along the lines of four distinct perspectives: financial (of course), but also customer, process, and learning. Figure 10-1 shows the conceptual framework. In the Balanced Scorecard approach, the organization creates measurable indicators in each of the four areas, which are used both to track progress as well as manage achievement toward its vision. Simple and easy to understand, the Balanced Scorecard has been applied in some form as a standardized system of measurement in over half of the world's companies.

Balanced Scorecard basics

The underlying framework for the Balanced Scorecard methodology is built on many of the same principles as Lean, including the following:

✔ Focus on the customer and, in particular, on the fact that the customer defines quality

✔ Structured application of measurements and controls

✔ Quality at the source

✔ Continuous improvement, through measurement and controlled feedback.

✔ Engagement, empowerment, and development of employees

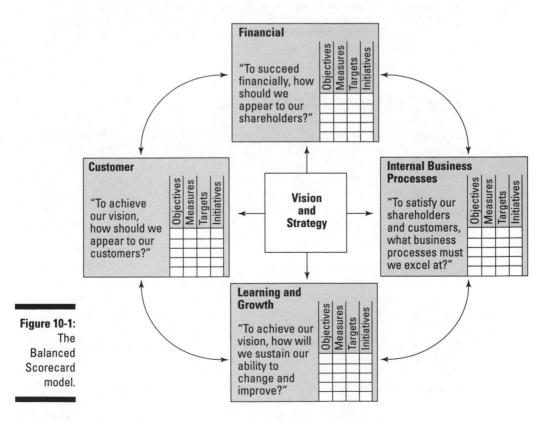

Figure 10-1:
The Balanced Scorecard model.

Consistent with *hoshin,* the Balanced Scorecard incorporates the outputs from internal business processes as well as from vision and strategy planning. It requires the organization to develop metrics based on strategic planning priorities, as well as the operational business fundamentals. This enables everyone to observe the outcomes of the measured processes and strategies and track the results to guide the organization and provide feedback.

Scorecard sections

The standard Balanced Scorecard contains four cards — one each for customer, financials, processes, and learning. They are purposely interdependent, forming a holistic view of the enterprise:

- ✔ **Customer:** The customer card focuses on the measures that demonstrate the ability of the organization to provide quality goods and services, effective delivery, and overall customer satisfaction. This includes both internal and external customers.

- ✔ **Financial:** The financials card mirrors that of most top-level financial reports, consistent with the nature of the enterprise (public, private, nonprofit, governmental).

- ✔ **Process:** The internal process card reports on the status and performance of the key business processes that constitute the core business functions (that is, what generates value for the customer).

- ✔ **Learning:** The final card is a report on the learning, development, and growth elements of the people, systems, and culture of the organization. This includes skills, communications, motivation, and agility.

You can easily see how the standard Balanced Scorecard would reflect the status and performance of a Lean organization. For this reason, the Balanced Scorecard is an acceptable tool of measure and works synergistically in a Lean enterprise.

Create your scorecard to fit your organization. Although the standard Balanced Scorecard is prescriptive, you may find it more beneficial to track categories like safety, people, quality, responsiveness, and cost. Find the right fundamental business metrics for your organization and review them on a frequent basis — at least monthly (see Chapter 9).

BAM! BAM! Management dashboards

The concept of the executive dashboard was first introduced in the mid 1980s. Known at that time as *executive information systems* (EIS), they were intended to provide a rollup of operating information for regular examination by company executives. Instead of having to wait for end-of-the-month reports, executives could see the information as it was happening, right there in full-color charts and tables on their PCs. Due to high costs and technology limitations, EISs were cumbersome and saw limited success at the time. But they were a great idea! They marked the first attempt at providing near-real time feedback from the far reaches of the shop floor to the lofty halls of mahogany row.

These have evolved now into the more ubiquitous and useful tool known as the management dashboard, also called BAM, short for business activity monitoring. Refer to Figure 10-2. These dashboards are now far-reaching tools that allow anyone in the organization to monitor key processes and track performance at nearly any level as it is occurring. Management dashboards are flexible and easily customized to provide anyone the view of what matters most to them — as well as what matters most to everyone else.

Figure 10-2:
Business
activity
monitoring.

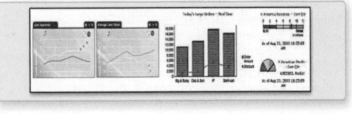

Courtesy of webMethods

A management dashboard can be as simple or as complex as necessary. Dashboards can display everything from pie charts, maps, and histograms to run charts and control charts with upper and lower spec limits.

In keeping with Lean, your dashboard should be simple to read and visual in presentation.

Dashboards help people in organizations quickly access information and apply analytics. Once strictly captive to the domain of IT specialists, business users can now quickly define, monitor, and analyze key performance indicators (KPIs) on their own. This enables an organization to not only monitor the fundamental business processes in real time, but also understand the context of local operations within the realm of larger strategic objectives.

Many organizations are now deploying management dashboards in more sophisticated and intricate application contexts, such as with a customized analytic application or even as an extranet that reaches beyond the corporate boundaries and provides views into the contributions of suppliers or deliverers to the value stream. This transcends standard analytical applications, which historically provided little more than modestly structured "buckets of reports."

Dashboards are useful in other ways as well:

- ✔ **Operational fulfillment:** Management dashboards can focus the entire organization on a core set of objectives and process indicators. Everyone can track indicators that exist beyond their function or work module, observing their local effects on broad-scale performance.

- ✔ **User needs:** Regardless of function — from senior-most management to shop-floor workers — everyone can easily absorb the highly visual presentation of a management dashboard. It is instantaneous broadband communication of everything from *andon*-like operational alerts to specialized analyses.

- ✔ **Supportable:** The IT function within enterprises can now more easily than ever provide the infrastructure and support needed to deliver this information. Dashboards are fast to construct and flexible for rapid modification. Middleware technology and the emergence of service-oriented architectures (SOA) enable connectivity and delivery that doesn't require extensive custom programming.

With the broad deployment of management dashboards and related performance-management tools, organizations are finding that their objectives and metrics are easier than ever to monitor, manage, and improve. This, in turn, enables *Kaizen* and permits organizations to strive toward even higher performance goals. Business performance becomes an upward spiral that enables an enterprise to strive for ever-higher performance goals.

Creepy, crawly spider charts

Spider charts, also know as *radar charts,* are radial plots of several performance measures in a single display. Spider charts are effective at showing the performance of several performance characteristics in a single graph (see Figure 10-3 for an example).

Spider charts are popular in Lean because they're graphical, they're visual, and they communicate information rapidly. With a spider chart, you can do things like:

- ✔ Graphically observe the performance of business metrics to a set goal.

- ✔ Observe the relative value of different suppliers.

- ✔ Make logical comparisons between competing strategies or approaches.

- ✔ Instantly see the strengths and weaknesses between alternatives.

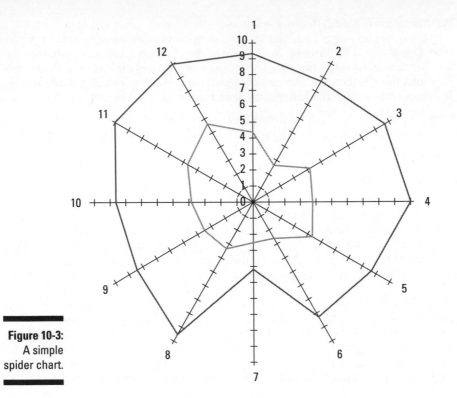

Figure 10-3:
A simple
spider chart.

Even if you've never used a spider chart before, don't worry — it's easy. Follow this quick process:

1. **Identify the information you want to compare.**

2. **Generate a list of approximately five to ten evaluation criteria.**

3. **Score the alternatives for each of the criteria.**

4. **Draw the chart, and identify as many axis arms (spokes) as there are criteria.**

5. **Label the spoke arms of the chart — one arm for each criterion, and put hash marks on each spoke that represent counts.**

6. **Score a given alternative on each axis arm — and connect the dots with a straight line.**

7. **Repeat for each alternative. When you finish, it looks like a spider web.**

When using a spider chart to track progress to a goal, fill in the space representing the actual performance. This will help you to visualize how far you have to go.

Now observe the results and analyze the chart. What do you see? Look at the balance, the extremes, and the total area within each score. Spider charts are a powerful and revealing graphical tool.

When using a spider chart to compare alternatives, limit the number of items you're comparing on any individual chart. It's easy to see a few, but when you get much past five or six, you'll get lost. Refer to Figure 10-4 for an example of a more complex spider chart. You don't want them any more complex than this.

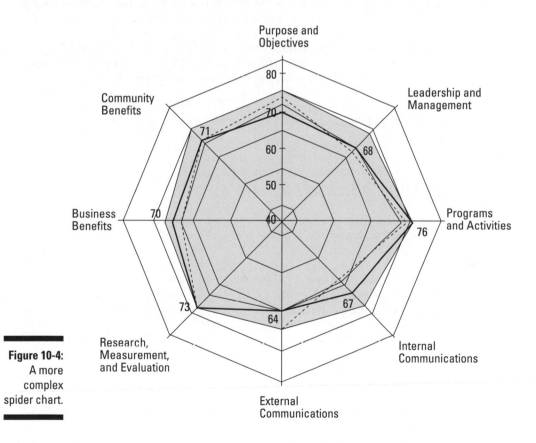

Figure 10-4:
A more
complex
spider chart.

Go and See

Lean managers know that they can't effectively lead their organizations from their office. They need to be where the action is — to build relationships, to understand the real issues, and to set performance expectations. You can create the most eloquent annual plan, but without the day-to-day activities and involvement, those plans will be mere pipe dreams.

However, leaving the office isn't enough. The tools of this section create a framework for these managerial activities. *Gemba* walks, for example, aren't random strolls through an area — they're focused on Lean implementation, safety, quality, or some other perspective. Whether conducted by an individual or team of people, the intention of a *gemba* review is clear.

Communication centers display vital information to the people working in the area as well as any visitors. Customer, performance, and company information are displayed in a visual manner and kept current by the team (see Chapter 9).

At any level, the best way to know what is going on in the business is to "go and see."

Genchi genbutsu

One of the fundamentals of the Toyota way is called *genchi genbutsu*. In short, this means "go to the actual scene *(genchi)* and confirm the actual happenings or things *(genbutsu).*"

Former Secretary of State Colin Powell returned from the ruins of the Asian tsunami of 2005. He said he had never seen such devastation and immediately pledged further assistance. After the visit, the pledge of aid increased more than tenfold from the initial U.S. White House statement released immediately after the disaster on December 26, 2005. Things look a lot different from ground zero.

The power of *genchi genbutsu* is in the firsthand knowledge that you gain. It's one thing to look at a report, see a bunch of numbers, and draw conclusions. It's a totally different experience to go to an area and see what the numbers mean. A purchasing manager may believe she's cut a sweetheart of a deal with a supplier, but not understand what that supplier's product does to the quality and reliability of the production process. Gaining the firsthand knowledge of the process will help that manager make better deals for the company, not just her department.

Gemba walks

Gemba is where you go when you "go and see." *Gemba* is where the action is — where value is created for the customer. It is the kitchen in a restaurant, the operating room in a hospital, or a retail floor in a store. *Gemba* is where the real business occurs. If you don't go to *gemba,* you'll never truly understand the business or its issues.

One management tool is the *gemba* walk or observation tour. This is not a "run through that area, wave hello, and get back to your office" tour. The key is to be observant and to ask questions about things you notice. During a *gemba* walk, you may focus on a single item, like safety, housekeeping, performance, or Lean implementation. For example, if quick changeovers are a priority to your organization, find out when setups will happen and go watch them. Can you suggest additional improvements?

Though *gemba* walks aren't scripted, you must set a main intention for the walk. If the theme of the day is safety, you'll observe everything about safety, from employee actions to metric performance to the condition and location of safety equipment.

You may be wondering, "What do I do on a *gemba* walk?" Here's a list:

- Build relationships with the organization and break down barriers to change.

- Learn to observe your organization with "Lean" eyes. Initially, go on *gemba* walks with your Lean *sensei* (see Chapter 12) to learn what and how to observe.

- Train others to observe by conducting regular and frequent walks — as a staff and with individual staff members. Have individual staff members shadow you — it's a powerful way of educating them.

- Review performance metrics as tied to the *hoshin* plan.

- Review A3s, team performance charts, *andon* status, housekeeping, and display boards (see Chapter 9) at communication centers.

An *A3* is a one-page report of an issue and resolution plan. It's named after the international paper A3 paper size. On one page, all the salient information is recorded in sketches or words: the issue, before condition, after condition, action plan, cost, responsible parties, and results.

- Talk to people. Seek to understand what they do and what their issues are. Ask about what you're seeing. — they're the experts at their job function. Most people love to talk about what they do.

- When possible, connect the global issues and strategy of the company with the issues of *gemba.* Help people make the connection.

You can build a rapport with your organization while you're on a *gemba* walk. Listen to their issues and take action to help them out. Over time, you'll earn their respect and build trust. Eventually, they'll look for you during the walks to recommend improvements and give you feedback.

Housekeeping tours are a good way for management to accomplish several goals:

- ✔ Stress the importance of the orderly environment.
- ✔ Practice a form of standardized work.
- ✔ Connect with the organization.

Management tours should cover the entire facility, inside and out. They should also follow a set process, including an established checklist of items to review, an agenda, and facility route (including restrooms and safety equipment). Nonconformances should be recorded and addressed. These items should be followed up on the next tour.

Software and Information Management

More and more software tools are available to facilitate all manner of business-process improvement, analysis, management, and whatnot. These tools are increasingly broad ranging and capable. Software poses a bit of a conundrum to the Lean practitioner, however, because software is complex, and complexity is an anathema to Lean. Furthermore, you risk becoming captive to the tool, which is also a Lean no-no. However, a well-designed software program can enable your staff to perform both tactical and strategic tasks faster and more accurately, thereby reducing several forms of waste.

Per Lean doctrine, keep your computer and software application usage as streamlined and simple as possible. That may sound like an oxymoron, but you can contain the size, scope, and proliferation of your computer applications. Use them where they're needed.

Lean facilitation software

You can apply software to the practice of Value Stream Mapping and related Lean activities. Leading tools include iGrafx Flowcharter (www.igrafx.com), eVSM (www.evsm.com), and LeanView (www.osgi.com). These tools also offer additional features, including process mapping, simulation, and some analytical capabilities.

These tools are "desktop" tools that run only on personal computers running the Microsoft Windows operating system. Some of these tools have networked versions with centralized repositories for shared file use and configuration management.

Statistics and graphical analysis

The seven basic tools of quality addressed in Chapter 9, as well as the larger universe of statistical and analytical tools, are aptly facilitated by well-established providers. If you look in the Start menu of your PC, you'll likely find one of them: Microsoft Excel which (http://office.microsoft.com/excel) performs most all of the basic statistical analysis functions for you. Excel can be programmed to do more, and add-on products like SigmaXL (www.sigmaxl.com) will provide nearly all of what mere mortals will ever need.

For more high-powered statistics and analysis, there's Minitab (www.minitab.com), the king of desktop data analysis and statistics software. If you need more than basic statistics, such as regression analysis, analysis of variance (ANOVA), statistical process control (SPC), measurement systems analysis (MSA), design of experiments (DoE), reliability analysis, multivariate analysis, and non-parametrics, Minitab is the tool for you! Minitab also comes with a Quality Companion tool that performs process mapping, Fishbone Diagrams, FMEA, Value Stream Map comparisons, and more. It has extensive online guidance, coaching, and tutorials.

As great as these tools are, SigmaXL and Minitab run only on the Windows operating system. Excel is available for the Macintosh. An excellent alternative for Mac and Linux users, as well as multiplatform environments, is JMP software (www.jmp.com) from the SAS Institute.

Business Process Management

One of the most powerful forces to emerge in the enterprise-level software world since 2000 is a suite known as BPM — Business Process Management. BPM enables you to define processes that cross functional lines, integrating numerous back-end systems like ERP, MRP, CRM, and others, and track them as they perform.

BPM systems support process modeling, data capture, data analysis, and process control functions. They perform andon, facilitate the development and real-time display of management dashboards (BAM), and even build Balanced Scorecards. In short, BPM will enhance the Lean enterprise.

BPM is at present an enterprise-class application and is not yet available for independent small businesses. The genre is new enough that it's crowded with startups, and the large well-known enterprise vendors have yet to establish a clear and present direction. Until the industry matures and consolidates, there are no obvious leaders. But make no mistake, BPM is a key enabler of the Lean enterprise of the future!

Part IV
The Lean Enterprise

The 5th Wave

By Rich Tennant

"I'm writing the corporate bylaws. How do you spell 'guillotine'?"

In this part . . .

The successful Lean transition is not only about the things you do, but also about how you overcome challenges. Some people will be resistant to change — as a group or as individuals. In this part, you discover how to address change, see how to implement Lean in different parts of the business, and understand how Lean organizations look across different industries.

Chapter 11

Lean in the Organization: Principles, Behaviors, and Change

In This Chapter

▶ Probing the current cultural climate

▶ Aligning behaviors to Lean principles

▶ Understanding the phases of organizational change

*Y*ou are part of one or more organizations. An *organization* is a group of people arranged and structured to achieve a purpose. It could be a business purpose (for example, to develop or provide goods and services to customers for a profit). It could be another purpose (such as education, government, or personal or nonprofit contributions to humanity); for example, a family is a type of organization.

No matter what the purpose of the organization, the people within that organization and their conduct collectively define the organization's principles and guide the individuals' behaviors. The people give the organization its culture.

An organization's culture and the principles that drive people's behaviors ultimately determine the degrees of an organization's performance, quality, and success. Think about famous organizational cultures — like J. M Smucker, Hewlett-Packard, Nordstrom, EDS (Electronic Data Systems), the Federal Emergency Management Agency (FEMA), or Enron — and how they've performed. In each of these cases — as in the case of every organization — people's behaviors have both steered and been steered directly by the principles and belief systems fostered from within and spread across the organizational landscape . . . for better or for worse.

Organizational cultures are deeply ingrained. The principles guiding the behaviors of the people within an organization are purposefully long-lived and slow to change. Organizational culture has mass: The larger it is and the faster it's going, the more momentum it builds. This trait is a good thing when that momentum is carrying you in the right direction, but not so good when you wander off-course.

Few organizations are born and raised as Lean organizations, so if you're now embarking upon a Lean journey, you're likely in the process of changing course. This means that in addition to applying the methods and techniques described in the rest of this book, you will also be changing the organizational culture by changing principles and behaviors. In order to determine just how much change is needed, first you have to understand how your organization's current principles and behaviors align with Lean principles and behaviors. The extent of the gap between the two will help you understand what changes are required and how to make them. As with any change, the methods, the frequency, and the messenger will influence the organization's response.

In this chapter, we tell you all about the organizational principles and behaviors that reflect a Lean organization. We show you how to assess an organization's true principles and behaviors versus its stated principles. You will understand how to compare your current organization's principles to Lean principles, and get a feel for a basic organizational change model. Finally, you will identify a road map to close the gaps.

Many analysts and pundits use the term *values* in defining and describing organizational culture and principles. In the Lean world, the term *value* is more directly associated with the concept of what the customer values and adding value within a process or work activity. To avoid confusion in this chapter, when we want to refer to organizational culture and principles, we use the word *principles*.

Assessing Organizational Culture

Before you can change your organizational culture, you have to understand the culture in reality. In this section, we tell you how to assess the current organizational climate, compare it to Lean principles, and identify the gap that exists between the two.

Will the real principles please stand up?

Most organizations have both a stated set of principles and an implied set of principles. Collectively, these form the foundation of virtues and beliefs that

Chapter 11: Lean in the Organization: Principles, Behaviors, and Change 213

reinforce the integrity and character upon which everyone — including employees, customers, suppliers, shareholders, analysts, and consumers — depends.

The *stated* principles are often a flowery list of words, hung on a wall or occupying a page on the employee Web site. Most organizations address such hallmarks as customer service, trust, teamwork, diversity, honesty, and respect for people in their cadre of principles. No doubt an expensive team of high-level people spent the better part of a retreat session precisely chiseling those idealistic words into a lofty statement of principles — only to find that, in reality, they're mostly unknown or ignored within the organization.

The *implied* principles are often not quite so formalized. They're typically not the ones printed and framed — instead, they're implied by the behaviors, attitudes, and words of the individuals who drive the organization's culture. New hires are infected with the implied principles and belief systems before they even finish the orientation class. The implied principles are the basis for the real belief system in an organization.

The implied principles are often at odds with the stated ones. This discrepancy causes tension and conflict across the organization. If "respect for people" is a stated principle, but people are poorly treated or fired indiscriminately, your principles are at odds. If "trust" is a stated principle, but people are constantly second-guessed and overruled, you have trouble. "Integrity" was one of Enron's stated principles, but it's pretty obvious that the real set of principles resulted in behavior of a different sort.

Getting the culture to the starting line

If you're beginning the Lean journey, you have to know where your organization stands as the journey begins. Identify the current principles and beliefs, and assess what needs to change before you embark. You have organizational baggage accompanying you on your journey. The culture fairy is not going to wave a magic wand and instantly change the entire climate and culture of the organization — you'll have to work at it.

Most organizations have undertaken many initiatives before trying Lean. An organization's normal reaction is to resist change, hoping that "this too shall pass" — you'll hear people grouse about needing to do their "real job." Keep in mind that these attitudes are part of your current state. Your past track record will influence your organization's acceptance of another new initiative. Begin by assessing the current state of the organization. Then you can identify the gaps that could thwart your Lean efforts.

Identifying the current state of the organization

Taking stock of organizational culture is a squishy task: By its very nature, it's imprecise. Even though organizational culture is difficult to define, as Supreme Court Justice Potter Stewart once said, "You'll know it when you see it." Seeing the condition of an organization's culture and its readiness for change isn't difficult when you know what to look for.

Begin your assessment of the current situation by asking questions. You can use several mechanisms to gather data; organizational questionnaires, observation studies, electronic surveys, and employing outside observers or interviewers are all options to gather information on the current organizational climate.

Here are some questions to start your assessment:

- What are the officially stated principles and beliefs of the organization?
- What organizational behaviors support those stated principles?
- What behaviors suggest a different set of beliefs?
- What implied principles can you identify?
- Where are the stated and implied principles at odds? Where are they consistent?
- How would you describe the relationship between management and non-management employees? Identify behaviors that typify the management/non-management relationship.
- Has the organization undergone mergers and acquisitions? If so, how many cultures currently coexist in the current organization?
- How has the organization handled change initiatives in the past?
- When is the last time a significant improvement undertaking occurred? How long did it last?
- Are any formal change initiatives currently active?
- How effective have these change initiatives been?
- How many members of the current organization have been involved in the undertaking?

You cannot observe and measure any of this from your office. As with Value Stream Mapping and *Kaizen,* you must go where the action is to see the true picture. You're trying to identify misalignments and incongruities before you introduce a set of Lean principles. For example, if one of your stated values is "quality first," but you observe defective product being shipped to meet a delivery deadline, this is inconsistent. If "continuous improvement" is another stated value, but every year the organization is fighting the exact same fires, what does this tell you?

The organization's stated principles may be close to Lean, yet the implied principles may be across a chasm as wide as the Grand Canyon. Knowing your gaps in your credibility will help you formulate a change strategy to support the shift from traditional operations to Lean.

Defining Lean principles in an organization

The overarching Lean principle is *continuous incremental change.* This is supported by to two additional categories:

- ✔ Customer satisfaction
- ✔ Respect for people

Many Lean programs and practitioners focus on the customer satisfaction and forget that respect for people is just as important — and just as fundamental to the Lean enterprise. Each area contains subordinate principles, as shown in Table 11-1.

Table 11-1	A Summary of Lean Principles
Continuous Incremental Change	
Customer Satisfaction	*Respect for People*
Perform value-added activities	Ensure personal safety
Operate just-in-time	Foster employee security
Eliminate waste	Challenge and engage everyone
Continuously flow (pull)	Celebrate wins
Create quality at the source	Continuous growth and learning
Live standardized work	Communicate effectively

Measuring the gap

To understand your organization's current culture and define what Lean principles mean to you, try creating a table comparing the current stated values and behaviors in the organization to Lean principles and behaviors. Also include the implied values and behaviors and how they line up to Lean principles. Table 11-2 is a reference.

Table 11-2   **Build Your Own Cultural Assessment**

Current Principle	Actual or Stated?	Observable Behavior	Does It Support Lean?	Which Lean Principle Does It Support?	What Is the Expected Observable Behavior?

A commonly used graphical tool in Lean for showing progress to a defined goal is the *spider chart*. In a spider chart, the outside circle represents full compliance or 100 percent attainment, while the center of the circle represents no compliance or 0 percent attainment. The objective is to fill in the circle as performance increases. The spider chart in Figure 11-1 shows progress for cultural transformation. In this example, the organization has rated personal safety at 90 percent and value-added at 20 percent.

Figure 11-1: This spider chart graphically depicts an organization's progress toward cultural transformation goals.

After you've assessed the organization's culture, you'll know where you're strong and where your challenges lie. The nature of the organizational strengths and weaknesses will determine your change initiative. Going forward, remember to continually assess the culture.

Changing the Organization

It's one thing to measure organizational culture. It's another thing to assess organizational culture relative to Lean principles and behaviors. And it's a whole different animal when you begin to initiate the cultural changes to bridge the gaps. That's when the fun begins!

Rarely are organizations naturally prepared to begin a Lean journey. Most often, organizations experience growing pains — organizational cultures twist, contort, and usually writhe in outright pain as they grow and mature into Lean practices. These contortions are recognizable and typically occur in five discrete phases with each turn through the cycle of improvement. As the Lean journey progresses, the organization generally moves through these phases more quickly.

Everyone in the organization progresses at his own pace. Some people are "change embracers," some are "wait and seers," and some are "resisters to the end." In the process of change, each of these factions must be treated accordingly.

The organizational-change aspect of the Lean transformation is often ignored. The soft side of change is too murky and political for most people. But if you don't pay attention to it, your Lean efforts are in danger of failure.

Going through the five phases of change

Independent of the nature of the change, an organization that's undergoing a transformation will move through five phases — most likely *not* in strict serial order. The organization is a collection of individuals, each of whom accepts change in his own time. So as change happens, the organization may sometimes have to go backward to go forward. As you take your next steps in the Lean journey, you'll go back through these phases again. The trick for management is to monitor the pulse of the organization to know in what direction it's morphing and evolving. When backsliding occurs, management needs to correct the course.

When embarking upon a Lean journey, the organization has to change — continuously. It can't expect to harbor its old ways and at the same time truly implement Lean. How quickly and how readily the organization adapts to Lean depends upon the past, the present, and how far away the organization is from its desired future.

Phase 1: Recognition and acceptance

Recognition is the beginning of change, and acceptance completes this first phase. Just like in your own life, an organization must recognize and accept that today's conditions are no longer workable.

Not until the pain of the present is greater that the pain of the uncertain future will an organization embark upon a change of any type. Opportunity alone will motivate only 5 percent of the population. The other 95 percent are motivated by a fear of loss or some other significant emotional event. The critical first step in the process is to clearly identify and communicate the need for change until the organization recognizes and accepts the premise.

Recognition usually requires letting go — letting go of a stale dream, an obsolete vision, or a nostalgia for the past. People are reluctant to let go — many people cling to memories of the good old days long after they're gone and irrelevant. And the bigger the organization, the more difficult letting go is.

Think about a family that has outgrown its current home. The lone bathroom is overcrowded in the morning, the kids are tripping over one another in the bedrooms, and there's no place to relax or do homework. But the mortgage is affordable, the neighborhood is comfortable, and there are all the memories. At what point does the family recognize and accept the need to make a change? Only they can decide when the timing is right.

Phase 2: Direction and planning

After a critical mass of the organization recognizes and accepts the need for change, the next step is to determine the new vision and set the direction for the future. Only then can you define the action plan to move the organization into that future.

Sometimes, the very act of painting the future vision helps cement the acceptance for change. When that vision relieves enough current pain and suffering, organizational buy-in improves. In the process, forward momentum begins to build, which attracts support and ideas for the action plan.

Consider the family in the cramped house (see the preceding section). After they accept the idea of change, the next step is to paint the vision of their future — a vision where they have enough space and sufficient facilities to meet their needs and better enjoy their lives together. The parents decide that the time has come for radical change — a move to a new house. As they discuss the move within the family, they receive input and considerations from all family members. They create a vision of their new home and set the direction — a target for what and where to buy. After the direction has been set, the detailed planning phase starts. The plans include the full range of activities required when you move into the new residence — from packing and changing schools to utility transfers and meeting new neighbors.

Overall, the family recognizes and accepts the change, and they define the vision and the plan. Yet each member of the family will deal with the changes in his own way. If Trevor has to leave his baseball team in the middle of the season, or Sara worries she'll have trouble making new friends at a new school, they may quietly hope that it won't happen. Even if the planning accounts for it, in reality, each family member will adapt in his own time.

Organizational acceptance of change is very similar to what the family experiences. The direction comes from the top, but those in lower positions may feel like they're being forced to change. They may see the potential for long-term benefits, but in the short term, they'll be uncomfortable — if not downright unhappy.

Phase 3: Charging forward

After organizational leaders set the direction make the plans, it's time to charge forward and begin to execute on the plan. If you're helping to lead the change, you'll look over your shoulder to see if anyone is following you. Some will be, but others will be staying put, waiting to see what happens.

When you start to implement Lean, a range of personalities will be present — hiders, naysayers, adapters, wait-and-seers, opportunists, and a host of other characters. They may cause your best-laid plans to be retooled. Facilitating organizational change requires

- ✔ **Proper communications:** The best way through the change is two-way communication — not only listening but being heard (see "Propagating the principles" later in this chapter)

- ✔ **Proper behavior:** Actions must match the new direction — this is vitally important. Actions must support the vision, adhere to the principles, and reinforce the plan. Just like in the family in the too-small house (see "Phase 1: Recognition and acceptance," earlier in this chapter), each member may need something different to adapt to the new situation. But by virtue of the move, the parents have said, "There is no going back."

Think about the family on moving day. There are boxes everywhere. The moving van is loaded up. Matt and Michele are hiding in hopes that mom and dad won't notice. Trevor is convinced that there won't be a good baseball team at his new school. Sara is anxious to meet new friends in the new neighborhood. The dog is waiting to see what happens. Meanwhile, the parents just want to get it over with!

Phase 4: Turmoil

The initial Lean implementation is underway. The first work area has finished its inaugural *Kaizen*. Despite its successes, the rumor mill starts to churn, full of dire predictions of job loss, doom, and gloom. The lunchroom conversation is colored with dark clouds and reasons why "it won't work" or "if everyone just waits five minutes, management will be on to something else." The first crisis hits middle management, and they're tempted to go back to their old ways. Turmoil is underway. Nothing is settled. Many still doubt management's resolve to the Lean undertaking. No one is comfortable.

This phase is like the family starting to sort everything out in their new house. Things invariably don't go exactly as planned. Belongings are misplaced because they don't have a place in the new house. Boxes are mixed up. Maybe the kids are waiting to see if the parents crack and decide they can go back to their old life. The kids will be closely watching how the parents handle the situation. The parents' actions will either enlist or alienate the kids in the whole moving process.

Similarly, in the organization, how management addresses the rumor mill, conducts themselves, and responds in the face of a crisis will either fuel the negative fire or extinguish it to a pile of simmering coals. It is during this tumultuous phase that the tone is set for the rest of the Lean journey.

Phase 5: Integration

Eventually, with commitment and consistency, proper communications and behavior, the organization absorbs the changes and integrates the new direction into its psyche. People climb onboard and buy in to the vision of a Lean organization. Management will have to handle — maybe even dismiss — the small percentage of the organization that refuses to join in.

Particularly because Lean is a journey and not a destination, integration includes an environment of continuous improvement and change. Full buy-in across the entire organization may take years.

Like with the family settling in the new location, unpacking the boxes is really the easy part. Everyone will find a place for their things. How each of the kids adjusts to his new situation will be as individual as the kids are. But with persistence, patience, and communication, eventually they'll all get settled into a new routine — until the next change.

Hurdling roadblocks to success

As with any new undertaking, organizational roadblocks develop along the way. Some of them are cultural, some historical, and some situational. All are rooted in the individuals of the organization and their corresponding perceptions, attitudes, emotions, and actions. In the following sections, we discuss some of the common roadblocks to successful Lean implementation and corresponding organizational change.

Roadblock #1: Rules are made to be broken

Lean is based on the implementation of standards and performance to those standards. It is based on processes being repeatable. Improvements can only be made if there is a measurable baseline for comparison. The attitude that "rules are made to be broken" is misaligned with the Lean thought process. If the organization embraces a countercultural attitude, you'll have challenges on your Lean journey.

Reframe this old adage to a new one: "Standards are made to be followed and then improved." Adopting this new adage will go a long way toward mitigating those challenges. You must be vigilant to ensure that the standards are being followed. When someone violates a standard, you must understand why. If his reason is legitimate, formally adjust the standards. If his reason isn't legitimate, you must take appropriate action to reinforce the importance of the standards and prescribe the consequences for violation.

Roadblock #2: Cowboy individualism

No man is an island in a Lean organization. Everyone in the value stream is connected in some way. Cowboy individualists who buck the system, for whatever reason, will inhibit everyone's Lean journey. There is room for creativity and individualism if it is directed toward the elimination of waste and improvement of the standards. There is no room for those who, on principle, refuse to operate to the methods of standardized work.

Roadblock #3: Fear of the unknown and job loss

If management has not made guarantees that employees won't lose their jobs as a result of productivity improvements, the Lean journey will be a very bumpy ride. People fear the unknown. You're asking them to have faith that, by actively participating in Lean, they won't be rewarded with a pink slip. It's one thing to get them to trust that the concepts will work — it's another thing to get them to trust that it won't negatively impact their quality of life.

Roadblock #4: Resistance to change — what's in it for me?

In general, people resist change that isn't their idea. They may be fearful when it's their idea, but if they still feel in control, they'll make the decision to change. But when change is foisted upon them, they feel like they have little or no control, and they may be uncertain about the outcome. Their collective resistance rises up like a tidal wave ready to crash down on the organization, stopping all forward progress. When they do not see a personal benefit or incentive to change, they won't.

Some of the employees will fight through; you don't need to worry about them — they'll be your trailblazers. It's the ones who can't overcome their resistance or fears that you'll need to either move forward or move out.

Roadblock #5: Been there, done that

A portion of your organization will be waiting for you to fail, especially if your organization has a track record of failed initiatives or flavor-of-the-month programs. One of the best ways to mitigate this reaction is to enlist some of the biggest naysayers early on in the initiative. By winning them over early, you create influential endorsers of the Lean process.

Forecasting the Future

Organizations are like supertankers: You can't make a left turn with a supertanker, or it'll roll over and sink. Turning an organization requires you to get out the tugboats and nudge, nudge, nudge. But when the new course is set and the engines are cranked up, you can go a long way.

The changes you make to develop a Lean organization must be constantly nudged, carefully pointed, and supported from within. The culture will resist at first, but with vigilance and guiding principles, the behaviors will change and the new cultural course will be set. To ensure success, you must maintain the watch.

The journey that never ends

The single most powerful attribute of a Lean organization is adaptability. The Lean journey is continuous; _Kaizen_ is continuous; change is continuous. By embracing the principles of Lean, the organizational culture develops the inherent ability to constantly adapt and respond to events — both internal and external. Independent of all the specific tools and techniques of Lean, this agility makes the Lean organization as competitive as any type of organization anywhere.

There are no measures by which the Lean organization can declare itself finished. There is no "Lean Land," where all problems have been addressed, everyone's knowledge is complete and all processes are optimized. There is always something else to improve — something better to strive for.

Certain organizational cultures are destination-focused. For them, initiatives are like projects — they have beginnings and ends. The idea that you never finish may be frustrating and difficult for such organizations to grasp. These organizations need to shift their perspective and alter their principles when they commence their Lean journey. They must adopt the cultural predisposition of _Kaizen_.

Propagating the principles

The most effective lever to change an organization is communication. Change requires descriptions, definitions, explanations, education and training, and questions and answers. Everyone in the organization has a mouth, eyes, ears, and a pen or keyboard. In this section we cover ways to propagate Lean principles through communication and action.

Everyone speaks — and hears

The team element of Lean requires everyone to participate in the process. Communication is multidirectional. Everyone in the organization has the responsibility to communicate and to listen. No one has either the monopoly on communication or the option to opt out of communication.

Management-speak . . . and action

Managers at all levels in a Lean initiative are responsible for ensuring that communications are flowing in all directions. For managers to create the vision — setting directions, defining plans, enabling events, measuring outcomes, and analyzing results — they must ensure that communications are flowing among all levels and across all functions of the organization. Without these communications, they can't ensure that the plans will be implemented and that new behaviors will emerge that support the overall Lean journey.

The first step is to send a clear message. If the organization has been involved in other continuous-improvement initiatives or major changes, management must clearly and continually communicate the new Lean principles to the organization and explain how Lean fits relative to these previous events. Next, managers must reach out to the staff with the what's-in-it-for-you message, to engage the early adapters. Additional messages must be crafted as the journey continues.

The organization will be waiting for management to put its money where its mouth is. It will be examining the behaviors of managers, looking for proof that management is committed to the principles and will walk the walk. Have their behaviors really changed? When a crisis occurs, are they reacting with the new principles? Is this initiative for real or is it a "flavor of the month?" Management must set the tone and lead by example.

Methods of communication

Everyone responds differently to different methods and modes of communication. Therefore, the messages must be broadcast on all frequencies (meaning: all the tools and techniques of communications must be invoked to move the organizational culture). A Lean transformation will impact the people working in the organization at a very personal level. Face-to-face, personal communication is recommended from the beginning. Communication includes ways to get the message out, as well as ways to listen and collect feedback from the organization — remember communication must be multi-directional.

As the journey unfolds, communications technologies as traditional as presentations and newsletters; as new-wave as Webcasts, podcasts, personalized e-mails, tip lines, newsletters, e-zines, and blogs; and as personal as hallway conversations and off-site seminars — all are appropriate. Methods of communication include anything and everything — whatever it takes to reach every corner of the organization, and vice-versa.

Mergers and acquisitions

When organizations unite as a result of a merger or acquisition, a blending of the cultures must take place for Lean to succeed. For example, Wiremold, which in the 1990s was on a Lean journey and grew through acquisitions, found success when it introduced the new company to Lean on day one of the merger. Initial *Kaizen* events occurred in the first week of the acquired company's union with Wiremold. In most, if not all cases, CEO Art Byrne led the initial events, which sent a clear message to the organization that Lean was not an option and that Wiremold would teach them how to start their journey.

Several instances of Lean derailment or outright failure have occurred when the dominant culture of a merger or acquisition was a traditional culture with no interest or understanding of Lean. The purchase was made to increase market share or because market conditions changed. Successful results from Lean implementations made the acquired companies attractive to purchase. However, under traditionally minded management, progress that took eight to ten years was undone in a matter of months.

Differentiating the parts from the whole

Human beings have their own unique reactions to change. They color facts with emotional responses. Getting this concept is critical if you want to understand, measure, and manage the cultural issues and culture change.

You must address the human element of change, both individually and collectively. Something happens in the alchemy when individuals become the organization — you have to address both.

This process requires hard work. You won't find a magic bullet or pixie dust that will miraculously change the culture overnight. To transform an organization's principles, behaviors, and attitudes requires diligence, discipline, patience, communication, and a commitment to the long-term vision. Implementation of tools and techniques is the easy part when compared with changing the core of an organization. And if you lose momentum, it's very difficult to regain it.

The organization will not move as fast as you want it to. The whole moves slower than the individuals who make up the organization.

Chapter 12

Power to the People

*O*ne of the oldest clichés in business — you've heard it a zillion times — is "People are our most important resource." From the Lean perspective, these words are both critically true *and* utterly false. On face value, it's true that an organization is powered by people more than anything else. Without the people, there is no organizational performance. People are more important than facilities, equipment, capital, or other resources.

But in the Lean world, you don't think of people as a "resource." You don't categorize, value, measure, and manage people the same way you would manage financial, capital, or intellectual resources. In Lean, people are not the most important *resource* in an organization; people *are* the organization. A Lean practice trusts and respects people to control resources in order to add value to the customer.

Lean will not happen without the people. Lean affects every single person in the organization — and each has his own unique response. Often, when embarking upon a Lean journey, managers and practitioners focus on the tools and techniques of Lean. They spend all their time advocating Lean, and not enough time inquiring — checking in with the people, getting their ideas and reactions, and bringing them along. Investing time and energy in the human side of change is not only a critical component of success; it also pays long-term dividends when the organization is fully engaged in continuous improvement.

In this chapter, we show you the human side of change, and let you know how it's manifested in a Lean implementation. You discover how managers act and support change at various levels of the organization. You find out about Lean teams. This chapter includes an in-depth examination of the individual's role in the transformation. You also discover the role of the Lean *sensei* and what it means to be a student of Lean.

The Human Side of Change

"Motivation is a fire from within. If someone else tries to light that fire under you, chances are it will burn very briefly."

—Stephen R. Covey

People love to change when change is their own idea — they have a sense of control, the feeling that they're in the driver's seat. Even if the control is limited, the feeling is there. Whether it's a big change (like taking a different job or moving into a new home) or a small change (like buying a new pair of shoes or upgrading to the latest mobile phone), when it's your idea, you're motivated. You determine the effort, the risk, and the rewards. You balance the equation — and you're willing to go for it!

Now alter one critical element of the scenario: the change is no longer your idea. Immediately, you don't feel the same sense of participation. You don't feel in control. You're not sure where it will all lead. Fear, doubt, uncertainty, and perhaps even anger are among the flood of emotions you feel. Do you still trust the opportunity?

Fight, flight, freeze, fake, fall in line, or fade away — the choice is yours. Each individual, facing the same situation, will have her own unique response. In the context of a Lean journey, people experience the total range of emotions — from excitement to resistance and everything in between. They experience stress. They need support. They need to be heard. They need to be educated.

Whether you're a practitioner, manager, or participant of Lean in your organization, you have to work through your own reaction to change. You have to adjust your actions and attitudes and evaluate your emotional responses. There is no magical incantation. It takes real work — and it's work people usually don't like to do. Ultimately everyone has the ability to become a Lean student, actively engaged in continuous improvement and lifelong learning. First, you have to get over the hurdles of resistance that appear as you move down the road of Lean.

Change and the individual

As an individual in an organization moving toward Lean, you have choices. It doesn't matter where in the organization you fit, what your title is, or what job you perform — you will experience change. The attitude you choose to adopt is up to you and no one else. You may choose to jump onboard immediately, becoming a change agent. You may wait and see. You may choose to leave rather than go through this. You may play the victim or you may play the trailblazer — or something in between. It's all up to you, but understanding the dynamics and science behind change helps you in the process.

The basics: Change 101

Independent of the circumstances of change, people experience change in their bodies and minds. In this section, we explore the basics of change and stress.

Perceptions are reality

Have you ever gone to a high school reunion and noticed that some of your classmates just can't seem to get over high school? It's as if their lives stopped at age 17. They long for the "good old days." They relive every moment of the big game. They wish they could go back. Other classmates never even think of coming back to a reunion because they're so over it — they've moved on and embraced the future like there is no tomorrow.

Perceptions create reality. Perceptions completely overlay a situation, causing a person to act, think, and feel in a certain way. What people can control is their attitudes, actions, and emotions. If a person believes her life was best in high school, this perception will have her stuck in high school — and it will be reflected in her attitudes, actions, and emotions.

When implementing Lean, you need to recognize that people are judging the situation with their own unique biases or perceptions. Part of the organization will want to hold on to the "glory days," and others will be so committed to the change that they run forward without a mere glance back to the old way of doing things. A whole range of people will fall somewhere in between. But eventually, they all need to get on the Lean path.

How people perceive the change colors their responses. During the initial communication, many people check out and don't hear most of the change message. Almost immediately they start thinking, "How is this going to affect me? Am I going to lose my job? Will I have to change? Are they really serious this time?" How each person perceives the change dictates how quickly that person overcomes her natural resistance.

The reality of resistance

If you want to create a truly Lean organization, you have to overcome individual resistance to change. Certain attitudes appear — these attitudes are symptoms of resistance. You may recognize some of them:

- ✔ **"Been there, done that":** If someone feels like this resembles something that failed in the past, she'll resist. She won't willingly jump on the train to Lean Land. Lingering trust issues, lack of faith, and sarcasm are just a few of the blocks that you have to remove. How? Through two-way communication, demonstrated commitment, and early results.

- ✔ **"A rose by any name":** This attitude manifests in several ways. If the most draconian of supervisors is now anointed a coach or mentor, no one is likely to believe it possible or sustainable. If you've had previous failed attempts at Lean or other continuous-improvement initiatives, you have to show how this time is different. Both of these situations require two-way communication, ongoing monitoring, and continual training and development. That supervisor will have to prove that he did more than attend "charm school" to win over the people who work for him.

✔ **"Not invented here" or "Doesn't apply here":** These attitudes have contributed to the failure of Lean in many companies. In the worst manifestation of these attitudes, people may understand how the tools and methods of Lean apply in an automotive manufacturing company, but they don't see how Lean applies in their company. Overcoming these attitudes can be very difficult. Constantly demonstrating how to find and eliminate waste in your processes takes creative leadership. You may need to adjust the language or demonstrate a concept to show people how Lean applies in your organization.

✔ **"Fear of failure":** This attitude prevents individuals from actively participating. Being a perfectionist is different from striving for perfection. Perfectionists will be stuck, stopped, or scared if you don't show them how important it is to try — independent of the outcome. In a Lean culture, when you try something new, it won't always be perfect the first time out. Remember the Plan-Do-Check-Act (PDCA) cycle (see Chapter 6). The Do phase of that cycle is all about trying — trying is built into the process.

It's okay to fail as long as you learn a lesson.

Stress: The natural response to change

Stress is a naturally human response to change. It's unavoidable. Stress happens on a continuum, from positive and motivating to negative and debilitating. In the Lean transformation, the stress you need to watch out for is the negative stuff.

When stress starts to go to the negative side, you may feel

✔ Tense

✔ Anxious

✔ Angry

✔ Depressed

✔ Distracted

✔ Frustrated

✔ Short tempered

✔ Apathetic

✔ Unusually tired

You may also find yourself eating or drinking more than you normally do. And you may not show up where you're supposed to.

You can manage stress in many ways. Personally, you can monitor your own behavior and choose to deal with your stress in healthy ways — through diet, exercise, laughter, and rest. You may also find a friend to confide in and to give support — talking helps you work through stressful situations.

Reactions beyond reason

In extreme cases of stress or change, your body can actually have a physiological response — fight or flight. Deep inside your brain is a tiny, almond-shaped cluster of neurons called the amygdala. The amygdala receives a fear or danger signal from the thalamus, which causes it to secrete chemicals in the body, even while the rest of the brain is trying to process the information for the appropriate response. As Daniel Goldman describes it in *Emotional Intelligence,* the amygdala can actually hijack your brain, preventing rational responses.

So what does this have to do with you and a Lean transformation? If you find yourself reacting irrationally to situations during the Lean transformation, you may be a victim of that emotional hijacking. One of the best responses is to walk away and cool down — it can take as long as a few hours — until your body can actually clear the chemicals and enable you to rationally think through the situation.

When undergoing any change, it's natural to experience strong, impulsive reactions from time to time. You can learn and grow beyond the knee-jerk reaction. With each change you experience and accept, you train yourself that the situation is okay and the amygdala doesn't need to charge in to save you.

Embracing change the Lean way

In the previous sections we covered the fundamentals of individual change. In the next sections, we show you what the individual can do to embrace the change to Lean.

Know yourself

Assess where you are personally with the change; this will help you move through the Lean transition. How are you feeling? Where can you contribute? What attitudes, emotions, or actions may be getting in the way of participating fully as an individual or a team member? How does working closely around people affect you? How ready are you to learn and stretch?

You're the only one who can change you.

Most people are uncomfortable with the unknown. In the absence of information, they anticipate the worst. This "pessimistic" approach is a form of self-protection. The solution is to learn how to be comfortable with ambiguity and find the courage within to try something new. Every individual has to go through a phase of letting go — the trick is for you to find your own way to let go of the old and move on to grab the new.

Some Lean practices — like taking before and after photos of an area — actually help people let go. Creating ceremonies or events to symbolize letting go can also help. The movement of a monument, burying an old manual, or throwing a party in new floor space — these are all examples of ceremonial letting go. Conducting ceremonies may sound hokey, but it works.

Think about other changes you have experienced in your life that were successful. Identify how you adjusted your attitudes, emotions, and actions to make those situations positive. Build on that track record to propel you forward into the Lean transformation.

When you start to see progress, you'll have an easier time adapting to the changed environment. The concept of Lean will become more concrete for you. This shift in perception usually happens after you've participated in *Kaizen* activities — it doesn't happen overnight. Small, continuous improvements in your perceptions will drive you to change your thoughts, attitudes, and, ultimately, your actions.

When you truly start thinking in a Lean manner, you look at life differently. You tend to see ways to improve any situation. You look at waste in a totally different way. You want to make things better — and you know you can! Whether you're standing in line at the money bank or volunteering at the food bank, you have ideas to improve customer wait times or more effectively pack food boxes. Ultimately your actions, attitudes, and emotions are colored by the Lean filter.

Personal principles: Alignment with Lean

When an organization shifts to Lean, its principles shift. For an individual to get behind the change, she needs to understand what the impact is on her and her principles. People whose principles are closer to Lean principles will have an easier time making the adjustment then those whose aren't.

How do you align principles? You start by knowing your own principles. Then you identify and understand the organization's Lean principles — stated and manifested. When you compare your principles with the Lean ones, you'll see where there is misalignment and how severe it is. Then you can choose how to close the gap.

While the majority of people enjoy working in a Lean environment, some people may decide that they would rather work elsewhere and choose to leave the organization. That is okay; the people who stay are the ones who want to live Lean.

Speak up, step up: The individual's role

So often, when people are told that there will be a change, they give their power away. They don't ask questions — through their actions, they abdicate their responsibility. What can you do as an individual in a company that's embarking upon a Lean journey?

- ✔ Ask questions.
- ✔ Clarify expectations and new roles.
- ✔ Stay positive — don't fuel the rumor mill.
- ✔ Actively learn about the tools and concepts.
- ✔ Identify what will change in your world.
- ✔ Request training.
- ✔ Volunteer to participate in early activities.
- ✔ Hold yourself accountable to your own thoughts, emotions, and actions.
- ✔ Identify and improve at least one thing in your area daily.
- ✔ Ask yourself questions about your perceptions, reactions, and behaviors in the workplace.
- ✔ Get comfortable with ambiguity. Realize that you can't control the situation or know exactly what is happening all the time.

Management can help by providing forums where people can ask questions and voice their concerns. To make these sessions beneficial, keep them real and keep them positive. People will need to feel that management will hear them, will act and will convey feedback or status of these concerns.

Acting Lean

In traditional organizations of all types, people are taught to do one task, as fast as they can, with or without a connection other parts of the organization or to what the end customer requires. Stockpiling, working in isolation, hiding mistakes, working at an erratic pace, and only bearing good news are all behaviors that have no place in a Lean environment.

In order to eliminate waste or wasteful behaviors, you first must admit that they exist. Have you ever been in a meeting where presenter after presenter discusses dire current business conditions, yet their future trend predicts a miraculous recovery? When you venture into Lean, you have to deal with reality — it's the only way that you can improve.

Many people (including managers) have learned to *create* crisis situations so they can become heroes who fly in like Superman to save the day. Management rewards this type of behavior to the point that if the company is not in crisis, no one knows how to act. In a Lean organization, you learn how to thrive without daily disasters. Managers learn how to reward problem avoidance, root-cause resolution, and continuous improvement.

Many organizations are full of individuals who stopped trying to learn after they left school. They don't take classes. They don't analyze mistakes or failures. After school, they checked the "education box" and checked out. Lean organizations reward and thrive on learning. Like the *Kaizen* philosophy of improving something everyday, Lean also promotes learning something everyday — learning from mistakes, learning to solve root-cause issues, learning new ways to eliminate waste, learning more about your customer.

Looking at different learning styles

Not everyone learns the same way — individuals have different learning styles. Most people have a dominant style, but may also exhibit other styles at times. The four commonly held styles are

- ✔ **Visual:** They remember what they see.
- ✔ **Verbal:** They remember what they hear and what they say.
- ✔ **Logical:** They conceptualize information.
- ✔ **Kinesthetic:** They learn by doing and explaining what they've done.

Because so many new concepts and changes affect the way you do business in a Lean environment, you have understand your style. The people, who are leading the charge and developing training materials, need to appeal to each individual learner. In order for management's messages and communication to be effective, you also need to appeal to each style.

Kaizen events may be a dream for kinesthetic learners, but a nightmare for logical learners. The verbal learners will want to talk about what's happening to grasp the change, and the visual learners may want to hang back and watch the first time, so they get it. When you have a *Kaizen* activity, try to identify each of the team member's learning styles. You may even hear them using language that reflects their styles.

Learning happens formally and informally along the Lean journey. Formally, you will hold classes, workshops, *Kaizen* events, or training sessions. Topics range from team building to quick changeover (known as SMED) and everything in between. Informally, you will learn from actions, mistakes, and interpersonal interactions.

Change and the team

Lean relies heavily on teams of people working together to improve the business. What is a team? A *team* is a collection of individuals working toward a common purpose. If you don't have that common purpose, you just have a group.

In a Lean environment, several types of teams exist. There are natural work teams, cross-functional teams, teams that come together for *Kaizen* events, teams that include members from upstream or downstream of the organization. The type of team formed and length of time the team stays together is dependent upon the reasons for the team's existence and expected performance objectives The team environment takes advantage of the synergies of the individual members to identify better solutions, accomplish an objective faster, and make bigger strides.

Characteristics of a winning team

Winning teams exhibit certain characteristics. Not only do they look a certain way, but they behave a certain way. High-performing teams have the following characteristics:

- **They're willing to share.** Sports teams are iconic when it comes to demonstrating this behavior. Teams with superstar ball hogs tend not to be as successful as those with players who pass the ball and set up teammates for the score. During the 2006 World Cup, winner Italy worked together as a team through match after match, while teams with celebrity players, like England and Brazil, fell in defeat.

- **They're constantly engaged.** Team members constantly look for opportunities to the overall success of the team. In the World Cup, even players who were sitting on the bench played a vital role for the team — as motivators, observers, and providers of moral support.

- **They capitalize on individual strengths.** Among all the team members is a breadth of knowledge and talent unique to each individual. Knowing how to bring out and use those talents will contribute to the overall success of the team. Not every soccer player can play every position. The coaches put the best goal tender in the net and their fastest players where they can take advantage of breakaway opportunities.

- **They're aligned to a common goal.** A group of individuals aligned to a common goal makes a team. You can believe that every team in the World Cup was aligned to the goal to win the cup!

- **They're able to learn together.** As teams face new situations, they have to adjust and grow in order to achieve their ultimate goal. As the different teams played each other during the World Cup, they had to adjust their playing styles and strategies each time they met new opponents. You can be sure that learning and adjustments were made when teams found themselves down at the half.

In addition to displaying the preceding characteristics, effective teams are usually made up of five to seven people. Each team member is a unique individual, who has something special to offer the team. Ideally, during the formation process, these unique traits are identified.

Many assessment tools — such as the Myers-Briggs Type Indicator (MBTI), the DiSC Classic Profile, the Kolbe A index, the Cultural Orientations Indicator (COI), or the StrengthsFinder found in *Now, Discover Your Strengths,* by Marcus Buckingham and Donald O. Clifton — can help a team understand who is playing. You want to find a qualified person to administer the assessment and help the team interpret the results. The best teams are ones that consist of very different types of individuals. You may find it difficult to work with people who are very different from your style. The assessment can help you understand how to improve working relationships, facilitate communications, and capitalize on strengths. Assessments provide the team with a common language, context, and understanding.

Teams must have a variety of perspectives, talents, and types in order for innovation and creativity to materialize.

Team formation

Dr. Bruce Tuckman, noted psychologist and organizational behavior expert, identified the now famous five phases of teaming:

1. **Forming:** People join forces to achieve a common goal. Members get to know one another, identify commonality, and begin to develop ground rules.

2. **Storming:** Members are trying to figure out where they fit. Hostilities and emotions may run high as people jockey for position, figure out who they can trust, and claim a role. Leaders emerge.

3. **Norming:** Members learn how to work together. Leadership and roles are understood. Principles and standards of behavior are established, but not necessarily the same as the overall organization's. Team identity is formed — formally or informally.

4. **Performing:** Members work together to get the job done.

5. **Adjourning:** Work is complete and the team will either disband or address a new scope of work.

Changes to the makeup or direction of the team can cause regression into earlier phases. As your team forms to eliminate waste and improve processes, remember that it will have to develop as an entity. The team will experience these phases. If the team is struggling to get to the performing stage, management may need to provide an intervention — such as facilitation, guidance, change of membership, or clarification of expectations.

Team leadership is determined during the formation process. Although there may be an official leader, a different leader may emerge as the team matures. Facilitators can help a team get off the ground. A *facilitator* is someone who guides the process of the team and ensures that all members are participating and being heard; ideally, the facilitator is not a team member and is not expected to contribute content to the team.

Collaboration

When people are used to working in a traditional environment, the idea of collaboration may seem a bit foreign. The result of a true collaborative environment is the win-win solution. It requires that team members contribute ideas, analyze the situation objectively, and negotiate a solution. It requires that the individuals be able to let go of an idea or position if better, alternative solutions are offered. It requires that an individual see a situation not only from his point of view, but from the points of view of others involved.

In a Lean environment, teams work to eliminate waste. But sometimes what one person views as waste may be vital to another — this is why type-1 *muda* exists. When collaborative skills are developed in an organization, individuals are able to see both sides of the situation and, with a Lean mindset, propose alternatives that can minimize, if not eliminate, non-value-added activities. Ideally, when you collaborate, you gain new perspectives about a situation, which then adjusts your perceptions and influences your attitudes, actions, and emotions.

Multifunctional workers

Lean advocates the development of multifunctional workers, especially in natural work teams. Each member of the area is trained in the activities of the others. Training is tracked and each employee must develop a level of competency before performing the task unsupervised. This is easy to envision in a manufacturing environment, but the same philosophy can be applied in non-manufacturing environments like accountancies, industrial kitchens, retail outlets, or title companies. By having a well-trained workforce, you're insulated against the effects of absenteeism and vacations.

Post a tracking chart showing job qualifications by person (see Chapter 9).

Change and the managers

Managers directly influence the change to Lean by their behaviors, decisions, and communication. They have the challenging position, as the face of Lean leadership, to lead the organization to success in spite of their own personal reaction to the change. In this section we discuss what managers can do to make the unknown more known and move the organization along the road to Lean.

Creating the vision

Declaring that the organization will be Lean is easy; actually making the change is the greater challenge. Managers start by creating a clear vision for the organization — not some lofty visionary statement, but a straightforward image of what it means to the company to implement Lean practices. This vision includes performance expectations, timing, expected outcomes, interrelationships to other company initiatives, and commitments to the organization.

If you don't want your Lean efforts to look like a Dilbert cartoon, you have to pay attention to the human element of change. Management must lead by example and with a constancy of purpose. Eighty percent of change initiatives fail due to human factors, according to studies by noted organizational researchers John Kotter and Daryl Conner.

Creating a sustainable Lean transformation requires that you move people from compliance (implementing because you tell them to) to commitment (implementing because they want to). You have to address each individual at some point in time.

Engage people early in the process after you make the decision to implement Lean. By involving them in the planning of how to implement Lean, you enroll them in the process.

Communications

People need two things to deal with change: They need to be informed and they need to be heard. The communication should be clear, consistent, multidimensional, and frequent. One-time declarations don't make a Lean transformation. Develop a communication strategy to support the implementation plan. The communication plan needs to be a two-way effort. One part is what you want to say; the other part is what your employees want you to hear. You're dealing with a collection of individuals, with different needs, learning styles, and perceptions.

Remember the basics of communication:

- ✔ **Who:** Who is the audience? Is it an internal or external audience?

- ✔ **What:** What is going to happen? What does the audience need to know? What do you expect them to do as a result of the communication? What does the audience fear? What could prevent them from embracing the change? What are they saying?

- ✔ **When:** When will the communication happen? How frequently will it occur?

- ✔ **Where:** Where will it happen?

- ✔ **How:** What method of communication will be used? How can the company make use of technology to get the message out? How will the message permeate all levels of the organization? How can you prevent the message from being changed as it's relayed? How can you engage the audience? How can you solicit input from the audience?

✔ **Why:** Why are you making this change at this time? What are the business conditions that are precipitating the change? Why this method at this time?

Feedback loops are vital to an organization undergoing change. You need to know how filtered by perceptions and misinterpretation your original message is. Based on the feedback of the response, you can adjust your message and delivery method in the next round of communication. Figure 12-1 shows a model of a feedback loop.

Figure 12-1:
How messages are transmitted and understood among people.

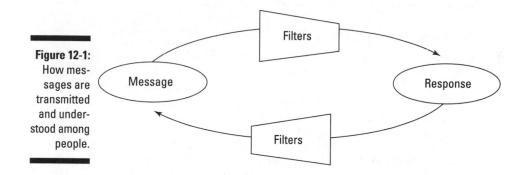

In the beginning, you cannot over-communicate with people. People need to know what they're in for. The formal communication plan needs to be supplemented with informal communications. Nothing can derail a change movement faster than misinformation and coffee-pot rumors. In the absence of information, people fill the abyss with speculation and fear.

Frequently, managers excited about a new initiative fall into the *advocacy trap.* They're so focused on telling people why they should be excited and the benefits of the change that they forget to listen and ask for input from the people. Practicing inquiry is vitally important to your long-term success.

Developing the ability to listen to and truly hear your employees is a critical skill for every manager. People need to be heard. Some may need to vent before they can move onto the new ways of doing business. Providing different forums for communication, including the following, will address the various needs of the individuals within the organization:

✔ **One on one:** Invest 15 minutes with your employees to hear what their thoughts, ideas, and concerns are around the change. Use this information to understand where blocks in the organization are happening, to monitor trends in the organization, and to craft follow-up group communication.

✔ **Small group:** Conduct regular small-group sessions to address issues and gather ideas. These groups can be diagonal slices across the organization, functional groups, project teams, or natural workgroups. Provide a mechanism for people to input questions before the sessions.

✔ **Large group:** Conduct regular large-group briefings. Recognize accomplishments, show the state of the business, progress to long-term visions, and recognize individual and group efforts. Provide a mechanism for people to input questions and concerns prior to the meeting.

Create a communications council with volunteers from various parts of the organization. This group becomes your eyes and ears into the organization. They can help with rumor control, act as an editorial board for your communiqués, keep the pulse of the organization, promote Lean within the organization, and become a sounding board for ideas.

Communications in action

Assume you're a manager who has just received news that your company has won a new contract, but you don't currently have the floor space available in your facility to accommodate the new work. After working with your staff on the right vision and strategy for the new contract launch, you start the communication process. Initially, you gather your organization together, tell them about the new business, and tell them that you need to free up 10,000 square feet of floor space in the northeast corner of the facility in two weeks. You tell them that they'll be involved in *Kaizen* activities to make this happen and that you expect there to be no negative impact on the customer during these *Kaizen* activities. It will require teamwork, commitment, and cooperation. You announce that Pat will be responsible to organize and oversee the activities. You tell them that you will be following their progress closely and that you expect the next gathering will be in two weeks in the newly-freed-up area.

Later that day, you go to the northeast corner of the facility and hang a sign saying "Future Home of Dizzo Production." You talk to employees as you walk through the plant, asking them what they think about the new contract and what they think it will take to free up the space. The next day, you and Pat walk the floor again, informally communicating with the employees. You both decide to add a sign showing progress to the 10,000 square feet. You may decide to personally lead or participate in the first *Kaizen* activity. After each *Kaizen* activity, you meet with the teams, recognize them, and thank them for their efforts. You may use a company blog to communicate the progress and recognize efforts. You may create a podcast, which can be accessed by employees 24/7, with updates on the new business.

Every day you walk the floor to review the progress. At the one-week mark, you gather all your staff and the supervisors in the area to review the status and subsequently make any adjustments to the plan. You record an update that is played in the cafeteria. Finally, at the two-week mark, you gather everyone into the area, recognize their efforts, and announce the next challenge.

Whatever you communicate, be prepared to back up the message with actions. If you say that you're going to do something by a certain date, do it, or explain why it didn't happen. Part of your population is expecting failure — don't let them win.

The changing role of management

Management has a unique role in the Lean transformation. Not only do managers have to lead the charge, but they have to deal with their own reactions to what's happening and adjust to redefined roles and expectations. Not all managers successfully make this change. Because they are members of management, they will undergo greater scrutiny by the members of the organization and be held to higher standards. People who don't want to change, managers and non-managers alike, will be looking for cracks in the resolve, so they can go back to their old ways.

When moving from a traditional manufacturing or business system, traditional Theory X management styles have to change. Managers have to shift from dictatorial stances to ones of collaboration. This doesn't mean that they abdicate their decision-making responsibilities — it *does* mean that they have to incorporate the synergies and ideas of the organization.

They have to develop new managerial skill sets. In the area of people management, this means the ability to listen, the ability to teach and guide, and the ability to learn and consider alternative viewpoints. It means developing the attitude that you don't always have to be right or have all the answers. These skill sets aren't usually taught at business schools, medical schools, engineering schools, and the like. Not having the skills can stop the Lean process.

Living Lean on the front line

First-line supervisors who have grown up in traditional organizations will have the greatest adjustments to make in the organization. Generally, they're used to giving orders, fighting fires, and making things happen. As self-directed work teams form, their role is very different. Now the team makes decisions, plans work, and does some of the tasks normally performed by supervisors.

The supervisors in a Lean organization are expected to coach, mentor, and advise the teams. Oftentimes, they feel as though they have the responsibility for performance without the authority they once held. Supervisors need training in new skill sets, particularly in the area of interpersonal communication, coaching, and Lean techniques. They need time to develop these new skills and mentoring as they change their behaviors.

Supervisors, too, have standardized work to perform. They're responsible for 5S implementation and the continuous improvement of their areas. They must create visual work areas and be more open with information than in the past. They may have to host more people in their areas as people start making pilgrimages to *gemba*.

As soon as more self-directed teams are working in the organization, an opportunity exists to flatten the organization. Not as many layers are needed. Supervisors are also freed up because tasks they previously had done are shifted to the teams. This enables them to support more teams. Remember, though, that as you change the organizational structure, you have to do it in a way that is consistent with Lean principles. If the management team has declared that there will be no job loss due to Lean improvements, the same applies to managers, too. How human resources and the management team handles the attrition must be consistent with the new values of the organization. The organization will use this situation as a gauge of management's commitment to the new Lean principles. It underscores trust, integrity, and credibility.

Living Lean in Cubicleland

Managers who are off the front line but not yet in the boardroom also have to change the way they work. They, too, have standardized work. They must drive the focus on the customer and unrelenting pursuit to eliminate waste in all areas of the company.

These managers develop a strong understanding of how their part fits into the value stream. They learn to look across the value stream and not solely in their areas of responsibility. They must become teachers and mentors to their organization.

Creating management-by-eye reporting areas (see Chapter 9) and implementing practical 5S in their area is also a new role for these managers. No longer is it sufficient to manage from behind a desk. *Gemba* walks are now part of their regular activities. Decisions are made with data and in context of the customer. Their job is to energize and motivate the organization to improve daily, as well as to actively participate in and support Kaizen.

These managers can be the glue that holds the Lean organization together or the barrier to forward progress. They can be a huge filter in the communication process from the senior levels of the organization. Addressing the needs of this group and ensuring that they're onboard is one of senior-management's primary responsibilities.

Living Lean on Mahogany Row

It used to be that executive alley was for the fat cats. Heady stuff like analysis and process improvement was for the working stiffs. An executive had "earned" the right to think on his feet, shoot from the hip, and react with his gut. And you know what? As long as corporate performance stayed high, and the executives' bosses — the board of directors, shareholders, distributors, key suppliers, employees, and customers — were all happy, nothing more was required.

That was then. That was before margin erosion, outsourcing, globalization, startups, brain drain, the Internet, and countless other new-era pressures welled up and required an evolved form of leadership from the top. Gone are the days of delegation — relegation, really — of programs to improve performance and the bottom line. The executives are in the mix, leading the charge.

You may not think that the same techniques that work on a factory floor apply in the boardroom, but they do. They just don't look quite the same. For instance, standardized work for an executive may consist of standard information reviews utilizing standard templates and timed agendas. Or it could be a set *gemba* walk within the organization. Maybe only 20 percent of an executive's job can be standardized, but that 20 percent should be standardized in the most effective way possible.

Lean, like any other strategic initiatives worth doing, must be led from the top. That's no surprise. (The role of senior management supporting the Lean journey is the subject of the last section in this chapter.) But the senior manager's personal behaviors are both individually meaningful and symbolically significant to everyone in the enterprise. They must "walk the talk." The following are a few ways that a Lean executive demonstrates she is living Lean principles and incorporating Lean tools.

- ✔ **Unrelenting focus on the customer:** Whether in personal discussions, questions, measures, reports, presentations, or briefings, the executive is focused on the customer.

- ✔ **Maximizing value added in all you do:** The executive ensures that personal activities, in meetings and briefings, travels, communications — and especially perks — all focus on the value added by both his own behavior and the collective effort of those directly involved.

- ✔ **Requiring visual management:** Performance reviews in the areas, regular *gemba* walks, safety tours, and simple measurement systems are all part of the Lean culture change. Senior management sets the tone and requirements for the organization to follow.

- ✔ **Living 5S:** Like none other, top executives should exhibit 5S in their personal conduct. (See Chapter 8 for more on 5S.)

- ✔ **Elimination of waste *(muda)*:** The crusade for waste reduction carries enhanced meaning when it's reflected in the top executive's personal behavior. This may mean letting go of perks like reserved parking spaces and executive dining rooms.

- ✔ **Consistency (reduction of *mura*):** People need to know their leadership is dependable and consistent. Variability in performance and action *(mura)* on a personal level should be eliminated.

- ✔ **Respect for people and systems (eradication of *muri*):** Leaders must show that they respect themselves and others, as well as the systems and equipment of the organization.

Can you think of other ways that senior leaders can personally exhibit behaviors consistent with Lean principles? How about cycle time reduction? Or the seven wastes? What would standard work for executives look like?

Read the latest business headlines and you'll find stories of executives abusing power and misappropriating resources, tales of egomaniacs making unreasonable demands for their own personal gain. These behaviors will not support a Lean transformation. Executives need to be able to park their egos long enough to truly listen to their organization and foster communication through all levels of management.

Bringing people along

"Motivation is the art of getting people to do what you want them to do because they want to do it."

—President Dwight D. Eisenhower

You have to bring individuals along by addressing their needs. Every organization, team, or department is still made up of individuals who all have their own needs, filters, perceptions, and timelines. In order to move the entire organization down the path of Lean, you still have to meet the individual where she is. Table 12-1 shows some of the differences that you'll have to consider in your communications activities, strategy development, and implementation steps.

Table 12-1	Organizational Development and Strategy Considerations to Evoke Change
Aspect of Change	*Impact on Change*
Cultural/organizational	People's perceptions are influenced by all the groups that they've belonged to — from family units to other business organizations. All of this will color their individual beliefs about the "right way" to do things and influence their willingness to change.
Generational	At least four generations are currently in the workplace, all with different values and guiding principles. Getting them to work together and communicate effectively within a Lean environment is vital. There may be a tendency to resist change as people progress in their careers and in position. Fear of loss becomes greater.
Educational	Your organization may have a broad range of people — from those who cannot read to those with PhDs. In this global world, you may not share the same first language as your coworkers.

Aspect of Change	Impact on Change
Learning styles	When introducing any new concept or change — and Lean is full of them — you need to present it in a multi-faceted way.
Personality styles	Understanding personality styles will help you evaluate how best to respond to the needs of the organization and how to get them to respond to the change.
Change motivators	Not everyone is motivated by money. Matching the motivators, like time off, money, or public recognition, to the individual will go far to bring people along.

Many organizations use economic incentives to motivate or buy change in the organization. Understanding what motivates each individual to change will enable you to employ a broader range of incentives to move a larger part of the organization forward.

One of the biggest fears employees have is that they'll lose their jobs. One strategy that has been successful in companies who have started to implement Lean is the guarantee that no one will lose his job as a direct result of performance gains made by implementing Lean improvements. This guarantee goes a long way to allay fears. The policy is clear that it's only in effect for Lean improvement. If the policy exists, then management must live up to their promise. They have to be very clear in their communications and open with information. If they aren't, they'll cause a credibility and trust problem — another impediment to change.

You may think that you shouldn't have to baby people or go to all this effort. Yet, if you want to succeed you need to address the needs of the individuals. What is the price of success? Is it worth investing time in your people for the long-term payoff?

The *sensei* of legends

Many of the earlier, well-known *senseis,* like Yoshiki Iwata, were trained at Toyota and were students of Taiichi Ohno. They have been known to play hard to get — not agreeing to work with a company unless the company was extremely persistent. When they agree, they have a reputation for being demanding, relentless, and unexpected. When things are not moving fast enough they have been known to move equipment themselves. Although their methods may be a bit unconventional, those under the tutelage of these *senseis* swear by the results.

The Master and the Students

One of the most famous *sensei*-student relationships was in the 1984 movie *The Karate Kid.* Daniel, the new kid in town, is getting his butt kicked by the local karate bullies. Mr. Miyagi, a handyman and karate master, steps in and saves Daniel by fighting off the lot of the bullies. Later and after much pestering by Daniel, Mr. Miyagi agrees to become his *sensei,* or teacher. When the lessons begin, Daniel does not understand Mr. Miyagi's unconventional methods. His lessons include washing Mr. Miyagi's car ("wax on, wax off"), painting his fence ("brush up, brush down"), and sanding his deck. After Daniel blows up in frustration because he feels like he's not learning anything, Mr. Miyagi points out to Daniel that he has been learning karate while doing these tasks. As a *sensei,* Mr. Miyagi has knowledge, experience, and his own unique way of passing on the knowledge. Mr. Miyagi demands that Daniel complete tasks in a precise way. He also has the understanding that karate is not just the external techniques and moves, but also the internal belief in the heart and mind.

Successful Lean organizations find a *sensei* or a master, not unlike Mr. Miyagi. The Lean *sensei* teaches and guides the organization on their path to Lean implementation. The organization may not always understand the *sensei's* methods at first, but eventually, with the right *sensei,* everyone in the organization finds themselves living Lean. In this section we will tell you not only about the Lean *sensei,* but also about Lean students.

The Lean sensei

The Lean journey does not mandate a Lean *sensei,* but if you want to be successful, having a *sensei* is highly recommended. Many companies have found it beneficial to bring in an external Lean *sensei* when starting the Lean journey. A Lean *sensei* has knowledge of Lean principles, methods, and implementation. They're there to guide and teach. Like Mr. Miyagi's methods, their methods may be unconventional by traditional business standards. They also have a broad understanding that Lean is more than just the external techniques — to truly get it, you must change your attitudes, perceptions, and actions.

Identifying the role of a sensei

The role of a *sensei* is to guide the Lean journey and teach the principles. The *sensei* does this where the action is in the organization. One of the main ways the *sensei* guides and teaches is through *gemba* walks with individuals and small groups of management. By pointing out what is un-Lean in the process and telling them how to fix it, the *sensei* teaches. *Senseis* may lead *Kaizen* events, and don't be surprised if you find them rolling up their sleeves and getting dirty. They oversee the short- and long-term vision. Think of the *sensei* as the wise master, who will do just about anything to teach a point.

What are the benefits of having a Lean *sensei*? A *sensei* can

- Jumpstart the initial Lean implementation.
- Serve as an independent party, ensuring the Lean efforts stay the course.
- Customize input based on the company's particular situation.
- Offer a broad view of the organization to ensure constancy of purpose.
- Provide tactical direction to support a long-term vision.
- Produce faster results.
- Set high expectations, allowing your organization to achieve more than it thought possible.

Hiring a sensei

No unique credential for a Lean *sensei* is currently on the market. So how do you find a *sensei?* You can find candidates by contacting consulting companies (Shingijutsu Co., one of the best known sources of *senseis* in Japan, also operates globally), hiring a former employee from a Lean company like Toyota, asking other Lean companies for references, searching the Internet, and so on. You will find an abundance of potential *sensei* candidates whose talents range from hack to expert. To find the one who is right for your organization, you need to be clear about what you are looking for and how much you can afford to pay.

Before hiring a *sensei,* your company will want to understand what its expectations are and what the background of the prospective *sensei* is. Here are some questions to ask of yourself and the *sensei:*

- Where did the *sensei* receive his training?
- What experience does he have?
- What expectations does the company have of the *sensei?*
- How long does the company expect to rely on an outside resource?
- What is the company willing to spend on a *sensei?*
- Does the company intend to develop an internal *sensei?*

How many *senseis* do you need? It depends on the size of your company or operating units. You're better off starting with one *sensei* and at one location. As your efforts increase, under the *sensei*'s guidance you may want to bring on more *senseis* as needed. No matter how many *senseis* you end up with, you need to make sure that they're all working in alignment with each other. There's nothing worse than too many cooks in the kitchen — or too many *senseis* in the company!

Organizations truly committed to Lean understand that they must continuously learn, stretch, and grow. To ensure that happens, you will need a teacher and guide to show you the next step in the journey. Over time, is that teacher the same person or always an external resource? Probably not. You may find that your organization responds better to a different *sensei* as the journey progresses — not unlike your school experience where your kindergarten teacher was different from your high school teacher.

The performance expectations of the *sensei* should be agreed upon as part of the original contract (for an external resource) or part of the performance appraisal (for an internal resource). At the end of the day, you're looking for performance improvement in your operations. Connect the *sensei*'s activities with the organizational performance metrics.

Senseis in the organization

Following the philosophy that you can't be a prophet in your own land, a *sensei* is usually external to the organization — especially during the initial phases of implementation. In some cases, the *sensei* is a member of the management team who has a broad and deep knowledge of Lean. The *sensei* may have experience from other companies and may have been under the tutelage of an external *sensei* before.

If the company goes the internal route, then that *sensei* needs to have the authority and backing of the rest of the management team. You don't want to deem a functional manager as *sensei*. The *sensei* needs to be focused solely on Lean and should report directly to the highest levels of the organization.

Lean students

Every member of the Lean organization is a student of Lean. In an unending quest to improve, everyone must learn — constantly. You won't spend hours in a classroom. In fact, the majority of learning happens where the action is. Every place becomes a classroom, every situation a class.

All levels of the organization learn new skills as the Lean journey progresses. You learn from classes, workshops, books, interactions with a *sensei,* on the job, from trial and error, from mistakes, from online blogs or other resources — the sources are countless.

In order to stay fresh and to be able to make daily improvements, an individual must continue to seek out knowledge. Particularly when you have worked in the same job or in the same area or with the same people for an extended period of time, you need a fresh perspective. But you can easily get comfortable and stagnate. As a student, your responsibility is to seek knowledge daily. You may learn a new job, apply a new technique, learn about a different part of the value stream — learning is all around you!

You'll know when you're an advanced student of Lean. You not only start applying Lean concepts beyond the workplace, but also look for Lean in everyday life. When you've taught your kids how to 5S their room and conduct *gemba* walks around your house, you'll know that you've changed your thinking.

The ongoing Lean curriculum

The curriculum of a Lean student is not fixed. Sure, you learn the basics — like Value Stream Mapping, *Kaizen,* forms of waste, 5S, visual management, *poka-yoke, kanban,* and all the other tools found in Part III of this book. But if you stop there, it's like dropping out of grade school.

To become a Lean student, you must have knowledge and competency in at least four skill areas:

- ✓ **Technical skills** including *Kaizen* to *kanban* and everything in between.

- ✓ **Interpersonal skills** including collaboration, conflict resolution, negotiations, teaming, and self awareness.

- ✓ **Strategy and planning skills** including project planning and management, goal setting, and problem solving.

- ✓ **Real world experience** (practical application skills) including demonstrated competency in the *real world* — where theory and practical application meet.

As time passes, more pieces may be added to the puzzle. ***Remember:*** Your responsibility is to become a lifelong learner.

Lean certification

Lean certification is a relatively new development in the field. Although several certifications are available, a common standard of certification does not exist for knowledge and demonstrated capability required. Lean certifications are sponsored by the Society of Manufacturing Engineers, the Association for Manufacturing Excellence, and the Shingo Prize (see Chapter 18).

Lean certification is a mildly controversial topic. Not all Lean practitioners agree to the value of certification. A certificate alone does not make you a Lean expert. Only you can determine the value of having a certificate. You may belong to an organization that esteems certificates and credentials; in that case, certification may be of value. At the end of the day, you'll determine the value of certification for you personally and professionally within the context of your organization.

Chapter 13

Go Lean: Implementation Strategy, Startup, and Evolution

A journey of a thousand miles begins with a single step.

—Lao-tzu

As you know by now, Lean is a journey. It is not a prescription, where you follow steps 1, 2, and 3 and — *voila!* — you're there. It is not a one-size-fits-all continuous-improvement methodology. Lean is like the quest for perfect health: Your pursuit is multifaceted — nutrition, exercise, rest, genetics, beliefs. It requires discipline. It's a way of life.

You have to assess your present state and determine the right Lean strategy for your organization, based on your own specific needs, objectives, experience, and the state of the organization.

In forming your strategy, don't just copy someone like Toyota. Although Toyota's history is a good reference, it's not an exact blueprint for anyone else. You have to follow your own path, make your own adjustments, and find your own way.

In this chapter, we offer strategies and tips to help you begin your journey. You figure out how to prevent the "program-of-the-month" trap. And you see how to evolve from your starting point to a place of living Lean.

Preparing to Go Lean

Lean implementation does not follow a prescriptive step-by-step scenario, like you might see in other continuous-improvement methodologies. It's rigorous, to be sure, but it's more of an *evolution* than a *revolution*. Lean focuses on the means just as much as it does on achieving end results. It's not strictly measured just by quarterly profit performance, although, over time, you will experience improved performance in your financial measures.

To be successful, Lean needs to be owned and encouraged from the top of the organization, and expanded to all levels and corners of the enterprise. Lean is a very action-oriented methodology, with all the projects, *Kaizen* events (see Chapter 6), and continuous learning. The planning process for a Lean initiative doesn't require an elaborate production, but it must be developed to the point where everyone in the organization receives a clear message about where they're going.

On the one hand, Lean is easier than other approaches, because you don't have to follow a prescribed rollout, where if you don't do things in a specific order, it won't work. You have a lot of latitude and leeway in your approach. On the other hand, Lean is more difficult than other approaches, because you don't have a firm prescription to follow and a precise road map to fall back on. You need to chart your own course and find your own way. The good news is that, with Lean, finding your way tends to happen naturally.

Starting from the top

Lean succeeds if and only if the management team is dedicated to the cause. You may start Lean in any part of the organization, but if you want sustainable results beyond a small portion of the company — and who doesn't? — the senior managers must endorse and actively participate in the effort. People respond to the cues they get from leadership — such as behaviors, recognition, and performance standards.

Senior managers must understand both the tools of Lean and the philosophy of *Kaizen*. They must practice Lean themselves in the course of their regular work routines. They must set a vision and communicate the messages of Lean. And they must follow up by performing Lean management actions (see Chapter 10).

Applying standardized work from the top down

Everyone in a Lean organization has standardized work. For people like the factory-floor assembler, most of their work is standardized. Senior managers spend much of their time responding to interruptions, crises, and exceptions — and the rest of their time they spend brainstorming how to have fewer interruptions, crises, and exceptions! But senior managers have standardized work, too — not as much as the front-line worker, but they have it nonetheless.

Examples of where standardized work applies in senior management include _gemba_ walks (see Chapter 10), routine meetings, briefings, reviews, and reports. This kind of work may amount to less than half the senior manager's time, but when standardized, it enables the managers to work more effectively, freeing up time and resources for more value-added activities. In the Lean world, the senior managers apply standardized work.

Focusing on the message and vision

The staff, directors, shareholders, analysts, suppliers, customers . . . all these constituents must know that you're embarking on this Lean journey. You can't take this journey and not tell anyone — they'll all wonder where you've gone, long before the new results kick in. You must set the vision for your new path and articulate the mission. Take the time to craft these messages, and convey them to the audiences as the journey begins.

The beauty of Lean for executives is that it provides the senior managers a toolkit that gives method and technique to back-up management's classic platitudes, for example:

- ✔ **We're customer-centric!** Management's been touting this for years, but how could they really make it happen? Lean gives the executive the techniques to examine value-added from the customer's point of view.

- ✔ **People are our most important resource!** That's the one you're used to hearing right before the next round of layoffs. Lean teaches executives about true respect for employees and provides the toolkit for safety, security, engagement, celebration, and growth.

- ✔ **Think win-win.** Unfortunately, without a method, this one's been only half-true: management's win for themselves. Lean techniques enable managers to create a win for all parties.

- ✔ **Do it right the first time.** (Also known as _Quality is Job #1;_ or, as they say in the software industry, _Quality is Job 1.1_ — the bugs will be fixed in the next release!) But, how do you actually do it right the first time? You can't test and rework products into submission. Lean, in conjunction with statistical methods and tools, provides the basis for making this real.

Leading by example

In addition to performing standardized work, the senior managers must also lead by setting the example. Managers translate the foreign and abstract concepts of Lean into practical behaviors that everyone can observe and emulate. They must change the way they think and react, especially in times of crisis. The people will be watching to see if the managers are legitimate or if they're just giving lip service.

Managers must use visual controls. Charts, graphs, trends, and reports should be highly visible and apparent to everyone. Take down some of those fancy framed photographs of faraway tropical islands and lofty mountain peaks, and replace them with images of the paradise of performance and pinnacles of success in your organization.

Managers must exemplify discipline and accountability. They must perform to the expectations they set for others. They must hold themselves accountable, just as they expect everyone else to hold one another accountable. The personal and professional discipline demonstrated by managers will be copied by everyone.

One of the most powerful showcases for Lean behavior is in meeting management. Managers should prepare for meetings and have a firm well-defined agenda, with the outcomes articulated explicitly. They must always arrive on time and finish on time — standardized work!

Managers must also conduct the same Lean practices that they expect of everyone else, including the development and analysis of Value Stream Maps, participation in *Kaizen* events and *Kaizen* improvement projects, partaking in continuous training and learning, and overtly demonstrating regular, continuous improvements.

Creating the Lean infrastructure

Although there's no standard recipe for a Lean deployment, you'll need to put in place a framework of support elements before you begin the trip. You must acquire certain specific Lean expertise and disseminate the knowledge across the organization in a controlled manner. You must also bring in cooperative human resource practices, set up certain financial and accounting practices, and put in place some specific IT infrastructure. This support framework is critical to a successful rollout.

Bringing in a master of Lean: The Lean sensei

The first step in creating the Lean infrastructure is acquiring Lean expertise in the organization. Lots of great references and books on Lean are out there (you're reading the best one, of course!), but you can't gain the necessary experience from a book. You must bring in a Lean Master or *sensei,* who guides your Lean journey by:

- Creating the itinerary
- Teaching your organization Lean skills

> ✔ Leading your teams through the process of discovery and understanding in the ways of Lean and *Kaizen*
>
> ✔ Guiding you toward your destination
>
> ✔ Knowing the best way to get the results you want

Companies rarely have this expertise in-house. The most common approach is to hire a Lean *sensei,* usually as an outside consultant. But if you do have a prophet in your own land, then the onus is on the managers to set up the internal expert for success. Wherever the Lean *sensei* comes from, the expert will need resources and authority at his disposal to launch the initiative.

Be very careful and highly selective about retaining a Lean Master. This person will have a large role in the Lean initiative and an even larger influence on the nature of the organization's adaptation. Bringing on the wrong Lean Master is a disaster. Make sure the Lean *sensei* has the credentials and fits the profile that your change requires (see Chapter 12).

Adjusting the people policies

When moving into Lean from a traditional environment, numerous personnel policies and practices have to change in order to be aligned with the people-centered principles of Lean. For example:

> ✔ Incentive systems that are traditionally focused on the individual require realignment in order to include a team perspective.
>
> ✔ Policies must support the realignment and reassignment of employees who are displaced due to productivity improvements.
>
> ✔ Organizational structures and labor agreements, if applicable, will have to be adjusted to support a Lean environment. Frequently, this includes a reduction in the number of organizational levels, the consolidation of job categories and flexible work rules.
>
> ✔ Recognition and reward programs will have to expand to include individuals and teams.
>
> ✔ Promotions will have to be based on performance, knowledge, and capability. The company may establish standard path progressions for multifunctional workers.

Acquiring training materials

Lean courseware includes formal training on the practices of *Kaizen* and the Lean toolkit (see Chapters 7, 8, 9, and 10). Additional courses are available on Lean people and organizational change management. These courses are offered by numerous practitioners and training and consulting firms (see Chapter 18 for recommendations).

Training firms typically prefer to perform the training for you, rather than license you the training materials. If you're embracing Lean fully and organically, you will want the materials and adapt them to your organization to use in a variety of settings and formats. But if you're just sticking your toe in the water, you can either send people to training or bring the trainers to you.

Putting the people in place

To initiate the Lean effort, you have to put in place the logistical support pieces. People at all levels of the organization will need training. In addition, *Kaizen* events must be scheduled and tracked. Outside resources like trainers, consultants, materials, and software tools will also need coordination. A core group of people will assemble to perform this work.

Putting the support tools in place

The Lean practitioner uses software application tools as part of his optimization work. These tools include process mapping, Value Stream Mapping (VSM), statistical analysis, and mapping and charting tools (see Chapter 10). Some of these are individual desktop-computer tools, while others are shared by workgroups. The IT organization must include these in its cadre of applications support. Other software tools include programs for facility layouts and graphics packages for visual aides.

In addition to software tools, the Lean practitioner uses more traditional tools:

- **Markers and flip charts** to record idea generation and team sessions.
- **Video cameras** record the processes, enabling the team to analyze the film for improvement.
- **Still cameras** record before and after shots of the areas, particularly in conjunction with *Kaizen* events.
- **Stopwatches** establish and verify performance standards; this data is then used for line balancing and takt time (see Chapter 4) comparison.
- **A toolbox** full of screwdrivers, wrenches, and hammers may come in handy for creating display boards, hanging visual aides or other improvement activities.

Beginning the Journey: The Lean Rollout

You can start Lean anywhere, in any place, and at any time. There's no special magic place to begin. Often, people just start the process by performing a 5S (see Chapter 8) or a *Kaizen* Event (see Chapter 6) in an area of need or interest. This action begins the journey; then you ensure it's progressing by executing to a plan or a framework. Don't make the rollout a big deal or burden it with bureaucratic management — keep it straightforward and simple. It is Lean, after all.

Minding the big picture

True Lean is a process of small, incremental improvements. Sounds simple enough, except that these improvements are happening all over the enterprise involving the entire organization, across multiple value streams, simultaneously. If you aren't careful, things can get out of control. In this section, we share strategies to keep your Lean efforts on track.

Understanding the enterprise value streams

Within the context of the high-level value stream of the enterprise, most companies have many, many internal value streams. They also may have single areas, or monuments, that services multiple value streams, such as a large piece of equipment or a hospital lab. When the organization understands the many different value streams it has, and how those different value streams interrelate, the organization is better able to coordinate the improvement efforts and avoid *sub-optimizing* (improving one part of the enterprise at the peril of another).

Avoiding the Kaizen blitzkrieg

Especially in the beginning of the Lean journey, people are motivated to get something done — and now! Many organizations respond to this urgency by hosting as many *Kaizen* events as they possibly can. They may instill a metric for the number of *Kaizen* activities performed. In response, everyone runs right out and checks off the "I did a *Kaizen!*" box — without coordination, without a larger scale vision, without connection.

When all these blitzes are happening at once, the results are minimized. One area may free up floor space, but it may be too small or in the wrong location to be useful or to amount to a true savings. In another scenario, one area may move the *muda* (see Chapter 3) to another part of the facility or value stream, without truly eliminating anything.

Don't turn your *Kaizen* blitz into a *Kaizen* blitzkrieg — where instead of improvement, you leave only devastation behind. Build into your process ways to coordinate the *Kaizen* activities, so that you yield overall improvements.

Kaizen events are a great way to start, but they need a proper scope, vision and tie to the performance objectives of the organization.

Connecting the pieces

The Lean toolbox has an array of different tools (refer to Part III: Chapters 7 through 10). The organization must understand how, when, and why the different tools are used. If you're trying to level schedules and implement *kanban* (see Chapter 8), yet your changeover times are still counted in days, you're implementing the wrong tool at the wrong time. By understanding each tool in the toolkit, you'll better match the implementation of the techniques to your particular situation.

Most organizations have other initiatives occurring in the organization. These initiatives may be continuous-improvement initiatives or large-scale projects like an ERP implementation or an acquisition. The organization must define how all these things fit together.

Neglecting to connect the dots for the organization will cause confusion and fuel the rumor mill. Some people in the organization will be waiting for Lean to fail and will jump to the conclusion that Lean is just another "program of the month." Showing the organization how it all fits together will help minimize the impact of these naysayers.

Keeping your finger on the pulse of the organization

As we discuss in Chapters 11 and 12, communication is the lifeblood of the Lean transformation. You need to take the pulse of the organization, continually. If the organization starts either reverting backward to un-Lean behaviors and tendencies or moving off course, you need to know this and correct it.

Enlist volunteers from various parts of the organization to act as a communication council. This strategy will help you keep the message real, keep the movement consistent, and keep you connected to the pulse of the organization.

Picking the starting point

As an actor studies a role to bring art to life, he asks the question, "What's my motivation?" When you're bringing Lean to life in your organization, you, too, should ask yourself this question: What's your motivation? Identify where you have the greatest pain points or the greatest opportunities, which will impact the organization in a strategic manner. Find your greatest motivation and you've found your starting point.

Impact on the customer

The first place to look is where you have the greatest impact on the customer. Evaluate where your relationships are strained with customers and identify the potential sources of the issues. Brainstorm all the potential causes. Then apply the right combination of improvements and monitor the progress. Build the relationship through action and communication.

The enterprise 5S blitz?

An easy way to start is to 5S (see Chapter 8) all the departments in a given facility. If you choose this path, you really need to understand your motivation. The 5S tool is a great one (your facility will be neat and clean!), but you must ask yourself if this is the best way to start your Lean journey. The answer is "not usually." The 5S tool is more powerful when used in combination with other tools or in conjunction with a greater vision.

Quick visual improvement

If your motivation is to build momentum, you want to find a starting point that has impact and is quick, visual, and relevant, like:

- Removing an inventory warehouse or storage
- Reducing setup times from hours to minutes
- Reducing repair time for vehicles needed to support soldiers in the field

Wide-open spaces

If your motivation is to create space in your facility to accommodate new business, eliminate lease payments, or bring workgroups together, you'll want to create wide-open spaces. You'll need to free up large concentrated spaces in your facility. Start by conducting a series of coordinated *Kaizen* and 5S activities to create the right space in the right location.

Creating awareness

In the beginning of your Lean journey, you want to create a buzz, get people excited, and engage them in your Lean efforts. As you progress, you want to keep the organization motivated and involved in the Lean transformation. Ultimately, you want your organization to live and breathe Lean. None of this will happen if your people don't know what is going on. In this section, we tell you ways to create the buzz, improve communication, and engage people for the long haul.

Communicating the rollout plan

Communicating the plan to the organization will help create a buzz in the organization. Giving people information about upcoming changes will help them to overcome any anxieties they may have about the change in the environment to Lean. Again, communicate in a manner that appeals to a variety of learning styles (see Chapters 11 and 12).

Leading by listening

Listening is one of the most powerful communication skills a person can develop. Whether you're on an intentional *gemba* walk or hanging out at the water cooler, listening will enable you to gauge the pulse of the people. Figure 13-1 depicts an effective listening model.

Figure 13-1:
Following an effective listening model like this one can go a long way toward improving your communication skills.

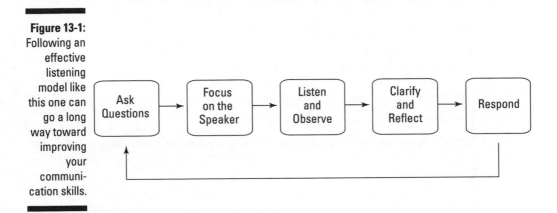

Highlighting progress

As you start to make progress, communicate! Let the organization know what has happened, why it's important to them, what is slated to happen next, and how that is relevant for them. Highlighting progress is your opportunity to celebrate wins — large and small.

Reinforcing the long-term view

Constantly keeping the motivation and long-term vision in front of people will make Lean real for them, even if their area hasn't yet started implementation. The message to the organization is that this is not about a *Kaizen* here and there — Lean is about the long-term sustainability and viability of the organization as a whole.

Lean by doing

The best way to create awareness and understanding of Lean is to get involved. Get on a *Kaizen* team, 5S your workspace, learn a new technique and find a pertinent application for it. There is no better way to grasp the concepts of Lean than by actively participating and implementing improvements every day.

Avoiding program-of-the-month syndrome

Since the beginning of continuous-improvement time, battling program-of-the-month syndrome has been an organizational challenge. As long as there are consultants, new methodologies will be introduced into the market. Or when movements lose steam in an organization, clever consultants or opportunistic leaders repackage tools and techniques with a twist. Companies that are truly committed to the Lean journey will find ways to keep the journey invigorated and determine how best to fit in new methodologies. In the following sections, we give you tips how to avoid the program-of-the-month syndrome.

Talking the talk

Communication is really, really important along your entire Lean journey. People need to know what's happening, how it affects them, and that you're truly committed to the trip. If you do not, people will make things up, start rumors or do nothing in hopes that "this too shall pass." (See Chapter 12 for more about the importance of a communication strategy to help people change.)

Walking the walk

If yesterday, you hailed the TLA (Three-Letter Acronym) Improvement Program, today you cheerlead the Charge for Lean, and tomorrow you're touting a new program called Ten Thetas, you'll feed organizational frenzy. You'll doom your improvement journey to a certain death at the hands of the cynics and naysayers. Your behaviors must reflect that you're a serious practitioner and leader of a Lean process initiative. If you're inconsistent and non-committal, Lean will be just another bygone program of the month.

Separating the wheat from the chaff: Handling new initiatives

As new initiatives rise to the surface, you will need to have a process to triage their impact and determine what to do about them. Whether it's a new whiz-bang IT solution or the latest incarnation of continuous improvement with a consultant's twist, you need to know how that initiative will affect your Lean journey. Ask yourself the following questions:

- Does this initiative have relevance to the organization? If so, where in the organization does it fit?
- What activities are currently underway in these areas?
- Is there overlap between this initiative and Lean?
- How does the Lean initiative facilitate the activity?
- How and when should the organization incorporate this initiative?
- How does it all fit together, and what does the organization need to know?

Great expectations

By setting the expectations with the staff, customers, stakeholders, and others, you support the Lean principles and establish the behaviors and tone for the organization. When you're clear about the performance and behaviors you expect, and when you hold all the people in the organization accountable, they know that Lean is here for the long term and isn't just a passing fancy. When you connect the dots for them in terms of Lean, you reinforce that Lean is the foundation and that any other activity or initiative has to be interpreted in the context of Lean.

Measurable outcomes

When you continually show measurable progress, you build momentum in the organization. As the momentum builds, you increase your progress. Staying the course with Lean — and keeping the momentum going — will show the organization that Lean is not just here for the short term.

 Put the outcomes in terms that any individual can see and understand. Translate the impact to a personal level. The outcomes are not necessarily direct financial measures; they could be freed-up floor space, decreased time to serve a customer, a reduced approval chain, or anything that the individual can observe and use to verify the longer-term performance.

Measurements: The enterprise at a glance

When you're rolling out Lean, you need to determine what the relevant measurements are for your organization. Table 13-1 shows an example of a Lean measurement matrix. Performance charts like this one are then displayed for people to see how the business is doing.

Table 13-1	Enterprise Performance Matrix												
	1	2	3	4	5	6	7	8	9	10	11	12	YTD
Safety													
Recordables													
People													
Absenteeism													
Turnover													
Quality													
DPMO													
Spills													

	1	2	3	4	5	6	7	8	9	10	11	12	YTD
Delivery													
On-time													
Premium transport													
Cost													
Inventory turns													
Actual cost per unit													

The closer you can tie your Lean implementation metrics to overall company performance metrics, the more meaningful the Lean implementation metrics are from a business standpoint. A double digit savings in floor space is great, but if you don't have work to put in it, then the freed-up floor space doesn't mean much to the business.

Localized within a value steam, you may want to add other measures — both process and outcome metric — relevant to Lean implementation. Example metrics could include:

- Percent of team cross-trained
- Performance to takt
- Actual setup reduction versus target
- Percent of *Kaizen* events complete versus planned
- Number of work orders completed to plan

Reading data in a graphical form is easier than reading it in a text form. Post graphs of these metrics in communication stations in your facility and on your intranet.

Living Lean

After your Lean initiative gets its legs and begins to run, your organization is changed forever. The positive effects of Lean are contagious, and the mindset of *Kaizen* has a certain dogged determination and undeniability about it. As a result, over time, your enterprise Lean initiative will evolve into an ongoing, sustaining phase. This is when you know you're *living Lean*.

The Lean evolution

The evolution of a Lean initiative begins with the rollout phase and moves into its sustaining phase sometime after everyone has been trained, *Kaizen* events have been performed across the enterprise, and the positive results have occurred widely enough and consistently enough that everyone begins to believe in its power.

After Lean has been validated through repeated successes over a wide range of applications, the cultural adoption will set in. Through everyone's combined behaviors, the Lean principles will be absorbed and the organization will begin to think of itself as a Lean enterprise.

What happens then? Are you "done"? Have you "become Lean"? Can you now put the Lean techniques and methods and tools aside — *thank you very much* — and move on with your business? The answer to these questions is "absolutely not!" You don't put anything aside.

The minute you declare your organization "Lean" is the minute you've lost your way!

Inwardly Lean

The first Lean activities begin with training and *Kaizen* events (see Chapters 6 and 8 for more on *Kaizen*), usually in a selected program area or workgroup. Successful events give rise to improvement projects. These projects address a specific challenge area in a particular value stream, and involve time and effort on the part of a project team and the Lean *sensei*, who together apply the Lean toolkit. After a few projects have been successful and the positive results become visible, the participants all begin to truly internalize the value, and they understand the power of the approach. Others begin to notice. People start initiating small projects in their work areas and as part of their workgroups.

The next step in the Lean evolution is the development of an enterprise project-oriented mindset, where challenges are addressed with Lean projects on a broader scale — both within their value streams and in concert with other value streams. At first, this may be a look over the wall at some closely related function or department in the organization (see Chapter 14 for an exploration of the relationship between two such groups: the development and production teams). Integrated enterprise value-stream activities will begin between organizations like marketing and IT or between design and customer service.

This is the point where everyone is "doing" Lean stuff. It's a very exciting time: The organization is growing and learning, people are improving their work processes and environments, and the results are showing — in improved business productivity and performance. Figure 13-2 shows how Lean organizations evolve over time.

In a large organization, it takes years to reach a level of ubiquitous enterprise-wide Lean practice.

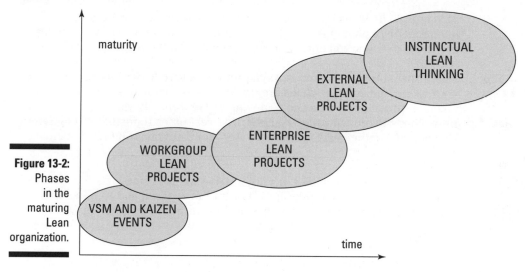

Figure 13-2: Phases in the maturing Lean organization.

At some point, someone in the organization climbs the next rung on the evolution ladder. Instead of creating a project team to approach a challenge, he just goes off and Leans-up a value stream on his own. No fanfare, no project team or official results — he makes the Nike marketing team proud and "just does it." At this stage, the mechanical formalities begin to drop away and the mindsets begin to change. People begin to see the world through different eyes. They're acting on instinct. They're *thinking* Lean.

Outwardly Lean

After people within their own work areas become comfortable with internal projects, they begin examining the cause-and-effect conditions that give rise to the waste in their segment of the value stream. Very quickly, this leads to an expansion of view: They begin to look outside their own world.

Groups begin to look up and down their value stream. They begin to suggest projects with suppliers, and other projects with customers. Eventually, this may lead to integrated value-stream projects involving suppliers, customers, and even the customers' customers. Meanwhile, groups within the enterprise have begun to explore the relationships between them more fully.

All these are examples of outward Lean behavior. Outwardly, Lean is important, because it represents the emergence of a systems view, the more holistic view of the organization and its life in the value chain. The external view provides the objectivity needed to adjust how the enterprise fits into the world. It promotes *adaptivity* — the ability to adapt and survive in the economic gene pool.

This adaptivity leads to a decrease in what's known as *functional sub-optimization* (a phenomenon where a lot of time and effort are spent fixing problems in a function or area that don't matter in the bigger picture).

Functional sub-optimization is a symptom of inward focus, where you think your world and your problems are the only ones that matter. Don't be mistaken: Improving any area and removing waste from any value stream are the right things to do, but diverting enterprise resources to further strengthening a strong link in the chain when there are weak links all around isn't a smart move.

Eliminating waste is just that. It's not moving waste. Using logistics tools like postponement, third-party kitting, distribution centers, and topping up to move your waste to someone else is nothing more than sweeping dirt under the rug. Sure, your room looks clean, but the dirt is still there. Don't move *muda*; eliminate it.

Building the learning organization

Maturing Lean organizations have a passion and zest for learning. Part of the culture of openness that accompanies the Lean mindset is a desire to continuously learn. It's part of the journey — the recognition that you're never done.

The learning organization is continuously curious. People recognize that what they knew yesterday may be outdated, and that new knowledge today will make them better tomorrow. They never feel like they know everything — there's a world of evolving knowledge out there and much more to learn.

In the learning organization, everyone has the mutual trust and comfort to examine mistakes and truly learn from them. Post-mortem examinations aren't finger-pointing sessions — they're improvement sessions. They seek to find cause, not assign blame. The learning organization has a continuous sharing of knowledge and a sense of need for shared or "tribal" knowledge.

Hallmarks of the learning organization are obvious and everywhere:

✔ **Education and training are a priority.** They're the last thing to fall victim to budget pressures.

✔ **Everyone participates in cross-training programs.** When workloads shift, people are quickly cross-trained and develop the proficiency to pick up the slack.

✔ **Contributions to increased knowledge and proficiency are supported and rewarded.**

✔ **People conduct early-morning education sessions and brown-bag lunch-and-learn sessions, and there is a full slate of well-attended evening classes.**

✔ **When necessary, people stop what they're doing to train and educate someone who needs additional knowledge for everyone to move forward at the proper takt.**

✔ **The organization has a formal mentorship program.**

✔ **Libraries and online reference materials are readily available, continuously updated, and used extensively.**

✔ **Everyone occasionally attends a book-review discussion, a conference, or a symposium, and they actively seek to present at these events.**

✔ **People in the organization write papers, publish articles, and author books.**

✔ **People actively monitor and participate in online chat forums and subject-specific blogs.**

The curiosity of the learning organization is naturally contagious, but the framework and support mechanisms must be deliberately and proactively supported. Senior management, middle management, and supervisors must all foster the learning culture by budgeting the time and expense to facilitate the learning organization. Also, in the spirit of leading by doing, managers must actively participate.

Creating the continuous-improvement mindset

Although learning is an important enabler, the other side of the coin is application. Knowledge is one thing; putting it into action is another. The Lean organization's thirst for knowledge is complemented by an equally strong continuous hunger for improvement. It's all about progress.

The continuous-improvement mindset is driven by the notion that no matter where we are or what we've achieved, we can always accomplish something better:

- ✔ We can find and remove more waste.
- ✔ We can balance the cycle time to the takt time.
- ✔ We can remove more defects, reduce variation, and improve the quality.
- ✔ We can delight our customers even more.
- ✔ We can make our value chain more effective.
- ✔ We can improve our use of technology.
- ✔ We can better apply ourselves, working smarter.
- ✔ We can make a difference and make it better.

Continuous improvement isn't a death march. It's not tireless drudgery. This isn't an assault on Mount Everest. The maturing Lean organization doesn't feed off Herculean victories; it thrives on constant progress. The Lean mindset, therefore, never has the need to rest on its laurels, because it never tires out.

The Lean organization is like a long-distance runner, rather than a sprinter. Lean is a sustainable aerobic movement, leveraged through fitness, disciplined through training, maintained by momentum, fueled by balanced nutrition, and spiced by endorphins.

Facilitating with finance

The finance and accounting functions directly support the Lean journey by providing financial measures of the benefits and effectiveness of processes and operations as they're transformed.

There's nothing like financial incentives to move the mountain. When Lean processes make money, everyone notices. The finance and accounting function is responsible for working with the Lean practitioners across the enterprise to define the key metrics that demonstrate the financial benefits that accrue from Lean process improvements.

Standard accounting practices and systems don't capture, manage, analyze, or report financial information according to Lean practices. You need to develop specialized applications first, and then tune the financial systems over time, in order to implement financial practices that align with your Lean initiative.

Because Lean operations cut across traditional functional boundaries and generate new types of metrics, traditional accounting systems and measures don't facilitate the Lean organization. Not having the right metrics can be a real problem. Remember the part about how the finance organizations are slow to change? When you ask them to change how the beans are counted, you may encounter some resistance.

Getting support from IT

The IT organization must provide the Lean enterprise with information-management resources and activities that support Lean processes. These include specific tools as well as certain integration and reporting capabilities. Oh, and then there's enterprise resource planning (ERP).

Lean and enterprise applications

Increasingly, specialized enterprise application environments support Lean information and management needs. Business activity monitoring (BAM) tools and business process management (BPM) tools are large-scale enterprise-class application software solutions that provide sweeping capabilities in the areas of data collection, analysis, reporting, monitoring (dashboards), and control. In some cases, these have evolved to real-time control systems that directly control such critical operational elements as inventory, supply, distribution, and more.

Lean and ERP

The promise of the truly integrated Lean enterprise is now causing organizations of all types and sizes to examine and reassess how they use their traditional enterprise resource planning (ERP) systems. Although ERP systems were pivotal in creating large-scale efficiencies and implementing cost-effective processes in a variety of industries, IT organizations are beginning to realize that the Lean enterprises require a different approach.

Some organizations are delaying or shelving elements of ERP implementations in order to institute Lean practices first. This way, they don't lock in software-driven operational frameworks that are counter to Lean techniques.

Now I am the master

As the initiative matures, Lean principles and behaviors are carried forth in an organization more by momentum and cultural predisposition than by impulse. It's not a matter of who carries the torch, because everyone is carrying his own torch. Lean behaviors become ingrained, and, because organizations are slow to change, those behaviors don't disappear. Continuous learning and improvement become cultural mainstays.

Still, management must maintain leadership and continue the Lean direction. They must continue to exhibit Lean behaviors and ensure the organization stays on course.

An enterprise doesn't need to maintain a significant organizational entity to support the long-term Lean initiative. However, a core group is required:

- ✔ To maintain and channel the organization's Lean practices.
- ✔ To integrate Lean practices into other organizations — such as new suppliers, merger or acquisition partners, and new distributors.
- ✔ To stay abreast of Lean developments and trends in other industries.

Chapter 14

Lean within the Enterprise

Most people equate Lean with Lean Manufacturing, because Lean practices were first developed for improving production processes in the automotive industry. During the 1990s, most businesses did concentrate their Lean efforts on manufacturing functions like fabrication and assembly. However, with such great successes on the shop floor, Lean practitioners have more recently applied their methods and techniques in other areas of the enterprise. Nowadays, you're just as likely to see *Kaizen* events, Value Stream Mapping, and cycle time reduction efforts in many other areas of an organization, including engineering, administration, and customer care. Lean isn't just for shop-floor processes anymore.

This spread of Lean practices across organizations is vitally important for several reasons.

✔ Because Lean principles apply to processes in general, nearly any process can be improved using Lean methods and techniques. Is there any process that wouldn't be improved by reducing waste?

✔ By applying Lean across the enterprise, the multidisciplinary views and experiences contribute to the practice, and benefit the science of Lean.

✔ Practicing Lean everywhere benefits the practice of Lean anywhere. As we stress throughout this book, Lean is not a sideshow — it's not just something done by the worker bees off in a corner of the organization. Lean is a philosophy, and the more widely it's practiced in the organization, the greater the understanding, acceptance, and support it will receive in each area of implementation.

In this chapter, you see how Lean can be applied from top to bottom and from wall to wall in an organization. From the executive suite to the engineering lab, and from the procurement office to the customer-service center, Lean practices reduce waste, time, and mistakes, and improve overall performance.

Lean Enterprise Management

In the Lean enterprise, people consider the whole business system. They conduct improvement activities at all levels with a complete view — seeing not just their own value stream and their own customers, but everyone's customers, the organization's customers, and the end consumers. Everyone examines the processes that influence outcomes — causes and effects — and sees the organization through two lenses:

- ✔ *Kaizen* **maintenance:** Following the policies and rules that maintain the performance levels set by the present operating standards

- ✔ *Kaizen* **improvement:** Efforts to continuously improve existing standards and processes or innovate new ones

Across the enterprise, all training, materials, tools, support, and supervision contribute to both the improvement and the maintenance of standards on a continual basis. This business philosophy calls for never-ending efforts that involve everyone — managers and workers alike.

It's a Lean, Lean, Lean, Lean world

Lean has grown up and moved beyond its roots in the production and assembly bays of industrial manufacturing. Now you can practice Lean anywhere.

Don't look now, but most of what happens in many organizations isn't in hard-core physical manufacturing at all. While Lean was growing up in places like the automotive assembly arena, many organizations were evolving. Nowadays, most — if not all — of many enterprises conduct their business above and beyond what's known as the "shop floor."

Transactional Lean

You can practice Lean in the *transaction processes* — business processes whose primary role is to transact information or data. This includes processes within finance and accounting, contracts, procurement, legal, human resources and information technology. Just because you're not making something physical doesn't mean your processes are free of waste. Transaction processes typically don't waste much direct material, but they can waste things that can be worth a lot more, including

- ✔ **Time:** Poor transaction management wastes huge amounts of time. The Lean practice of cycle-time reduction is a strong focus in these areas.

- ✔ **Facilities:** Transaction processes use facilities just like physical processes do — office buildings and data centers, mostly. Poor transaction management consumes excess square footage.

✔ **Energy:** When you're wasting space, chances are, you're wasting energy, too. Offices are big energy consumers, and data centers are even bigger energy consumers. Overtime, excess travel, rework — these all consume energy needlessly.

✔ **People:** Worst of all, by not properly utilizing people, organizations fall well short of their potential.

Waste is harder to see in transactional areas. You can easily see waste in the physical areas: parts, inventory, material, people who aren't working, and so on. But waste is harder to recognize in transactions. Is that person sitting in front of his computer adding value? Is the computer program he's running adding value? Is the process that's consuming the results of that program adding value? You have to really look.

The value-stream manager

Lean organizations have a role called the *value-stream manager*. This person is responsible for the end-to-end Lean improvements and maintenance of one or more value streams. The role of value-stream manager is multifunctional role — it integrates multiple disciplines and functional areas to optimize a given value stream. The value-stream manager role might be played by a product-line manager, who owns the profit and loss (P&L) for a family of products or services, and who would oversee the many value streams for those products or services. The value-stream manager role could also be played by a project or program manager, with a focus on a single program or project. The value-stream manager might also be an assigned role within an operational area.

Leaning up the support functions

Lean practices within an organization's support functions have a huge positive outcome. Long dubbed the *overhead groups,* these are the departments that, in general, add little or no value directly to the customer. In a high-level Value Stream Map (VSM), there's no value-added in a contract, an accounting procedure, or business travel. It's all *muda.*

How ironic that these business functions don't receive a lot of process-improvement attention! They get all kinds of budget pressure, and the IT vendors have a bandoleer of silver bullets for them, but efficiencies alone are the wrong answer. These functions generally don't receive much help in focusing on change, because enterprises tend to save their improvement energy for their core processes. As a result, these functions tend to grow out of date and become self-serving and replete with waste. Across the enterprise, Lean practices tend to have big impacts in these areas.

It's important for these functions and departments to be Lean. However, in an overhead organization, it's not just about Value Stream Mapping to reduce inefficiencies and lower costs. You have to conduct Lean efforts within a framework that aligns these organizations with the organization's strategic objectives and customer needs. Never lose sight of what creates value for the customer!

Lean finance and administration

Most people think those penny-pinchers do things about as Lean as you can imagine. But the financial and administrative departments in organizations are naturally conservative and slow to change, so over time they tend to build up and carry forward arcane procedures and excess baggage. This buildup results in slower throughput, higher labor costs, and increased difficulty satisfying their customers.

The results returned from initiating Lean practices in finance and administrative functions are often swift and significantly positive. Because these functions consist of many independent processes, beginning focused incremental improvements within them is less daunting than it is to ponder large-scale overhauls, top-down reengineering, or big technology initiatives. These departments have been told for years that they need to be more customer-focused; the Lean toolkit enables them to deliver on that mantra.

The scope of Lean practice facilitates improvements in all the finance and administrative functions, including:

- **Accounting:** Traditional accounting conventions and practices can be rethought from the viewpoint of what truly adds value to the customer, as well as reducing waste and cycle time. Eliminate unnecessary accounting and control transactions. Create business measures in terms of customer value.

- **Contracts:** The business contracting function has suffered in recent years from an onslaught of legal "protections." All customers, partners, contractors, and suppliers suffer under the principle that the extra effort is worth it if it prevents one failed lawsuit. Without unduly sacrificing protection, considerable waste can be culled from the contracting arena. Think customer value and cycle-time reduction.

- **Legal:** Corporate legal services believe their customer is the corporation and they work to protect the corporation from onslaught and exposure. However, corporate attorneys spend their days working with people whose needs are immediate and direct. Cycle time is money.

- **Travel:** Travel is mostly a non-value added activity, although Lean practice calls for *genchi genbutsu* (the practice of going out and seeing it for yourself). Standardize work for travel arrangements and Lean up the travel function. From the Lean viewpoint, which is the better option: having everyone waste their time making their own arrangements, or wasting a central office or agent's time making the arrangements for them?

✔ **Copy center:** Paper is waste. Documents are pure *muda*. Creating paper, printing and binding documents, shipping them, carrying them, storing them — these are all traditions that have less and less relevance in the modern world.

✔ **Mail room:** The iconic first rung on the corporate ladder, the mail room, is a showcase for Lean. Standardized work, waste-reduction, and cycle time are hallmarks of Lean and all apply perfectly to the mail room.

You can introduce Lean in these areas by facilitating *Kaizen* events, coupled with a modest amount of training, supported by the following management behaviors:

✔ Use performance measures that motivate Lean actions, reward Lean behaviors, and incentivize the elimination of unnecessary overhead.

✔ Define and measure standardized work processes.

✔ Build VSMs that show how the processes generate direct internal customer value.

✔ Facilitate understanding of its role in the organization as a whole and how it delivers value to its customers.

✔ Cross-train, enabling the shifting of work for rotations and peak load management.

✔ Define internal business measures in terms of customer value.

Lean in human resources

Human resources (HR) departments have experienced enormous staff and expense growth in recent years, due to increased personnel support needs. Lean HR helps better align the HR function to the core needs of the business, reduce expenses, and shorten the time to support the organization's HR needs. The HR function also has a critical role in supporting Lean initiatives across the enterprise.

Lean HR improves the performance of its internal processes through value-added, customer (staff) satisfaction, process cycle-time reduction, and a measurable high quality of results. Lean areas of focus in HR include

✔ **New-hire cycle time:** The time lag between a business area identifying the need for additional personnel and the time that an individual is onboard can run from weeks to months. Requisitions, postings, résumé reviews, interviews, background checks, follow-ups — all these routine activities have built up in the effort to ensure a quality hire. How can this process be streamlined for greater effectiveness?

- ✔ **Recruiting:** What's the Value Stream Map for the recruiting process? The recruiting process is a form of marketing; how do your future employee "customers" see it?

- ✔ **Benefits administration:** How are benefit programs structured? How are benefit packages defined? How are the options communicated? How are changes communicated? How do employees select and manage their programs? All of these are part of the benefits "product" offering to the employee "consumer."

- ✔ **Training and development:** By closely aligning with the lines of business, understanding strategic directions, and supporting the staff, HR plays a key role in organizational readiness and performance through its training and development function. The goal is knowledge. How effective is HR in getting knowledge into the heads of the staff?

- ✔ **Satisfaction and retention:** Although the rest of the organization often exploits the talents and energies of the staff, HR is the watchdog for the staff's ongoing satisfaction and for ensuring long-term retention.

Think about other HR processes that can benefit from Lean practice. How can Lean help in managing workplace diversity? How about outsourcing? Compensation plans? Change management?

Lean in information technology

The words *Lean* and *information technology* (IT) haven't been spoken together often in the past. IT has been anything but Lean in nearly every sense — non-value-added work, considerable nonstandard work, batch processing, redundant processing, push flow, over-capacity, disconnection from customers and consumers — you name it. IT has been the un-Lean. And the vendors haven't helped, having provided expensive and brittle systems.

The IT function can help contribute to the Lean enterprise in several areas:

- ✔ **Customer focus:** Customer focus is a broken record in enterprise IT. For over 25 years, the users have been too disjointed and disconnected from IT. Of all the classic gulfs that have divided the enterprise, this rift ranks near the top. But Lean provides methods and tools for bridging this gap. And it's not just about the immediate internal customer; it's also about knowing the organization's customers and the role of the organization in the value chain to the end consumer.

- ✔ **Reducing non-value-added activity:** Streamline all IT processes, and eliminate outdated processes, paper reports, multiple handling of information (both internally in IT and externally in the business), redundant processing, and other processes.

✔ **Single-piece flow:** Because IT shops traditionally work as project shops, the concept of single-piece flow is pretty-well understood already. Applications, integrations and database programs are conceived, designed, developed, tested, and integrated as single units and delivered as they're built. This is an important basis to build on!

✔ **Customer pull:** In times gone by, applications and systems were simply too big and too chunky to support customized individual needs. As a result, they got even bigger and chunkier in an attempt to be all things to all users. IT now has the tools to support customer needs on an individualized basis. Moreover, these tools can support individual needs by end customers and consumers. Information can now be processed and delivered at the rate of customer demand.

✔ **The end of batching:** Batch runs have been a trademark process of IT for decades. Even with the advent of modern systems that can support more real-time integrated and continuous-flow data processing, however, batch processing is still commonplace. But it's on its way out.

Vendor-led improvements in technology and software architectures, coupled with significantly lower price points, and advances in systems engineering, development processes, and IT practices, have combined to change the IT equation. And that's critical, because a key leverage point in Lean comes from IT's role in the integration between core business processes, the internal supply chain, and the larger external supply-chain environment.

The IT organization can improve its effectiveness by embracing Lean practices and the philosophy of *Kaizen* within its operations.

Many organizations attempt to fix broken business processes with IT. However, no matter how Lean your IT solution is, it will not fix a broken process. Simplify and/or eliminate processes before you automate and integrate them. Eliminating waste before you automate a business process will save you time and money in the long run.

Lean Product Development

More than ever, businesses of all types and sizes are pressured to develop and bring innovative, high-quality products and services to market rapidly. New product development efforts are now characterized by ever-shortening product-development cycles, lower budgeted development costs, and increases in levels of product quality. More demanding customer requirements are pushing the envelopes of features, customization, energy efficiency, environmental compatibility, reliability, maintainability, and life-cycle cost of ownership.

Lean product development processes enable the enterprise to produce products and services faster, with fewer resources, and at higher levels of quality, while using less capital and making happier customers. Lean product development practices help designers address a myriad of challenges that conspire against them, such as:

- Lack of a detailed understanding of customer requirements
- Haphazard work standards, with low process standardization
- Inability to effectively reuse previous designs
- Time and cost to produce expensive prototypes
- Unnecessary product and process complexity
- Use of uncommon or nonstandard parts and practices
- Last-minute design changes
- Large-scale validation testing
- Designs driven by tradition, politics, or perception

What happens during the development process affects what happens in the manufacturing and production processes. Product development is the headwaters of the company's performance. Well-integrated designs lead to greater efficiencies, reduced variation, and higher quality outcomes on the production end.

Table 14-1 summarizes techniques of Lean product development.

Table 14-1	Lean Development Techniques
Technique	**Description**
Kano modeling (must/should/could)	Understand customer requirements in terms of needs, wants, and delighters
QFD	Capture and translate voice of the customer; value-based designs
Design limits	Set high and low limits for performance, features, quality, or price
Task linking	Manage the links and interrelationships among development tasks using templates and checklists
Delivery road map	Envision the schedule development deliverables

Technique	Description
Standardized work	Produce recipes for performing functions identically and consistently
Reference standards	Follow best-practice guidelines
Short-cycle approvals	Manage by exception, providing value-added approvals
Reuse	Identify where reuse of designs, production, and other life-cycle elements reduce time, complexity, or cost
Meeting management tools	Hold standing briefings with defined outcomes; conduct waste-free meetings
Complexity reduction	Optimize product quality, cost, and manufacturing by reducing complexity
Visuals	Use status boards, Gantt charts, intranets
	Create visual pull systems for Engineering Change Notices (ECNs), Change Review Boards (CRBs), and so on
	Apply help sheets for exceptions to plan
Formal freeze points	Implement change control to enable parallel task execution
Critical path management	Pull the development project through the critical path points on the development schedule
Critical core management	Focus resources on core tasks that drive overall schedule, cost, or quality
SWAT teams	Form teams quickly and temporarily to attack and solve a specific problem
Interruption filters	Screen sources of interruption to completing work — meetings, phone calls, e-mail, and so on
Brainstorming	Conduct one-time events to address challenges and improve processes and outcomes
Work protocol	Follow guidelines for behavior in the development environment
Periodic process assessments	Continuously improve the effectiveness of the development process

The following sections describe the practices of Lean product development.

Product development: The systems approach

The first rule of Lean development is to bring a complete, holistic view to the development process. The three major components of the development world — people, processes, and technology — must be fully integrated and mutually supportive. Furthermore, they must be in alignment, not only with one another, but with the goals and strategies of the organization as a whole.

When these three fundamental system components are made coherent by design, they create a type of synergistic systems effect, each balancing with and playing off the other.

Hearing the voice of the customer

Every developer should hear that little birdie on his shoulder . . . *chirp-chirp!* That's the voice of the customer, singing in your ear, as you contemplate your next move. Are you listening? Can you hear the customer talking? What do you hear the customer saying?

The Lean development process should be closely bonded with the customer. The Lean process hears the customer's voice first, foremost, and louder than any other voice. The customer voice not only tells the developers what to design, but the customer's notion of value reveals much about the design process — and thereby helps the developers eliminate non-value-added steps and activities.

Refer to Chapter 3 for information on how the customer defines *value,* and refer to Chapter 7 for the tools used in the design/development process. The Lean system enables the developer to understand the customer requirements and systematically translate those requirements into functional products and services.

Lean development comes from an intimate understanding of customer-defined value. The system components — people, process, and technology — must be tuned to understand customer-defined value from the start. Product development must deliver a product design that accomplishes two goals — meeting the customer needs and manufacturing effectively — if you expect to actually deliver this value to the customer.

Front-loading the engineering process

Most of the cost of any final product or service is locked in long before the product is formally launched. Overly complex designs cannot be "Leaned out" in the manufacturing process. Slow design efforts delay market readiness, negatively impacting market share and profitability. And you can't market and sell your way past products designed without the voice of the customer.

Poor design and development planning undermines Lean Manufacturing. However, designs arriving late to production, with poor yields, major manufacturing deficiencies, and lingering engineering problems have been more common than not. This is because sufficient time and energy were not allotted to the design and development phase. This short-changing of the engineering cycle is counterproductive, because rushing to production creates more problems than it solves.

Applying Lean tools and practices during the product-development process will certainly reduce the development time. But by taking the broader view of development, the design and development efforts can also reduce manufacturing lead times, maximize product performance (from the customer's viewpoint), and maintain the target cost. The earlier in the process these efforts are applied, the more leverage is gained.

Concurrent engineering

Designing products has always been part of mass production. Early on, the work was divided between the designer, who created the design, and the manufacturer, who made the actual product. Over time, this division widened, until the product designer worked more or less in ignorance of the manufacturer — and his constraints.

A design thrown over the proverbial wall is often difficult and costly to produce, resulting in higher production costs, poor quality, and lost time to market. And yet, this is more the norm than the exception. In fact, the design function is not the only organization living in a functional silo; many organizations along the product life cycle often operate with minimal communications between them, including marketing, development, manufacturing, distribution, sales, and service. Traditionally, most products go to market in a serial fashion.

Concurrent engineering (also sometimes called *concurrent product development* or *simultaneous execution*) is the rational practice of having the design organization and other enterprise functions become more aware of the activities occurring beyond the borders of their own department. Concurrent engineering (illustrated in the bottom part of Figure 14-1) replaces a traditional product development process where functional tasks are performed serially. In concurrent engineering (CE), everyone collaborates on each aspect of a product's development process. This facilitates faster and more thorough reactions to changing conditions.

Concurrent engineering isn't unique to Lean, but Lean product development naturally performs these functions in a concurrent and integrated way. Lean practice requires early and continuing consideration for every aspect of a product or service as it is developed and brought to market. Compared to serial or "stove-piped" processes, it requires more collaboration and involved leadership, management, and direction. It may also require some organizational restructuring — involving finance and accounting, HR, and IT for integrated data management.

Serial vs. concurrent development

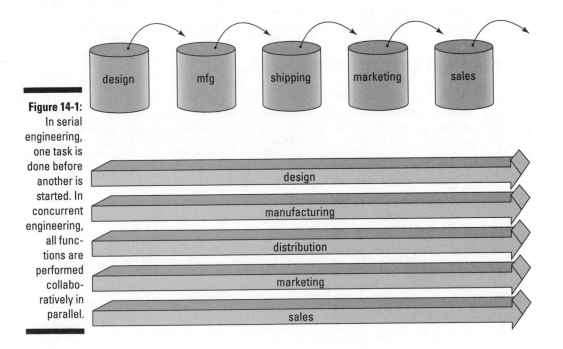

Figure 14-1:
In serial engineering, one task is done before another is started. In concurrent engineering, all functions are performed collaboratively in parallel.

Often different parts of your organization are not co-located in the same facility. Operations may span the globe. Location is not an excuse for not participating in the concurrent design process. Use the latest technology tools to bring the different organizations together virtually.

Genchi genbutsu: Go and see

In the modern, technology-enabled work environment, people seldom feel compelled to wander beyond the space between the conference room, break room, and their cubicles (or, for the telecommuter, it's the space between the kitchen, back porch, and home office!). Everything is learned via e-mail, conference calls, meetings, and presentations. The world seems large, but in fact it's very small.

Kelly Johnson, the famous head of Lockheed's legendary Skunk Works once said, "An engineer should never be more than a stone's throw away from the physical product." That's *genchi genbutsu*. Other examples of *genchi genbutsu* include:

- Visiting the manufacturing facility prior to beginning design work
- Seeing the showroom floor before developing the marketing materials
- Experiencing the product in action before designing the next generation
- Spending time with customer service to better understand warranty
- Visiting your suppliers — and their suppliers — to understand capabilities and constraints

Next time, before drawing premature conclusions based on hearsay, opinion, or even all that hard data, consider *genchi genbutsu* — go and see for yourself.

Rigorous standardization — for maximum flexibility

A constant knock on rigorous methodologies like Lean is that they're supposedly too rigid. Especially in the quirky, inventive culture of the design world, isn't it true that standards and processes do nothing more than take the art out of the practice? After all, where's the creativity, if all you're doing is following someone else's best practice, right? Nothing could be more wrong.

Lean is not about becoming a robot, programming yourself to perform repetitive tasks with machine-like precision. Lean work standards, best practices, and waste-reduction initiatives in no way imply you're limiting creativity and flexibility. In fact, just the opposite is true.

The development processes in Lean organizations are far more predictable, effective, and value-added than is otherwise possible. This is because the development teams are supported by tools and resources (refer to Table 14-1). They eliminate the noise factor of unnecessary randomness and chaos in the support frameworks, enabling teams to focus more time and energy on the creative elements. Redeveloping infrastructure on every project or at every step is wasteful and distractive — it saps creative energy. Such elements as work protocols, reference designs, and standard processes enable designers and developers to spend their creative time and energies on the value-added tasks. Such standards are also crucial to downstream Lean Manufacturing capabilities.

People fear that these support resources are somehow confining or limiting. They're not — they're enabling and supportive. Without these resources, developing anything would take more time and effort — and time and effort are exactly what's in short supply. Sure, you could have turned loose an infinite number of monkeys and they would have worked up the iPod. But who has an infinite number of monkeys?

Designing for manufacture

The practice of Design for Manufacturability (DFM) — or Design for Assembly (DFA) — isn't unique to Lean. DFM is part of concurrent engineering — it's recognizing that it doesn't matter how beautiful and elegant a design is if you can't actually build it. DFM is a collaboration between the design and manufacturing functions of an enterprise that ensure the product as-designed can be developed within reasonable manufacturing limitations.

Designing for Manufacturability greatly improves product quality and reduces fabrication costs. It's a matter of involving the manufacturing folks early in the design process. After completion of preliminary designs, meet with the manufacturing team (including Lean experts) and review the product requirements and design intent. Then, determine the manufacturing process requirements. The manufacturing staff should determine the process capabilities that are implied by the design in order to meet product quality, cost, and availability targets.

One of the most harrowing problem areas is *tolerancing* (the practice of defining tolerance limits for components, parts, and assemblies). Historically, designers define tolerance limits too casually — and in the process inadvertently dictate the capital and process needs of production. The designers should be careful to avoid unnecessarily tight tolerances that are beyond the natural capability of the manufacturing processes. In addition, the manufacturing team should identify to the designers any manufacturing tolerance challenges and suggest design or requirements revisions. When new production process capabilities are needed, identify these needs early. Figure 14-2 shows how a company ensures DFM through a formal "production preparation process."

Simplify design and assembly so that components can only be assembled in one way; they cannot be reversed.

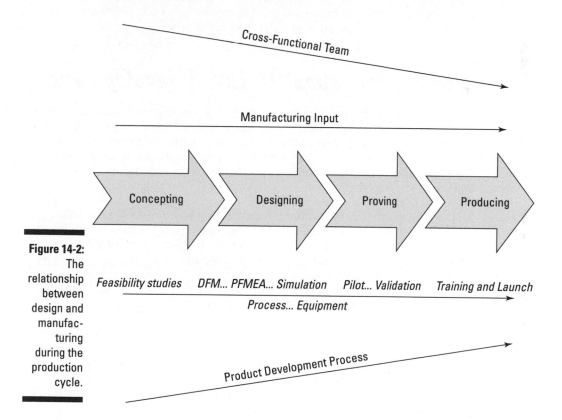

Figure 14-2: The relationship between design and manufacturing during the production cycle.

Built-in learning

In Lean, learning and continuous improvement are fundamental parts of every job. Although certain work skills require special outside training, Lean process and improvement skills can be acquired and refined as a regular and routine part of everyday work. Build in learning into your organization by including such practices as:

- ✔ During projects, real-time reviews and learning events encourage everyone to learn and update their work standards and practices.

- ✔ At project milestones and completion, so-called post-mortem reviews provide additional opportunities for learning.

- ✔ Learning and continuous improvement are also part of the problem-solving process. Multiple potential solutions focus on root cause, and solutions are designed to stop future reoccurrence.

A few words about software development

Lean practices apply to the process of software development, just as they do to the development of physical goods and services. Developing so-called virtual products, like software, has its idiosyncrasies, but remember that *Kaizen* is an all-encompassing philosophy, and that Lean improves *all* processes. Strictly speaking, Lean has nothing specifically to do with hardware or software.

All the behaviors, practices, characteristics, and techniques of Lean that enable the continuous improvement of hardware apply to the way software is developed as well. These include the focus on the elimination of waste, customer value-added, reduced cycle time, and quality.

The most important Lean technique for software development is to simplify before you code — in other words, fix in design first.

Some of the other important Lean software development techniques include

- ✔ **Avoid bloatware.** Pareto's Law applies to software utility: 80 percent of the value in most software is provided by 20 percent of the features. Don't waste time and energy designing and developing features no one's going to find useful.

- ✔ **Feel the need for speed.** How quickly can you respond to a customer's need for new features or functionality? How much non-value-added activity churns while the clock is ticking? Software should be modular, flexible, and extendible; teams should be small, fast, and focused.

✔ **Maintain "agilability".** Software development teams should be agile — able to work on any layer, feature, or capability. The goal is just-in-time software; information available on demand by any customer.

✔ **Simplify the interfaces.** The key to modularity and extensibility is to keep the interfaces clean and simple. Examples include: interfaces between code modules; functional interfaces between applications and systems; usage interfaces between departments.

✔ **Hear the customer, hear their customer!** Particularly in corporate software environments, it's critical to understand the customer. And understand what your customer is doing for *their* customer. Capabilities, timeframes, cost — understand your customer's issues and what's important.

✔ **Work continuously, incrementally.** Add capabilities and new features that your customers need regularly. Lean software continuously develops and deploys software in small feature sets.

✔ **Maintain standards and standard practices.** Software shops really struggle with internal discipline, and yet it's an environment where discipline and control is as important as anywhere. Everything from filenames to coding standards, documentation practices, configuration management, change control, backups, upgrades and release management, and 5S in the workplace.

✔ **Provide visual feedback.** The visual status, reporting, metrics, and controls are fully applicable in software environments. Use them liberally!

Lean practices are not in conflict with programming methodologies like spiral, iterative, agile, and extreme. Lean practices harmonize well with software quality approaches like the Capability Maturity Model. Lean software development acts as a foundation upon which other methods and standards apply.

Lean Supplier Management

The Lean journey within the enterprise is just that: It's *within* the enterprise. However, supplier performance significantly and materially affects the performance of the enterprise. The goal of Lean supplier management is to make the Value Stream Map organization-independent. *Lean supplier management* is a pursuit of seamless integration across a complex interface — the interface between organizations.

Lean supplier management requires involvement from multiple functions and departments within the organization. Sometimes, it requires a redefinition of the entire architecture of the supply process. The goals of Lean supplier management are

- ✔ **Value-added:** Products and services provided effectively, without waste, defects, or undue cost.

- ✔ **Rapid information flow:** A smooth, complete, bidirectional flow of both developmental and operational information

- ✔ **Effective administration:** Easy contractual arrangements, effective change management

- ✔ **Uninterrupted material flow:** Goods and services connected and delivered without interruption as scheduled to support your facility

- ✔ **Inventory management:** A strategic balance of inventory across the supply chain

Behaving like one entity: The architecture of supply

Supply chains tend to tier. The automotive industry, for example, has a first tier of suppliers that provide major components and assemblies to the vehicle brands. In turn, those suppliers have a second tier, that provide subassemblies and smaller components. A third tier provides piece-parts. The computer industry is similarly tiered, as are most industries.

The number of tiers in an industry, and the number of providers in each tier, is based on the complexity of the product and the volume of product in the market. Consequently, there are many players in each tier of industries like automotive, fewer in the computer industry, and very few in an industry like running shoes.

Supply architectures naturally balance according to a variety of pressures and constraints, including

- ✔ **Drive for simplicity:** Towards the fewest number of suppliers to manage; fewest number of parts to design, assemble, and support

- ✔ **Strategic competencies:** What you choose to make versus what you bring in from outside experts

- ✔ **Pricing:** What you can make it for versus what the supplier can provide it for

- ✔ **Availability:** What commodity or near-commodity parts and supplies are readily available in the marketplace

Binding the links

Supplier relationships should be bound with the longest possible contractual instruments. Short, re-competed contracts were in vogue in the 1990s, but supply chains are most effective when everyone is part of a stable consortium.

This collaborative approach enables the supply players to lower their fixed costs and focus on continuously lowering variable costs. That, in turn, enables performance measures based on quality and delivery. Longer-term contracts and trusted relationships also facilitate improved demand management and production smoothing.

Let it flow

Flowing information freely with suppliers is a core principle of Lean and is required to build and optimize your Value Stream Map. Both development information and demand information are part of the customer-supplier relationship. The more free-flowing the information, the more effective these relationships can be.

Development information involves the sharing of design data, manufacturing information, expertise, consumer data, and other background information that assists the players in the supply chain in developing effective products and services. Often, this information is proprietary, and sharing requires trust — trust that you won't share it with one another's competitor or use it maliciously. However, sharing of information is one of the key leverage points of Lean supplier management.

Demand information is critical to the ordering and delivery of materials and services. For many years, electronic data interchange (EDI) facilitated the flow of demand information. More recently, online exchanges and other electronic systems have facilitated the nearly real-time flow of demand data. This includes long-term forecasting and replenishment data, as well as order and delivery data.

Logistics

Logistics management in the Lean world means managing the flow of supplies to minimize stocking, inventory, or cycle time — anything that would waste *your* resources. Lean logistics include the following:

- **Top-up systems:** Have commodity items delivered and managed at the customer's site — right at the point of use. Have the customer manage stock-outs.

- **Third-party kitting:** Subcontract the kitting process, usually to one of the commodity suppliers. This requires effective traceability management. Third-party kitting is popular in the aerospace and automotive industries.

- **Milk runs:** Instead of having multiple supplier deliveries to your facility, you send one truck to collect from several suppliers according to a set schedule and route. You control the flow of materials to your facility.

- **Distribution centers:** Have suppliers deliver to a central facility where the redistribution can occur in a way that best suits the customer. This provides a type of buffering against shortages, but it also enables assemblers to kit more effectively.

Positioning stock strategically in the chain

One of the concerns about Lean is that, when it's taken to its extreme, there's no stock; therefore, if there's a hiccup anywhere in the system, the entire supply chain falls apart. You head off this doomsday scenario by positioning stock strategically along the supply chain.

In Lean, you prefer to hold stock toward the customer end of the chain — so that it's available immediately on demand. But keep in mind that this limits your flexibility, because the stock tends to be committed to that customer. However, if you hold it early in the supply chain to increase flexibility, it has less added value.

Through techniques like lead-time analysis and commodity trees, and strategies like postponement and mass customization, you can satisfy nearly any combination of stock management according to almost any given industry details.

Lean Production Processes

The Lean movement began in the production arena, on the shop floor, in Japanese automotive manufacturing and assembly plants. This is where the Lean philosophy, Lean behaviors, and Lean techniques were first developed and later honed. There's a reason why so much of the language of Lean sounds like you're making a new Toyota!

Although the rest of this chapter addresses how you can apply Lean to the many different functional areas of an enterprise, this section is about production processes — that infamous shop floor. This is the historical core of Lean.

Lean in the production area has always been about doing more with less — improving quality and effectiveness while at the same time consuming less time, fewer resources, less energy, time, inventory, people, and capital. The classic title "Lean Manufacturing" has been applied to the greater movement that eliminates waste *(muda)*, streamlines processes, and speeds up overall production, while enabling and respecting the people.

In a Lean Manufacturing environment, production workers use the broad set of tools and techniques described in detail in Chapters 7 through 10. Lean techniques a) lower production costs, b) improve product/service quality, c) shorten time to delivery, and d) improve employee morale — all while delighting the customer! Lean Production techniques are different from those used for 20th-century industrial mass manufacturing.

The key tenets of Lean Production are

- The customer defines value, and all production people, systems, and processes are focused on adding to that value.

- Reduce and eliminate waste — wasted time, energy, space, people, and capital.

- Instead of focusing just on outcomes, focus on the processes across the entire value chain that produce those outcomes. Use Value Stream Mapping, *Kaizen*, and standardized work as key enabling tools.

- Practice continuous flow — even if you have to rearrange facilities and systems and put in new control and measurement systems. Produce to a cadence, as measured by takt time.

- Through shortened equipment setup times, move to producing small lots, "every product every day", and to single-piece flow.

- Reduce and eliminate inventory and storage. Move to a demand pull system that's initiated by customer action.

- Practice *Kaizen*, develop a Lean way of thinking, and continuously improve processes.

Production is that place in the value stream where the product or service is created for the customer. It's where the action is — and where it's easiest to see the process in action. Lean practice applies the visual tools for quickly seeing status and reference.

The production arena is where most companies start their Lean efforts. Unfortunately, it's also where many stop them. Don't let this happen to you!

Lean Customer Management

Lean principles lead to changes in organizational behavior in many ways. At the epicenter of this change is the customer. In Lean, the customer is the primary focus — it's not that the customer is *right,* it's that the customer is *everything.* The customer defines value; the customer stimulates the demand for a product or service; the customer defines the requirements; the customer evaluates the results. All processes and activities within the enterprise are oriented toward the customer and optimized for customer value.

Within this philosophy, the Lean toolkit facilitates the flow of information from the customer to provide the products and services throughout the enterprise. Design information, demand information, operational information — it all flows to and from the customer.

But what about the direct relationship with the customer. How is that managed in a Lean environment? Who touches the customer? What's different about Lean customer management?

In short, Lean customer management is conducted to the same rules and protocol, and the same *Kaizen,* as other enterprise activities. Take the waste out of customer relationship activities; optimize the value stream of customer-facing functions; shorten the cycle time of customer response; take a holistic systems view of the customer; and understand the customer's customer. Optimize the customer-facing functions just as you would each of the other functions across the enterprise.

Most organizations suffer from similar customer management challenges, including

- Too many front-end processes and systems interacting with the customer
- Too many contacts, too many interfaces, and too many handoffs and delays in managing customer relationships
- Errors in selection, configurations, pricing, quoting, and fulfillment of customer orders
- Transactional customer relationships without intimacy or longevity.

Lean customer management woos customers for life. The customer relationship is where their expectations meet your abilities, where their goals and desires are addressed by the outcomes of your enterprise and the capacity of your systems of development and production. Lean solutions deliver high levels of satisfaction for both the customer and the enterprise. The direct relationships are facilitated through the primary processes of marketing, sales, and service.

Selling the customer

Customers need to quickly evaluate options in order to make selections and buy. Their ability to select and configure a solution quickly and easily is not simply a matter of efficiency; it's the enabler to a buying decision. Think about the experience of shopping for anything from shoes to computers. You need to find what you want quickly and easily, or you'll just become exasperated and go elsewhere. Lean sales ensures the customer a fast, accurate, and focused path through the maze.

In the online world, tools like product configurators and guided selling tools enable the customer to move quickly and easily through this process. These tools match supply and production capacity with customer buying preferences. Computer companies exemplify this process. If production of 60GB laptop hard drives is temporarily halted due to a typhoon in Malaysia, the Dell online configurator tool will quickly entice buyers to select the 80GB drive through special pricing and incentives. The customers are getting a deal, while Dell turns a production problem into a marketing opportunity.

Lean selection management also reflects a company's strategic balance between standard packaged offerings and mass customization.

Companies struggle with quoting and pricing their products and services. Pricing sheets, price lists, complex bills of material, pricing changes based on options and configurations — these issues confuse both the customer and the sales team. Management approvals, end-of-the-quarter deals to make quota, and lot reduction pricing all complicate matters, as do the overlaid enterprise effects like cost of inventory and cost of delivery. Lean sales is the practice of removing waste and cycle time from the quoting and pricing processes.

Servicing the customer

Service after the sale is the make-or-break function of the long-term customer relationship. It's likely the longest period of direct customer interaction — longer than the spikes of marketing or sales activity. It brings the customer back for more — or it drives the customer away, never to return. Because poor service kills the customer relationship, the customer service function must be optimized. Design your customer service process to best serve your direct customer. Once again, Lean practices and techniques apply.

The customer service function is markedly different in business-to-business (B2B) environments than it is in direct business-to-consumer (B2C) relationships. Design your customer service process to best serve the needs of your direct customer.

Lean and the Quality Organization

The Lean enterprise sees the quality organization in an entirely different light. The quality function has often been relegated an afterthought role — reactively inspecting products for defects. Quality in the design arena involved inspections of designs and drawings.

In the Lean enterprise, the quality function shifts from reactive to preventive, and looks to develop quality at the source. The quality group analyzes cause and effect, works to predict failure modes, and prevents them from happening. This is a key role shift — from one of reaction to one of prevention. The focus shifts to be active in *poka-yoke* (mistake-proofing) as well. As a result, the quality organization will move from inspection of product to a process/product auditing focus.

Chapter 15

Lean across Industry

• •

In This Chapter

▶ Seeing how Lean applies in any industry, not just manufacturing

▶ Recognizing that Lean works especially well in service businesses

▶ Identifying how powerful Lean is in government

• •

L ean is now practiced in every industry — from hard-core manufacturing like automotive and aerospace, to construction, logistics, pharmaceuticals, healthcare, banking, retail, high-tech, education, and even government, *especially* government (more on this later in the chapter). But what industry *wouldn't* benefit from focusing on the customer and eliminating waste?

In this chapter, you discover more about Lean in manufacturing and other industries, including, possibly, your own industry. But there are no revelations here. Lean is Lean — meaning that Lean is so fundamental that it's basically the same for services or in government as it is for manufacturing. The same philosophy and principles apply; the same methods and techniques apply; all the same tools apply. The language is sometimes adjusted to reflect the language of the industry, but at the core, Lean is the same in every industry.

Starting with What's Common

Every business in every industry has issues — for-profit or nonprofit, public or private. All ventures have customers, in some form. They all have processes — whether formally documented or not. All employers have employees who generally want to do a good job, use their knowledge and skills, improve their quality of life, and feel good about what they do. All ventures have a place where they conduct their business — an office, a factory, a car, a computer, or even a table at Starbucks.

The commonalities are important, because they help you to translate Lean from its manufacturing roots to "Wow! This all applies to me!" Follow this starter framework to translate and begin your path to Lean implementation, regardless of your industry:

- ✔ **Understand the current issues.** What are the mistakes? What's going wrong? What are the challenges? What are the priorities?

- ✔ **Understand your customers.** What do they want and need? What's their rate of demand? What constitutes their satisfaction?

- ✔ **Map your value streams.** Even if you're a custom provider, you have certain activities that are routine. What are they?

- ✔ **Calculate *takt time.*** This may seem foreign, but if you have a customer, that customer demands what you provide at some interval of time. That's your takt time and you need to know what it is.

- ✔ **Be clear about your goals and objectives.** Be specific about what you're trying to accomplish.

- ✔ **Identify wastes — and reduce them.**

- ✔ **Implement *Kaizen.***

- ✔ **5S your work environment.** Have the intention of permanently eliminating waste.

- ✔ **Evaluate the Lean toolbox.** Use a broad interpretation. Pick the right tool for what you're trying to improve.

Think of the Lean toolbox as a golf bag with a full complement of clubs. If you're a beginning golfer, you may only use a few clubs out of your bag. As your game improves and the courses you play become more difficult, you'll develop the ability to pull those more refined and specialized clubs out of your bag. The starting framework for Lean is like your driver, 5-iron, and putter — good clubs for starters.

Lean Manufacturing

Manufacturing is Lean's heritage, its bread and butter. TPS is the automotive manufacturing incubator where all the principles and practices of Lean were hatched and have matured over the past 50 years. If you're in manufacturing, it doesn't matter what your product is, how many you make, or how sophisticated your processes are (high tech, low tech, or even no tech): Lean is a highly effective manufacturing operations strategy.

Everything we cover in this book directly applies to the manufacturing environment. The following sections highlight some key aspects of how Lean applies specifically within manufacturing.

From batch to flow

The traditional methods of production work with batches, usually large in size, and usually organized by functional operations. This method of production is wrought with the seven wastes. Lean is not traditional. Lean is based on flow — single-piece flow, ideally. To achieve single-piece flow, you must organize how you do business differently, and you must remove all obstacles to flow.

Creating work modules

In Lean, you organize manufacturing by product groups or families. The recommended layout is a work module that flows counterclockwise. Inside work modules are all the pieces of equipment and fixtures required to manufacture a part or family of parts. The equipment is as small and as flexible as possible.

In the best module designs, all material replenishment and equipment repairs can occur without support personnel entering the main production area — usually from the backside of the equipment. This approach improves safety and productivity, because no one but the trained production team is in the direct production area. The operating pace is based on takt time.

Quality at the source

Instead of having large inspection stations at the end of the process, quality is everyone's job. Within each operation, you find standardized work, including steps to verify your own work and the work of the previous operation. Error-proofing "gadgets" are installed on equipment to prevent operations from being performed incorrectly and poor quality from being passed to the next station.

An error-proofing gadget, or *poka-yoke,* can come in many forms. It can be a physical guide that helps material positioning. It can be software code that monitors key characteristics and stops the equipment if they're out of spec. Or it can be a high-tech solution like infrared cameras, or whatever you can dream up! If it prevents errors in any form, it's *poka-yoke.*

Working in teams

Lean operators work as a team, based on standardized work methods. The team is responsible for customer satisfaction and quality. They're responsible for production and routine maintenance of their equipment and tools. The team runs the show!

Changing from batch to flow affects not only the physical layout of a facility, but also the organizational support structure. Lean organizations tend to use fewer layers of management, fewer supervisors, and fewer support people. With the hands-on team responsible for some of the tasks traditionally associated with first-line supervision or maintenance, the roles of the individuals in those areas change. Supervisors act as coaches, mentors, and roadblock removers. Maintenance workers focus on preventive maintenance, equipment improvements to support *Kaizen,* and error-proofing mechanisms.

Safety: "The sixth S"

The core Lean philosophy of "respect for people" has a special meaning in the manufacturing world with regard to worker safety. Lean and safety go hand in hand. Many manufacturing processes involve the use of dangerous equipment and machinery or otherwise expose workers to hazardous materials and conditions. Obviously, a safe worker is ultimately a more productive worker. But it's more than that: Lean workers contribute to improvements in worker safety, within the context of waste reduction and customer value. The net result: quality improvements, productivity gains, better safety awareness, and a safer workplace.

Any injury or loss of productive effort is waste. When an injury occurs, production halts. Time is lost on administrative tasks, such as locating replacement workers, paperwork, and insurance. Other workers are distracted and perform less efficiently.

Everyone is responsible for taking the initiative and becoming part of the process. Managers and workers alike must be familiar with Lean philosophies and articulate the value of safety interventions in terms of productivity. Better safety means less waste.

Incorporate ergonomic analyses into your operational processes to reduce *muri.* Conduct cause-and-effect analyses on the sources of loss to see where accidents are happening. Then analyze the production process from an ergonomics perspective and find the root causes of injuries. Finally, apply ergonomic design principles to reduce or eliminate the sources of injury.

An outdoor power equipment manufacturer discovered through ergonomic analyses that excessive reaching by production workers on an assembly line was causing shoulder injuries. One line alone suffered over $300,000 in lost wages and insurance payments from injuries. They conducted a *Kaizen* event and implemented simple adjustments, eliminating the injuries.

Reducing inventory

Flow manufacturing causes you to change how you treat inventory. Inventory is waste. It ties up cash, and it's at risk for obsolescence. Every time inventory is touched, it can be damaged or destroyed. Inventory stops the flow of production.

For instance, when you transition from traditional department-oriented manufacturing to cells, you no longer need the work in process (WIP) inventory that waited until it could be transported to the next transformational step. The machines are next to each other, not far away. Pull systems also lower the levels of inventories required in a process. "Point of use" becomes the design philosophy for in-process material storage. What is the absolute minimum amount — based on takt usage — that can be stored where you use it?

Sometimes process constraints prevent perfect cell designs and you need in-process inventory stores (type-1 *muda* — see Chapter 3). In that case, you install controlled inventory stores or supermarkets. The goal is always to reduce inventory, but until you can figure out a different way to remove the constraint, the solution is well-controlled, planned, standardized, minimized in-process stores, located as close to the point of use as possible.

To handle inventory, you need material handling equipment. But instead of fork trucks to move large gondolas weighing tons or conveyor systems connecting buildings housing different functional areas, go smaller: Consider using bins, hand trucks, and push carts. Safety improves — no more speeding lift trucks ready to run you over or take out a building column! Costs go down — no building repairs and fewer high-tech pieces of equipment to maintain. And quality improves — less risk of transit damage.

Kanban, just-in-time, and the pull system

The Lean system of consumption-driven replenishment has proven itself in manufacturing, across tiers of supplier and distribution networks. It is fast becoming a compelling alternative to traditional material requirements planning (MRP) for multiple reasons. Chief among them are

- **Push-style systems rely on forecasts to determine what and how much to replenish.** Forecasts can be useful indicators of overall demand in general, but they're poor predictors of precisely which products will be needed and when. Also, in multi-tiered supply chains, push-systems distance manufacturers farther and farther from their customers and, as a result, forecasts are pushed farther from reality. In addition, information is diluted by each layer in the system. As a result, excessive inventory builds and costly last-minute change orders ripple through the supply chain.

- **Manufacturers often incur large inventory-carrying costs with push-style systems.** And yet they still run out of parts. Stock-outs wreak havoc in production, delaying customer shipments, increasing premium freight charges, and disrupting plant operations by forcing unnecessary and expensive changeovers. In the MRP environment, you often have no clear record of how many times stock-outs occur or which parts repeatedly stock-out. Stock-outs often lead to an over-buying of parts, creating excess inventory, which can be carried for months after a stock-out. Errors in MRP also cause people to work outside the system to expedite materials and to conduct repeated physical inventories. It becomes a vicious cycle.

Lean pull-type systems are not like MRP forecast-driven replenishment systems. A *kanban* system reorders parts and components based on actual consumption at the point of use. Consider two Lean methods:

- ✔ **The "two-bin" method:** An operator has two bins of material: One is being consumed and the other is full. When the first bin empties, the operator keeps working, using the second bin. The empty bin is sent out for replenishment. A full one returns before the operator runs out.

- ✔ **The *kanban*-card method:** A *kanban* card travels with the inventory, containing information such as the description of the item or part number, and its location. Each card triggers replenishment when the inventory is consumed.

Pull-based manufacturing synchronizes production with consumption in real time, increasing on-time delivery performance, and reducing stock-outs and costly last-minute changes. As orders arrive, material is pulled from the end of final assembly, which instantly sends an order to the final assembly production module to produce more.

Volume and variety

Lean applies in manufacturing whether you make one a month, a hundred a day, or thousands every hour. In all manufacturing cases, certain steps repeat. A custom cabinet facility may look different from a commercial wood bookcase manufacturer, but both use wood, cut to a specific dimension, are sanded, and finished — and they both do it over and over again. The starting place for implementation is the same: Map the flow, 5S, identify value, and standardize work. Beyond the basics, the manufacturers may choose a different tool to apply first, but it all applies.

High volume, low customization

The bookstores are full of tomes about the traditional application of high-volume production of Lean. Implementing work modules, pull systems, or error proofing is easier when you make the same thing every day the same way. This is not to say that the organization doesn't struggle with the change, because it does. But Lean was developed and perfected in high-volume, standardized environments. Therefore, you can easily translate Lean from high-volume gadgets to your high-volume widget.

Low volume, high customization

In contrast to the high-volume production environments of Toyota, Motorola, or Dell, thousands of companies specialize in low-volume custom activities. Whether your company is a machine shop, sign maker, cabinet maker, or salad maker, the concepts of Lean apply to your business. It's not a question of how few you make, or the differences from one item of design or production to the next. The details may include different ingredients or different dimensions, but you're still performing similar processing steps each time.

Look for elements of commonality and repetition in what you do — there are more than you may think. Standardize all that is common, and compartmentalize the unique. If you focus only on how different you are, and how new everything is, you'll make it difficult to see how standardized work can help your situation. The more you can define standardized work, the more benefits you can begin to accrue from Lean practices.

Lean Services

Nearly 80 percent of the U.S. economy is now based in services, rather than product manufacturing. Lean provides some of the greatest opportunities and most powerful results in service businesses. Although service organizations have different processes, key metrics, and root causes of problems and challenges as compared to manufacturing businesses, Lean methods are just as effective.

In the past three decades, due largely to initiatives like TQM, Lean, and Six Sigma, productivity among U.S. manufacturing firms has nearly tripled. However, U.S. service company productivity is up only about 40 percent (see Figure 15-1).

Problems with products and with product development are not the fault of the products — the root cause is in one or more of the processes that designed and developed them. Lean addresses these problems as a *process* improvement system. What are service businesses? The service industries are pure *process* businesses. Lean principles and techniques are, therefore, directly applicable to service businesses. Lean practices improve service business performance, by

✔ Reducing the time spent performing business activities

✔ Reducing the total cost of doing business by eliminating wasted time and effort

✔ Increasing customer satisfaction by improving the timeliness and quality of deliverables

✔ Improving employee morale and increasing enthusiasm by engaging staff in the development and implementation of improvements

Exhibit: **U.S. Labor Productivity Growth**

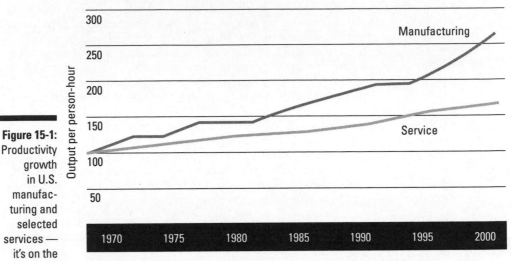

Figure 15-1: Productivity growth in U.S. manufacturing and selected services — it's on the rise!

Note: Service industries are financial services, insurance, and real estate.
Index 1970 = 100. Source: U.S. Bureau of Labor Statistics; Booz Allen Hamilton

By applying concepts that until recently had been alien to most service businesses — attacking speed and quality, simplifying complexity, scaling differentiation, and empowering employees — service organizations can share in some of the productivity gains already enjoyed by the makers of autos, planes, trains, appliances, and other products. Savings will vary significantly by company and industry, but it is realistic to expect reductions of 25 percent in costs and 50 percent or more in response times and in-process errors by implementing Lean practices in service businesses. In addition, revenue gains of 5 percent annually are not uncommon.

Commercial services versus internal services

Commercial services are those businesses that offer their services to other businesses and the general public. The services they offer represent their core competence and form the basis for their profit and loss (P&L). By contrast, internal service providers are company overhead departments and functions that provide support to other profit-generating departments. (We address the internal group in Chapter 14.)

Examples of commercial service businesses include everything from airlines, communications (voice, cellular, data) companies, cable and satellite TV providers, computer services, and mail and shipping services, finance and mortgage companies, education and training services, repair and maintenance services, and much more. Some of these services are labor and equipment based, while others are transaction based. In addition, most government agencies are in the service business, but they're a special case and we address them later in this chapter, in the "Lean Government" section.

In all service businesses, Lean is an attitude and approach that anyone can understand and everyone can apply. The Lean techniques don't require extensive employee training or complex technical support. In a service context, going Lean means getting back to the reason why everyone got into the business in the first place: to help people.

Embedding Lean practices within a service organization is not a quick fix or rapid overhaul. It requires the same diligent and holistic approach to transformation as in manufacturing or any other industry. Lean in services means:

- ✔ Improving service processes to focus on the customer and deliver more customer value
- ✔ Decreasing waste in the service value stream
- ✔ Reducing batch processes and moving increasingly toward a flow of activities to deliver the service
- ✔ Striving for the perfect service

Because service businesses are often even more labor intensive and dependent than manufacturing businesses, the respect for people in the service value chain is of utmost importance.

A service is a product, too!

Services are like products in many ways. They begin with a customer need or want, and they end when it's delivered to them in a satisfactory manner — at the right time, in the right way, and at the right price. The service is the result of a process or series of processes acting in a coordinated fashion to produce the desired results. There's a value stream of activities and support information. The service is a result of design, development, and delivery. And the service is prone to defects and rework — just like products.

However, services are often not as tangible and indelible as products — they're more flexible. After all, retuning your engine is a lot easier than remaking your car. Rebilling you for your mobile phone service is simple, but rebuilding your mobile phone isn't so easy. There's a natural tendency to confuse this flexibility with less focus and discipline. But if services are your business, this tendency can be fatal. Indeed, you would be very much mistaken if you thought that service rework was any less problematic for a service provider than product rework was for a manufacturer.

You must think of a service as a product, because

✔ Services have specifications — for quality, performance, timeliness, and price.

✔ Services are architected and designed to meet customer requirements and to fit the "manufacturability" of a production and delivery system.

✔ Services have a value chain comprised of components on both the supply side and delivery end.

The seven forms of service waste

Service process waste is waste, just like product or material process waste is waste. Service-business waste may look a little different, but it happens the same way:

✔ **Transportation:** Service transportation waste is the unnecessary and non-value-added movement of people, goods, and information in order to fulfill the service obligation to a customer.

✔ **Waiting:** If people, systems, materials, or information are waiting, that's waste.

✔ **Overproduction:** Are your services producing sooner, faster, or in greater quantities than the customer is demanding or requiring?

✔ **Defects:** Defective services are those that do not deliver the correct requirements to the customer.

✔ **Inventory:** Are certain services half-finished?

✔ **Movement:** Are activities, paperwork, and other efforts unnecessarily juggled?

✔ **Extra processing:** How much extra effort do people go to in order to deliver the service? Could any of these steps be eliminated?

Improving services the Lean way

Services naturally can benefit from one of Lean's fundamental tools: a pull system. In most cases, the delivery of a service to a customer is based on the action of the customer requesting the service, which stimulates the value chain to assemble and deliver it. A key to a Lean service is the development of common services — the building blocks that permit flexible assembly in real time as the customer requests it. All other Lean fundamentals also apply.

5S in services

The 5S of the workplace applies to service businesses:

- ✔ **Sort:** Workplace organization is universal. Sorting office materials, maintenance materials, or other tools is fundamental to the delivery of quality and timely services.

  These days, many service businesses are computer-based or computer-facilitated. Sorting your computer environment — your e-mails, your files — is a Lean activity. Keep your computer desktop and file system Lean and clean.

- ✔ **Straighten:** The tools of services should be arranged in standard locations for consistent and easy access. This includes desk items, databases, repositories, references, operating procedures, or process definitions. Information, including file and system names, should be consistent.

- ✔ **Scrub:** Maintain service tools in a neat and clean condition. This includes any work areas, whether in the office or in the field.

- ✔ **Systematize:** As always, don't wait for it to build up. As part of your regular routine, go through your work environment and maintain it. Define a certain time or regular event as the basis. This includes both private and common areas.

- ✔ **Standardize:** Exercise discipline in maintaining your workplace, and institute processes that ensure that this regular maintenance occurs, in a standard manner to standardized levels. Don't overdo it — just do it.

In the American "cowboy" culture, the 5S workplace could easily be considered too conformist, too conservative — even anally retentive. Subliminal cultural messages bombard most westerners with themes of independence and defiance to such schemes. "Being yourself" and "just letting it all hang out" are not 5S behaviors. However, the 5S workplace doesn't have to be at odds with individual expression. Although conformity is a part of Lean, it's more a culture of personal consistency and personal discipline.

Speed and quality

As in all Lean businesses, the goal is to increase both speed and quality at all times. The balance between them is just as important in a service business as any other business. But too much or too little of either is detrimental.

The Lean service organization is always moving to deliver customer value ever more quickly. By consistently increasing the speed of operations, service businesses are more flexible and can respond with greater agility to changing customer demands and market conditions. Faster services are delivered by fewer hands, and by streamlining and eliminating unnecessary steps. In processing more quickly, the organization reduces opportunity costs. And, of course, the customers are more satisfied to receive services faster.

By focusing equally on quality, service businesses can significantly reduce the time spent on reworking deliverables. Establish specification limits and collect metrics on quality, applying tools to reduce variance, prevent failures, and attack root cause.

Both strategies lead to sharply lower cost structures. Just as important, improved products cement customer loyalty, which increases revenue potential.

Checking variety and reducing complexity

In service businesses, variety increases complexity and should be vigilantly examined and reduced whenever possible. Service complexity can develop from providing a well-meaning effort, to offering highly-tailored, intimate customer service. However, any increases in complexity directly increase the risk of both slower and defective services, and indirectly increase support and maintenance costs, in the form of overtaxed back-office processing procedures, too many customer-service systems, and too much staff training.

Analyze service processes for variety and complexity. Sort the routine, commodity services from the specialized services and treat them differently. Standardize the routine services, and manage the lower-volume, higher-complexity services as specialty items. Where necessary, assemble these services in a value chain.

Credit-card issuer Capital One is an example of a service organization that separates common services from unique services, and it gains value from each. Through analysis, the company divides consumers into micro-segments. It offers customized lending rates to a person's credit history by leveraging a single cost-effective platform. In this way, Capital One offers a wide array of rates and lending limits — an alluring feature for customers, through a Lean set of processing systems, back-office infrastructure, and call centers.

Frontline power

To enable services to deliver on the promise of both quality and speed, the decision-making must shift closer to the customer. The segmentation and production of highly structured service components enable frontline staff to engage customers more independently — with less management oversight.

Empower frontline staff to operate, instead of having to seek approval for decisions. This setup also frees staff from focusing solely on basic transactions and allows them to give more personal attention to customers and have a more direct impact on increasing revenue.

Nothing better exemplifies frontline empowerment than the Ritz-Carlton Hotel Company chain, where every member of the staff has a discretionary budget for settling disputes. Each staff member has the personal authority to provide such perks as room upgrades, complimentary food, and other amenities on a case-by-case basis. When a guest has an issue, staff is both enabled and required to break away from regular duties and immediately address the customer concern.

Lean Transactions

Transactions are a specific form of service business, where the product is purely data and information, and it's processed according to specific procedures. Transactions are often performed as an outsourced back-office internal service function — the supplier and customer are the same entity. Examples include certain banking functions, accounting, payroll, and insurance claims. Success in transaction processing businesses is based on speed and accuracy. How can Lean help?

Once again, the fundamentals of Lean apply: focusing on the customer, improving the value stream, focusing on flow, striving for perfection, and maintaining a high respect for people.

Transaction businesses are typically professional office environments, with a highly educated workforce, using computers and data processing capabilities to perform the tasks. Lean transaction businesses do the following:

- ✔ **Explicitly map the value stream to understand precisely what is required to complete the process task for the customer.** Use this map as the basis for continually eliminating wasteful practices.

- ✔ **Move beyond the misconception that "information transactions are not like products."** Design, develop, source, assemble, and deliver transactions.

- ✔ **Regularly employ *Kaizen* to examine and optimize your transaction processing processes.** Keep the changes small, local, continuous, and practical. Ensure that management responds and implements changes quickly, and rewards the employees quickly.

- ✔ **Perform paperwork processing in an assembly line, with people in sequence along tables.** Visual signs hanging over the tables identify that these are work areas for accounts receivable, travel, and so on, rather than individuals working at desks. Team leaders set goals; the process is designed to flow.

Cubicles are based on a philosophy of work that is command and control rather than empowering. Cubicles deny collaboration, optimize around individual processes rather than around customer-centered workflow, and seek to bury problems rather than make them visible and fix them. Factories don't have walls — why should offices? Remove cubicle walls so that the staff handling the transactions works side by side and can see each other. Flow the process step by step down the line. To push the envelope, try arranging the office layout in work modules (see Chapter 8).

Lean Government

Of all industrial sectors outside of manufacturing, Lean practices are taking hold in government as strongly as any other. At first, this might seem a paradox. After all, most governmental entities seem to be the opposite of Lean! But in this section, we give you a closer look.

Leaning the military

Not traditionally known for doing more with less, the U.S. military has found great success with the application of Lean, particularly in the areas of maintenance. Especially during wartime, operating resources are at a premium. The faster a vehicle, aircraft, or system can be repaired to the proper working level, the faster it can be out in the field protecting and supporting the soldiers who need it.

The customer of the units responsible for repair is the soldier in the field. Their product is a top performing, well-maintained vehicle. The risk of not doing a timely quality job could be loss of life.

In one such facility, a horn sounds every 23 minutes (takt time) to signal the vehicle should move to the next station. Lesser skilled workers support the more highly trained mechanics by bringing tools and parts to them, so the mechanics can stay with the vehicle. They have also started to work with their suppliers. Implementing Lean practices in this nontraditional environment has yielded a tenfold increase in vehicle repair rate in less than two years, while cutting the repair cost per vehicle by half! These and other successes have prompted the U.S. military to specify Lean as a practice and roll out Lean initiatives in each of the branches.

Like any institution, governmental agencies face constant budget restrictions. At the same time, they're being asked to fulfill greater needs on the part of their constituents. Sounds a lot like doing more with less, doesn't it?

The choices are limited. Doing less with less isn't an option that sells well to voters. And it's not a matter of simply working harder. The challenges also are not solved by any singular approach like defect reduction, constraint management, or measurement and reporting, although those are all useful tools that have a role. More important, any solutions must be a workable cultural fit into the nature of the government environment.

And this is where Lean is the perfect fit. Governmental entities — like the Japanese corporations that developed TPS and Lean practices — have the long-term view. Unlike Western corporations that are driven by short-term performance measures, governmental agencies are in it for the long haul. They can afford to implement continuous, incremental change. They can readily embrace the approach when the methods and techniques are proven. Perhaps most important of all is Lean's accessible nature, enabling anyone to participate, embracing everyone equally, and empowering all participants through *Kaizen* events, cross-training, improvement suggestions, and respect for people. In the longer-view world of government, Lean is ideal.

In the public sector, Lean practices help organizations:

- Shorten cycle times to completing and delivering services
- Improve service quality
- Increase productivity
- Dramatically increase customer (constituency) satisfaction
- Reduce waste in all forms, including bureaucracy

The largest barrier to implementing Lean in government exists only in terms of providing the appropriate skills, capabilities, and experiences to those responsible for carrying out the processes.

Lean in Healthcare

The healthcare field is one of the most exciting frontiers of Lean. In an environment where patient care needs are climbing, and the availability of skilled resources and reimbursement for services are shrinking, Lean practices are helping. Lean healthcare focuses on the needs of the patient (the customer) and strives to improve turnaround time, contain costs, reduce space, increase speed of delivery, and improve the quality of care.

Improving healthcare through Lean

Lean healthcare is not about cutting people or eliminating assets. Lean healthcare is improving activities and processes within the system. This is accomplished by identifying and removing wasteful activities and focusing on patient value-based activities.

Health industries applying Lean principles across their organization are experiencing increases in benefits and performance, such as:

- Reduced incidents of mistakes
- Improved patient education
- Reduced wait times for patients
- Improved clinical outcomes
- Increased staff productivity
- Reduced clinic and management costs
- Improved employee satisfaction for nurses and staff

Defining waste in healthcare

Open any paper in just about any country and you'll find an article about healthcare. Public or private, they all have issues. If you've ever encountered a healthcare establishment, you know some of these issues firsthand.

Here are some ways that the classic seven forms of waste translate into a healthcare environment:

- **Transportation:** Samples and specimens needing analysis travel excessively to reach the labs and within the labs. Patients are moved excessively for testing and treatment.
- **Waiting:** Patients wait for diagnosis, treatment, discharge, beds, or testing. Physicians wait for patient lab results. Teams wait for specialists.
- **Overproduction:** Excess testing is performed for the convenience (liability protection?) of the healthcare organization, not based on customer demand.
- **Inventories:** Inventories include medicines, testing mediums, patients needing bed assignments, lab samples and specimens for analysis, lab results awaiting distribution, and dictation ready for transcription.
- **Movement:** Staff spends time looking for patient's charts, medicines, missing meds, missing charts, variation in procedures, sharing of equipment, and so on.

✔ **Defects:** Mistakes are widespread, including wrong patient, wrong procedure or medicine, misdiagnosis, unsuccessful treatments, re-sticks, redraws.

✔ **Excess processing:** Staff makes multiple bed moves, retest, complete excessive paperwork.

Lean Everywhere

The future of Lean across all industries is limitless. The principles, methods, tools, and techniques apply in any situation. Looking at a business, organization, or industry through Lean eyes will open up new pathways for improvement opportunities. In the following sections, we offer a couple more examples.

Nonprofit organizations

Nonprofit organizations are a growth area for Lean practice. They have business processes just like any other business or industry. Nonprofits provide services to the community. Whether the organization is packing boxes of food, making lunches for homeless shelters, or delivering clothing bundles to new mothers, they can use takt to balance the line, standardized work to quickly train volunteers, and customer demand data to request the right supplies from donors. Applying Lean principles to fundraising events and silent auctions can generate more money for the cause by improving logistics, minimizing costs to yield more funds, and obtaining more items targeted to their bidders' tastes.

Retail

Retail is a strong emerging application area for Lean. The retail environment is where the rubber meets the road between products and consumers. The retail chains are the direct connection with the ultimate customer — the consumer. Retailers know customer demand firsthand. They're also the main point of customer interface for issues with the product or service. Through their ordering practices, sales campaigns, and customer service, they feed the value stream.

Lean is powerful in the retail industry as a method of optimizing the supply chain. Lean practices also improve customer service, by decreasing wait times and ensuring that the right products are on the right shelves at the right time. Some retailers are using point-of-sale data to stimulate supply and delivery based on real-time customer purchases. Lean helps them with flow to the store shelves and minimizing inventory levels.

The next time you go to a retail store, look for evidence of Lean practices, and you'll be likely to find it. Figure 15-2 shows an example of a visual standardized work instruction for something as simple as cleaning the restroom. See what other Lean techniques you notice, from customer service to products on the shelves.

Whether you're watching a television show where they build a house in a week, you're in a retail store, or you're eating in a restaurant where you order before you're seated, you'll find evidence of Lean. After reading this book, you'll see opportunities for improvement all around you. The potential for Lean is limitless.

Diagram of Area to Be Cleaned
with Process Step

Process Steps

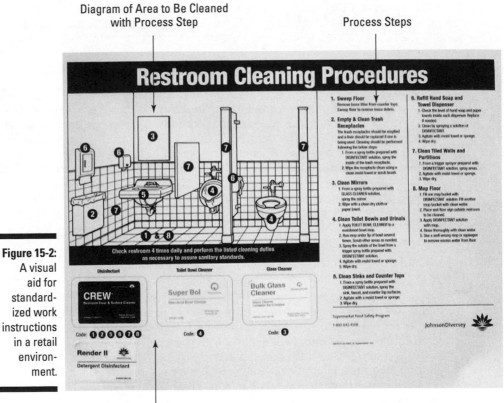

Figure 15-2:
A visual
aid for
standard-
ized work
instructions
in a retail
environ-
ment.

Cleaning Products by
Process Steps

Part V
The Part of Tens

The 5th Wave   By Rich Tennant

"For a more aggressive approach, we have our
'Or Else' series of motivational posters."

In this part . . .

In this part, we steer you toward some excellent resources for more information on Lean. We also fill you in on best practices to adopt and pitfalls to avoid. If you're pressed for time and you want to get some key information quickly, this part is for you.

Chapter 16

Ten Best Practices of Lean

In This Chapter

▶ Satisfying customers and delivering value is at the heart of successful Lean practice

▶ Looking at Lean as a journey, not a destination

▶ Keeping things simple, people-focused, and visual

Most every best-practice list begins with something about leadership. Leadership — in the form of unwavering guidance and support from top management, as well as the everyday inner leadership of individuals — is so fundamental to the success of any initiative that it precedes a place on a best-practices list. Leadership is the "zeroth" law of success. Bring it on or stay home — it's that simple.

The previous chapters chronicle a collection of principles, methods, tools, and techniques that comprise a Lean system. If you recognize the ten best practices in this chapter, in addition to following what we outline throughout this book, you'll keep your bearings over the long haul of the Lean journey.

Feel the Force (of the Customer), Luke

The Lean *sensei,* Obi-Wan Kenobi, is calling out to you: *Feel the force.* Do you hear him? Do you feel it? That force is the will of the customer — calling out to you, pulling on you, stimulating you, aligning your action. Your mission is to align all your brainpower, your energy, and your might to answer this call.

Successful Lean practice has the customer at its core and the center of your universe — the customer's wants, needs, and idea of value. Feel the customer's force like the force of gravity. It is constant, undeniable, and unrelenting, but it is also your grounding and your base.

Step by Step, Inch by Inch

Success is not a big bang. You can have big wins along the way, but no single breakthrough event or project victory will sustain achievements over the long term.

Lean is a journey, not a destination. You live Lean every day, through successes and setbacks alike. Lean is the force of a million little things, all the time. Lean is trying, doing, learning, and trying again — and again.

Lean is the tortoise and *The Little Engine That Could.* Lean is "small ball" — scoring again and again by hitting singles, bunting, and stealing bases. Lean is the Lexus tagline: *The Relentless Pursuit of Perfection.*

Follow the Value Stream

Value "flows" downstream, toward the customer. You can easily find yourself in an eddy current or a side pool, swirling 'round and 'round, spending energy but going nowhere. All the Lean techniques — for reducing waste, organizing into cells and teams, performing standardized work, and applying quality and control tools — are intended to align your efforts to the center of the value stream.

Use the tools of communication, leadership, and visual management to help people see alignment to customer value. Design your environments, your tools, your practices, and your habits to keep the value stream flowing and to recognize when it's not. Support people and processes in centering themselves, using tools like tugboats to nudge them back into place.

Eat Your Vegetables

The wide array of Lean tools and techniques may seem like a smorgasbord, enticing you to pick and choose whatever looks inviting and tastes yummy. You could be tempted to select too many sweets, and not enough fruits and vegetables; however Lean requires a balanced diet and complete nutrition. You're healthy only when you're whole. Don't neglect any of the parts.

You must not just follow lofty principles of Lean — you must also use the tools. But you can't just apply technical tools — you must apply the people tools as well. Short-term projects are effective, but only within the context of the long-term view. Lean applies to the whole body of the organization — and not just your organization, but all of the organizations in the value stream.

Turn Over a Rock

Manufacturing or line work is where companies like to direct the focus of quality-control tools and rigorous analyses, because people can easily *see* the results there. Confining an initiative like Lean to manufacturing or line work may be tempting, but don't do it!

Turn over any rock, in any part of the organization, and you'll find opportunity. Actually, most companies find greater waste when they start flipping those rocks — in places that they've ignored or thought that Lean doesn't really apply. For example, Lean practices often provide the most significant returns in areas like new product development and back-office functions.

Lean is everywhere — everywhere you turn. Neglect nothing.

People First!

Commerce, organization, enterprise, service — they're all about people. They're led by people, they're staffed by people, and they serve people. People are constantly tempted by the leverage and economies offered by technology and tools, but don't forget what tools are for: Tools are to aid and assist people!

People come first. They *always* come first. No matter where you are on your journey, you'll only sustain Lean if your people are onboard and supportive. Your people are motivated and rewarded by success, not their tools. Tools don't "win"; people do. People change their thinking and behaviors and use tools accordingly. You need them both, but the people are what make or break you.

Genchi Gambutsu

This poetic expression says it perfectly: Go and see. Or, more bluntly, get up off your butt, get out there in the world, and see for yourself! E-mails, reports, conference calls, hearsay, even video — they can't tell the whole story. You must see it with your own eyes. And not just your eyes — you must experience it with all your senses.

The world is subtle and full of nuance. Nothing's black and white. And these subtleties are often not just important, but the critical difference. Reports and data only tell one part of the overall picture. There's nothing like being there to get the whole picture.

Some people may label these efforts as boondoggles — or worse, outright *muda*. But you're adding value when your firsthand observations and experience enable faster and more effective processes and procedures.

The Art of Simplicity

It's a famous cliché: "Keep it simple, stupid" — but this is one of the best practices of Lean. Indeed, keep it simple. When in doubt, simplify and eliminate. When confronted with a decision, ask yourself "Which option is simpler?" And unless you're compelled to do otherwise, choose the simplest option.

Lean guides you to take on challenges in small bites. To make continuous improvement continuous, you don't implement complex and convoluted solutions. Increased complexity increases the risk of failure and lowers reliability. *Kaizen* is surely simpler.

At a Glance

Lean environments are high-sensory environments. Design your environment to convey critical information with a glimpse of an eye or a turn of an ear. Use simple techniques like *andon boards* (see Chapter 9) to show where trouble is brewing or has boiled over; have horns honk to signal *takt time* (see Chapter 4), or tool boards to illustrate when something is out of place or missing. Use customer information centers, cross-training boards, and performance trend charts for key metrics to present information about the business in a way that you can respond to nonstandard situations.

A Lean environment should enable everyone — even an outsider — to understand the status and state of affairs. Are you running to standard? Is there an issue? How are you doing? All at-a-glance.

Standardize Something — Standardize Everything!

Standardize your work: Define a segment of work, standardize it, work to that standard, and measure its effectiveness. Say you've just completed a *PDCA cycle* (see Chapter 6). Find areas of improvement, eliminate waste, and redefine the standard. Now work to that *new* standard, and measure *its* effectiveness. And on and on and on — across the entire organization. That's *Kaizen*.

Standardized work provides the basis upon which Lean operations are built. After standardized work is in place, you can depend on it, build on it, train to it, delegate it, or even outsource it. You don't have to reinvent it each time you do it, or suffer performance variances because it's, well, nonstandard. Standardized work becomes a building block that enables to you move forward and accomplish more.

You'll find that certain practices are custom by definition — they don't seem to fit a standard. Standardize the parts that can be standardized. Allow the custom parts to be defined as "custom" until you can see a way to standardize them. In an ideal Lean world, everything you do follows a standardized work scheme.

Chapter 17

Ten Pitfalls to Avoid

In This Chapter

▶ Thinking differently because Lean is different

▶ Knowing what to watch out for

▶ Avoiding the most common mistakes

Because Lean is different from traditional western-style thinking, organization, and management, keeping your bearings can be difficult. The rewards don't come without risk. Many people — some well-meaning, and some not so well-meaning — can quietly conspire, either accidentally or purposefully, to knock you off course and kill the initiative. Many large and well-meaning companies have fallen prey to one or more of these traps, and suffered mightily for it.

In this chapter, we fill you in on the most common causes of problems with Lean initiatives, and tell you how to avoid them. These issues are real — and they can be real trouble if you're not careful. Pay attention to these pitfalls, and stay alert for signs of disaffection or discontent. Doing so can save your initiative and, ultimately, your organization.

Yawn

Complacency is the number one killer of Lean initiatives. If things are going even moderately well, there's just not a lot of organizational willingness to change course, take on a new initiative, or expand an existing one. Proactively stimulating change is very difficult. If there is no crisis demanding action, people often can't see the reasons. Tellingly, over two-thirds of companies now practicing Lean are doing so because they felt compelled to act.

Even if you've started a Lean initiative in the face of trouble, it still will be difficult for the areas not directly affected by the problems to see why they should adopt Lean practices. After all, if it's somebody else's problem, why should they change?

In addition, because Lean is a continuous, incremental-change process, it may be difficult for certain people or business areas to perceive the significance of small changes occurring from the adoption of Lean practices in other organizations or work areas. And if they can't see it, and if it doesn't appear significant enough, they're going to wonder why they should do it.

Resistance to change is natural to any change initiative, and it's no different in Lean. But Lean almost intensifies this resistance through its incremental, baby-steps approach.

How do you get people to adopt Lean practices if they can't readily see the results? You fight complacency with several weapons:

- **Communications:** Have a strong communicator who's unrelenting and convincing in the purpose and goals of the Lean initiative, as well as its proven, time-tested methods and tools.

- **Information updates:** Be sure to communicate the results and benefits from Lean improvement activities as they occur — both in your company and elsewhere.

- **Competition:** People need to know what your competitors are doing, what industry practices are, and what it takes to keep pace.

- **Lean measurements:** Create performance measures that reinforce Lean behaviors.

- **Punitive measures:** Sometimes, you have to use the stick. In every group, there are some who will not board the train.

Same-Old Same-Old Senior Management

If the senior managers aren't fully embracing Lean, you have a very, *very* difficult road ahead. Many in the industry would tell you that your chances of a successful Lean initiative are nil without senior management's full support. Why? Because the initiative is so all-encompassing and life-changing, that without management support, it simply won't happen.

Senior managers can't go on living the old ways and expect a new initiative to take hold. Not only must they be supportive, but they have specific roles to play and regular actions to take. The management functions can't be delegated or handed off; they must be practiced and performed by the managers themselves. Senior managers have to participate in *Kaizen* events; they must take the *gemba* walks. No free tickets.

Furthermore, senior managers must regularly communicate the nature of the initiative and reinforce its purpose. The senior managers must be visible and available to talk to people at all levels inside and outside the organization.

The revolving door of senior managers, particularly through merger and acquisition, has also been the source of Lean initiative failures. Replacing enlightened Lean leaders with traditionally minded ones has caused the demise of some very noteworthy companies in record time. You cannot have a successful Lean journey unless all the leaders understand and are committed to its success.

Quick Fix!

Do not sell yourself or your organization on Lean as a quick fix. You can realize short-term benefits and gain momentum through a special Lean project or a *Kaizen* blitz event. However, the true success of Lean does not come through short-term special events. The true power of Lean is through continuous, incremental improvements over the long term.

If your organization is so severely damaged that you must take immediate action and slamma-jamma a miracle overhaul in order to dramatically improve results in the upcoming quarter, Lean is not the right method. If that's your situation, best of luck to you, but shop elsewhere.

Use Lean as a long-term solution. Use Lean to more patiently, orderly, and consistently change people's thinking and behaviors, change the culture, and improve continuously and incrementally forever. You don't create that kind of change overnight.

Cherry-Picking

One of the most common faux pas of Lean implementations is the piecemeal application of individual tools. Companies who believe that a couple of tools will solve their world-hunger problems are grossly mistaken.

The piecemeal efforts always backfire. Because Lean is a complete system, picking up a few tools and hacking away is a recipe for disaster. Without the holistic understanding, adoption, and support of the principles and methods of Lean, the tools are out of context. Of course, you never implement all the elements of Lean at the same time, but not losing sight of the interrelationships of the elements in the overall system is critical.

The most flagrant abuses have lacked the respect for people, attempting to implement Lean tools within traditional management, accounting, and operations frameworks. It just doesn't work.

With Lean, do it, or don't do it. But don't think you can do it halfway.

Beans Are Beans

Do not expect traditional accounting methods and systems to reflect the improvements accomplished through Lean practices. Eventually, results will hit the bottom line, but even these results don't properly account for the whole picture. Of all the nemeses to befall Lean initiatives, this is perhaps the most insidious: believing that the old ways of accounting for the business are the only ways to account for it.

A Lean implementation will redefine boundaries, breaking down traditional functional walls and changing the nature of how cost and value are defined in the organization. They will further change how people's contributions are measured, incentivized, and rewarded. Floor space will be reduced and cycle time will improve. You cannot make all those changes operationally and continue to perform accounting the old way — all the numbers don't overtly show up with traditional cost accounting.

The accounting managers may tell you how difficult it is for them to change, or even wave the risk flags (think Sarbanes-Oxley). Help them understand how they can be part of the solution, instead of the problem. Show them the results and challenge them how best to account for the improvements you make. Bring them onboard, and they can make a key difference!

Playing the Shell Game

Let's say that a nugget of waste is sitting there on the table, under the shell of your organization. Your operations manager — fully trained in Lean practices — deftly pulls out two additional shells: one for a supplier, and one for a distributor. He starts moving shells around and, suddenly — presto! — the nugget of *muda* is no longer under your shell. It's now under one of the others. He's eliminated waste from your organization, and aren't you the better for it?

You've just committed a Lean infraction: You've moved the *muda*. Moving the *muda* doesn't count in Lean, because improving yourself at the expense of someone else isn't really improvement. You're all interconnected through the value stream. Ultimately, the aim of Lean is to improve the *entire* stream. You have to eliminate the waste — period.

The Grease Monkeys

Many people around you will happily pick up a tool and use it — Lean tools included. A new technique, a new form of analysis, a new software program — they're all good. People love tools. They seem like toys. When you get a new toy, you get to play with something different that you haven't had before. You look for opportunities to show off your new toy, er, tool. But you need to remember to pick the right tool for the job.

A carpenter cannot build a bookcase with just a hammer, and you cannot build a Lean organization with just a *kanban* card. One tool does not a transformation make. You need to figure out how to use the full compliment of tools in your toolbox and pick the right tool for the job.

Busy Bees

Activity ≠ Progress. Everyone knows that people can be busy — very busy — without being at all productive. Bureaucracies are replete with useless activity, wasting people, time, and effort without producing anything of value. Make sure that the Lean improvement activities you undertake really add value.

When you have *Kaizen* events, make sure that they're well organized, with defined objective and teams creating lasting results. Be certain that managers are participating in them, to ensure the results are understood and supported by the people with authority and accountability. For example, if the objective is to free up floor space, then make sure it is freed up in usable, collective areas, not isolated pockets that don't create value for anything.

Busy bees should be busy making honey. Make sure your bees are making honey, too.

Stuck in the Middle Again

Traditional middle managers really are in the middle: They get it from both ends. The senior managers are forever beating on them to increase productivity and performance, and to "lower overhead" (that is, reduce headcount). Meanwhile, their subordinates are often like a herd of cats, who won't always do what they're asked to do and, furthermore, don't necessarily like being "railroaded" into yet another new initiative that they didn't ask for. They think of their immediate managers more as roadblocks than enablers.

Welcome to classic middle management — a lot of pressure, often in a thankless position, struggling to satisfy two disparate constituencies, and trying to make do with inadequate tools and insufficient support.

The roles of middle managers and supervisors are very different in Lean from traditional hierarchical, order-giving organizations and systems. In Lean enterprises, the supervisors become coaches and mentors. They relinquish considerable authority and decision-making to the employee teams, who find their own solutions to problems and challenges. The middle managers become listeners and enablers. Their job is to break down walls that inhibit team success.

These roles of middle management and supervisors are different from traditional western-style systems. Managers and supervisors must be properly trained, equipped, and supported in order to perform within a Lean system. It's not an easy transition for people. Some of them just don't make it.

Lean Six Sigma

The final pitfall to avoid is the distraction by the latest continuous-improvement fad. The consulting industry will continue to re-brand, re-badge, or repackage tools and techniques into the latest and greatest whiz-bang solution. Like the millions of fad diet and exercise programs, these new methods can give false hope and distract you from the Lean lifestyle changes proven to create healthy organizations over the long term.

After you've chosen your Lean path, take the time to understand how best to include new or existing methodologies to complement your Lean journey. Take Six Sigma for example: The statistical tools of Six Sigma can be very useful in the reduction of variation *(mura)* and eliminate particularly nagging defects. However, the short-term, big-project mentality and highly structured infrastructure of Six Sigma is incongruent with a true Lean organization.

As a fundamental method, Lean cannot be easily subjugated into other methodologies or frameworks. Lean tools can be borrowed by another framework, but that's all it is or will be: borrowed. Lean has a successful track record as a whole system in organizations that don't get sidetracked by bright, shiny objects.

Chapter 18

Ten Places to Go for Help

. . . .

In This Chapter

▶ Browsing on the Web

▶ Entering the Lean blogosphere

▶ Joining associations and societies

▶ Using the services of facilitators and consultants

. . . .

*T*here's a lot to learn about Lean. Between all the tools, applications, methods, jargon, projects, planning, leadership, change management, and support — *whew*! — Lean is involved. It's all-encompassing, and it's everyday — and you need to stay on top of it to make it all work.

This book is a great introduction to Lean. We provide you with a broad understanding and working knowledge, showing you the principles and practices, the methods and tools, the language and jargon. But as complete as this book is, there's so much more to Lean than could ever fit in 384 pages.

Fortunately, Lean is so broad and ubiquitous that many, many sources of help — on every aspect and element of Lean — are available. Researchers and practitioners, businesses and organizations, blogs and Web sites, societies and associations, authors and historians — they're all out there, accessible, and available to help. Whether you want more knowledge, education and training, consulting and project assistance, tools and technologies, or reference publications, you've got it. In this final chapter, we introduce you to the greater world of Lean support that can pick up where we leave off.

Books and Publications

Believe it or not, *Lean For Dummies* is not the only book about Lean! (It may be the best one, but it's not the only one!) There are hundreds of books on Lean, written from every angle. Whether you want to know about a particular tool or technique, or about implementing Lean in a certain business or industry, chances are there's a book for you. You can search for these at any of the major online bookstores.

Check out Productivity Press (www.productivitypress.com), which offers the broadest selection of books and learning tools about Lean and the methodologies based on the Toyota Production System (TPS). Many of their books are translated directly from the Japanese versions.

Online Information

In this age of the Internet, you can find an almost limitless amount of reference material online. Use your favorite search engine to find information on nearly any topic. If you want more direction, check out the following sites:

- **Wikipedia (www.wikipedia.com):** This site has general information on Lean, as well as info on the history of Lean and the people behind it.

- **The Improvement Encyclopedia at Syque.com (www.syque.com/quality_tools/index.htm):** UK Quality consultant Dave Straker has implemented an extensive online reference library that includes useful information on Lean and other quality tools.

- **The Lean Library (www.theleanlibrary.com):** Founded by Jamie Flinchbaugh of the Lean Learning Center, the Lean Library is a clearinghouse for book reviews, papers, links, and industry news.

- **The Lean Enterprise Institute (www.lean.org):** Founded by James Womack, the Lean researcher, this site provides Lean resources, products and event information.

- **Gemba Research (www.gemba.com):** Gemba is a training and consulting firm whose Web site contains outstanding reference information.

- **The Lean Manufacturing Resource Guide (www.leanqad.com):** The ERP vendor QAD maintains an extensive on-line Lean library and reference center under this name.

- **Daily *Kaizen* (www.dailykaizen.org):** There's nothing quite like your friendly daily reminder.

Blog Sites

Want to stay apprised of ongoing trends? Have a specific issue you'd like to address? Want to participate in discussions with the real experts in the Lean community? Check out the following blog sites:

- **The Lean Blog (`http://kanban.blogspot.com`):** Senior Lean practitioner Mark Graban maintains one of the most active Lean blogs on the Internet.

- **Kaikau (`http://kaikaku.typepad.com`):** Lean guru Norm Bodek's blog site.

- **The Lean Insider (`http://leaninsider.productivitypress.com`):** This is the blog site of Productivity Press, the company that translated most of the Japanese quality books into English.

- **Evolving Excellence (`http://superfactory.typepad.com/blog`):** Bill Wadell and Kevin Meyer, founders of the Superfactory knowledge products company, host a lively blog.

- **Lean Reflections (`http://leanreflect.blogspot.com`):** Karen Wilhelm, the Society of Manufacturing Engineers editor of the *Lean Directions* newsletter, hosts.

- **Innovation Weblog (`http://innovationtools.com/Weblog/innovation-weblog.asp`):** PR and marketing maven Chuck Frey hosts on his Innovation Tools Web site.

- **Gemba Panta Rei (`www.gembapantarei.com`):** *Gemba* consultant Jon Miller hosts.

Professional Societies and Associations

Several professional societies and associations have dedicated Lean efforts, and you can contact them for additional information:

- **The Society of Manufacturing Engineers (SME):** SME is the world's leading professional society supporting manufacturing education. SME promotes an increased awareness of manufacturing engineering and helps keep manufacturing professionals up-to-date on leading trends and technologies. The society has members in 70 countries and is supported by a network of hundreds of chapters worldwide. Lean certification information is found on their Web site. *Web site:* `www.sme.org`.

✔ **The Association for Manufacturing Excellence (AME):** AME is a not-for-profit organization dedicated to cultivating understanding, analysis, and exchange of productivity methods and their successful application in the pursuit of excellence. AME is practitioner-based, and events and workshops focus on hands-on learning. AME publishes the award-winning *Target* magazine and puts on several regional and national events each year. *Web site:* www.ame.org.

✔ **Shingo:** The Shingo Prize was established in 1988 to promote awareness of Lean concepts, and recognizes companies across North America that achieve world-class manufacturing status. The Shingo Prize is administered by the College of Business of Utah State University. *Web site:* www.shingoprize.org.

✔ **Manufacturing Extension Partnership (MEP):** Sponsored by the U.S. National Institute for Standards and Technology (NIST), MEP is a nationwide network of over 350 centers, funded by a combination of federal, state, and private monies, providing resources, expertise, and services to manufacturers. It helps companies to compete globally, improve supply chain integration, and gain access to technology for improved productivity. *Web site:* www.mep.nist.gov.

Conferences and Symposia

Numerous organizations regularly sponsor conferences and symposia around the United States and the world on Lean, quality, and business process improvement. These conferences are outstanding forums for meeting with peers, surveying product and service providers, and attending seminars on current topics of interest. Major Lean conferences and organizations include the following:

✔ The Society of Manufacturing Engineers (SME) hosts a variety of technical events and expositions. Check the events section on its Web site (www.sme.org).

✔ A number of Lean Summits are sponsored by the Lean Enterprise Institute (www.lean.org/Summits/Index.cfm).

✔ Productivity, Inc. (www.productivityinc.com/events) holds a variety of conferences and workshops throughout the year.

✔ Ixperion (www.ixperion.com) hosts quality conferences across Europe.

✔ Lean Enterprise China (www.leanchina.org) a Lean Enterprise Institute sponsored event for Asia-Pacific.

✔ Lean Summit UK (www.leanuk.org/#summit) a Lean Enterprise Institute sponsored event for Europe.

Consultants, Facilitators, and Trainers

If you're embarking on a Lean initiative, or you have an initiative underway, you may need assistance — in the form of expert advice, training, and experienced facilitation of *Kaizen, Kaikaku,* or other events. Worry not! The Lean community has experts available to help you in all of these areas.

You can find and apply expertise in several forms:

- ✔ **Methods and tools:** Most training and consulting organizations specialize in the methods and tools of Lean — everything from Value Stream Mapping and Kano modeling to performing statistical analysis and conducting *Kaizen* events.

- ✔ **Change management:** Leading an organization through the change process to understand and practice the philosophy of *Kaizen* is very different from learning and applying the tools. Look for a different kind of expertise to help you through the change process.

- ✔ **Rent-A-Sensei:** Sometimes, you just need an expert who can facilitate your team through a project or phase of an initiative. Certain consultancies have such experts, in the form of experienced leaders, or *senseis,* who can assist you.

To find people to help you, just enter "Lean consultants" into your favorite search engine.

Interview consulting organizations carefully, to ensure that they have applied experience in the areas of your greatest needs and interests.

In addition to private consultancies, an increasing number of academic institutions are teaching and training Lean practices. An organization known as the Lean Education Academic Network (LEAN) is group of university educators who are pursuing Lean education in U.S. higher academia, as well as continuous improvement of Lean education in the classroom through sharing of knowledge and teaching materials, collaboration, and networking among colleagues. You can find out more at www.teachinglean.org.

Lean Periodicals

Subscribing to Lean periodicals will bring you regular joy and knowledge, via your mailbox! The following established periodicals are manufacturing-oriented:

- *Assembly Magazine* (`www.assemblymag.com`; subscription: free; 12 issues/year)

- *The Manufacturer Magazine* (`www.themanufacturer.com`; subscription: free; 12 issues/year)

- *Industry Week* (`www.industryweek.com`; subscription: free; 12 issues/year — yes, it's called *Industry Week,* but it comes out monthly!)

- *Lean Directions,* an SME e-publication (www.sme.org/leandirections; subscription: free; 12 issues/year)

- *Target,* an online AME publication (`www.ame.org`; free access; 4 issues/year)

- The Superfactory online newsletter (`www.superfactory.com`; subscription: free; 12 issues/year)

Software Providers

Technology vendors are building increasing knowledge in the methods and tools of Lean. In addition to their products — which have considerable online help and tutorials — they provide education and support services.

Practitioners

Chances are, you know someone who has been involved in Lean, perhaps even a specialist of some type. If you're working in a Lean company, you're surrounded by experienced professionals. They have the expertise and reference material available for you.

Even if you don't know of anyone personally, you may be surprised by just how few degrees of separation lie between your interest and a Lean expert. Ask your friends and associates, ask the people at your church or synagogue, or the other parents at the ballgame. Try shouting "Lean" in a crowded theater! You know people who know Lean — you just have to ask around.

Related Genres

Lean is so broad and all-encompassing that it touches and affects many related disciplines and genres. Conversely, Lean in and of itself does not have all the answers. You must maintain a broad perspective to and a complete picture. Look into these related disciplines for important supporting information:

- ✔ **Ergonomics and industrial engineering:** How consumers use products and services, and how workers use machinery and tools

  - Usernomics: www.usernomics.com/ergonomics-standards.html

  - The Institute of Industrial Engineering: www.iienet2.org

- ✔ **Supply chain and logistics:** Optimizing supply, delivery, inventory, and readiness

  - The Council of Supply Chain Management Professionals: www.cscmp.org

  - The Association for Operations Management: www.apics.org

- ✔ **Project and program management:** Controlling project scope, schedule, and resources; configuration management; getting the most out of project teams

  - The Project Management Institute: www.pmi.org

  - The Project Manager's Homepage: www.allpm.com

- ✔ **Statistical analysis:** In-depth understanding of the behaviors that influence outcomes

  - The American Society of Quality: www.asq.org

  - The Online Statistics Textbook: www.statsoft.com/textbook/stathome.html

- ✔ **Six Sigma community:** Because defects are a form of waste

  - The Online Six Sigma Forum: www.isixsigma.com

  - The International Society of Six Sigma Professionals: www.isssp.com

- ✔ **Business Process Management:** A rapidly growing field that is becoming a clearinghouse of all things process

  - The Business Process Management Initiative: www.bpmi.org

  - Business Process Trends: www.bptrends.com

- ✔ **One Page Business Plan:** Concise descriptions of goals, mission, and strategies; not just for small, startup businesses anymore — it's applicable as the one-page description of any project or program plan.

  - The One Page Business Plan: www.onepagebusinessplan.com

✔ **Organizational Development (OD) and Training:** Training, facilitation and Organizational Development resources and professionals

- Organizational Development Network: `www.odnetwork.org`
- American Society of Training & Development: `www.astd.org`
- International Association of Facilitators: `www.iaf-methods.org`
- Free Management Library — OD Information: `www.management help.org/org_chng/org_chng.htm`

Glossary

5S: The principle of waste elimination through workplace organization. Derived from the Japanese words *seiri, seiton, seiso, seiketsu,* and *shitsuke,* which have been translated into English as *sort, straighten, scrub, systematize,* and *standardize.*

5 Whys: A method of root-cause analysis that entails the progressive asking of "Why?" at least five times or until the root cause is established.

5 Ws and 1 H: A tool of inquiry in which you ask, "Who?", "What?", "When?", "Where?", "Why?", and "How?"

Affinity Diagram: An organization of individual pieces of information into groups or broader categories.

andon: A signal to alert people of problems at a specific place in a process; a form of visual management.

A3: A one-page reporting format, named for the international paper size. It contains, on one page, critical information about an issue, such as description, cost, timing, data, planned solution, and planned resolution.

autonomation: Automation with a human touch. Autonomation is related to *jidoka.* Intelligence is added to equipment to prevent the production of defective products, eliminate overproduction, and automatically stop the process when abnormalities are detected. This type of automation frees people to perform more valuable activities. *See also jidoka.*

backflow: The return of a "product" to an earlier step, usually to the source of the issue, for reprocessing or repair.

Balanced Scorecard: A framework for identifying business metrics beyond the basic financial measures normally used. The framework includes customer, internal, people, and financial measures, and ties together strategic goals with operational metrics.

Bar Chart: A graphical method of depicting data, grouped by category. The values are depicted in vertical or horizontal bars.

batch and queue: A method of processing where material is accumulated into a *lot* (batch) and pushed through the process independent of demand or requirements. This is also known as *mass production* or *traditional manufacturing.*

bottleneck: A process that constricts or limits the flow of the overall process.

buffer stock: An amount of inventory accumulated between processes to protect a process from starving due to uneven capacities. Buffers are a form of inventory, one of the seven forms of waste. *See also* inventory; seven forms of waste.

bull-whip effect: The progressive magnification of demand upstream from the customer in the value stream.

Cause-and-Effect Diagram: A pictorial diagram that shows the variable causes that can affect a given process or output. Also known as a C&E Diagram.

cell: *See* work module.

Check Sheet: Any standard way you can gather data and view an activity as it happens, normally on a piece of paper or chart on which someone indicates an activity and checks it as it occurs.

changeover: Elapsed time between one activity or product and a new one. In a production environment, changeover is the time between the production of the last part of one type to the production of the first good part of the next type. Another example is a racing pit crew: The time between the moment the car rolls into the pit for tires and fuel to its entrance back into the racecourse is changeover.

consumer: The person or entity who obtains goods and services for his or its own use. In Starbucks, the person drinking the Venti half-caf, nonfat White Chocolate Mocha Frappuccino with extra whipped cream is the consumer. *See also* customer.

continuous flow: The ideal state where products move through a manufacturing process — or people move through a service process — one at a time, without stopping or waiting.

Control Chart: The most powerful tool of statistical process control, the control chart is a time-series run chart, with statistically determined upper and lower control limits and a centerline.

Current-State Map: A Value Stream Map that depicts things as they currently exist within the value stream. *See also* Value Stream Map.

customer: The person or entity who is the recipient of what you produce, either within your organization or outside your organization. For Starbucks suppliers, the customer is the retail store that receives the espresso beans, milk, syrup, and blender, in order to make that Venti half-caf, nonfat White Chocolate Mocha Frappuccino for the consumer. *See also* consumer.

cycle time: The total amount of elapsed time from the time a task, process, or service is started until it is completed.

defects: The output of a process that fails to meet the required specification or performance standard. One of the seven forms of waste. *See also* seven forms of waste.

demand amplification: *See* bull-whip effect.

Deming Cycle: *See* Plan-Do-Check-Act (PDCA) or Plan-Do-Study-Act (PDSA).

downtime: The stoppage of a process due to planned or unplanned causes, such as equipment maintenance or failure, material or quality issues, training or staffing constraints, and so on.

effectiveness: The utilization of the minimum number of resources, with the least amount of waste, to create a defined value for the customer.

efficiency: The optimization of a process that results in minimum resource use. Efficiency is not necessarily tied to customer value. A process can be efficient but not effective.

error-proofing: *See poka-yoke.*

excess processing: work being performed beyond what is required to satisfy the customer standards or requirements. *See* seven forms of waste.

Failure Mode Effects Analysis (FMEA): The method used to identify, assess, and mitigate risks associated with potential failure modes in a product, process, or system.

FIFO: *See* first in first out (FIFO).

finished goods: An inventory of products in a completed state awaiting shipment or sale.

first in first out (FIFO): A process to manage orders or inventory so that the oldest is processed first. The goal of FIFO is to prevent earlier orders from being delayed unfairly in favor of new orders.

Fishbone Diagram: *See* Cause-and-Effect Diagram.

flow: The movement of a product or service along the value stream, from its inception to the customer.

flowchart: The graphical representation of all activities in a process including tasks, delays, decisions, movement, and so on.

flow production: *See* continuous flow.

FMEA: *See* Failure Mode Effects Analysis (FMEA).

freed up: Resources or floor space made available through continuous improvement or *Kaizen* efforts.

Future-State Map: A Value Stream Map that depicts an improved view of the value stream. *See also* Value Stream Map.

gemba: Where the action occurs.

genchi genbutsu: Go and see.

group technology: The process of analyzing and categorizing products, parts, and assemblies in order to simplify design, manufacturing, purchasing, and other business processes. The resulting categories form the basis of work-module development.

heijunka: The technique of smoothing or leveling schedules.

heijunka **box:** A tool used to control the volume and mix of production through the controlled distribution of *kanban* at standard, fixed intervals of time.

Histogram: A Bar Chart that depicts the frequency of occurrence — by the height of the bars — of numerical or measurement categories of data.

hoshin: A system of planning, forms, and rules that engages everyone in addressing business at both the strategic and tactical levels. It is also known as *policy deployment* or *hoshin kanri.*

hoshin kanri: *See* hoshin.

Ideal-State Map: A Value Stream Map that depicts a value stream comprised of only value-added activities. *See also* Value Stream Map.

information flow: The uninterrupted progression of supporting data and instructions along the value stream.

inspection: The act of comparing a product to a predefined performance standard. Inspection is a non-value-added activity, especially when it occurs after the transformational step in the process.

inventory: The raw materials, purchased parts, work-in-process components, and finished goods that are not yet sold to a customer. Inventory is one of the seven forms of waste, when the amounts exceed the minimum level to maintain the pull system. *See also* seven forms of waste.

inventory turns: Financial measure of the Cost of Goods Sold (COGS) in a given period (annually) divided by the Average Inventory for the same period.

Ishikawa Diagram: *See* Cause-and-Effect Diagram.

jidoka: Transference of human intelligence to machines via automation. The automation enables the equipment to detect defects and stop until someone comes to fix the problem. This supports quality at the source and the prevention of defects from progressing along the value stream. Additionally, the person in charge of the step in the value stream is responsible to resolve the issue or stop the flow to get outside assistance.

just-in-time: Providing what is needed, when it is needed, in the quantity needed, and the quality level needed.

Kaikaku: Radical improvement activity to reduce waste.

Kaizen: Incremental continuous improvement that increases the effectiveness of an activity to produce more value with less waste.

kanban: A signal that triggers replenishment or withdrawal in a pull system. *Kanban* is often in the form of a card on a container in production environments. The signal regulates the production flow in the value stream.

lead time: The elapsed time from the initial stage of a project or policy and the appearance of results. In the case of a product environment, the time from order receipt to shipment to the customer for one product.

Lean: An improvement methodology based on a customer-centric definition of value, and providing that value in the most effective way possible, through a combination of the elimination of waste and a motivated and engaged workforce.

left-hand/right-hand analysis: A method to analyze the motion of an operator's hands to perform a process step. The analysis is then used to eliminate the waste caused by unnecessary motion.

level production: *See* heijunka.

level scheduling: The practice of averaging out both the volume and mix of products in the production schedule. Leveling allows a consistent workflow, reducing the fluctuation of customer demand with the eventual goal of being able to produce every product every day according to demand.

level selling: A sales method characterized by the elimination of artificial demand spikes, created by sales incentives and promotions. The resulting sales process coupled with a Lean production process can respond to real fluctuations caused by customer demand.

line balance: The process of aligning the cycle times and operator staffing of a process to takt time. *See also* takt time.

mass production: *See* batch and queue.

material flow: The movement of raw materials and product through the process steps of a value stream.

metric: A measure that is considered to be a key indicator of performance.

milk run: A method of consolidating material shipments that includes the routing of trucks to collect materials from various suppliers based on *kanban* signals, fixed routes, and fixed times. Milk runs help to control the incoming flow of materials into a facility.

module: *See* work module.

monument: A unit or piece of equipment that cannot or should not be moved due to process constraints.

motion: Any movement of people's bodies that does not add value to the process. One of the seven forms of waste. *See also* seven forms of waste.

muda: Any activity that consumes resources, but creates no value. *Muda* is categorized in two forms: Type-1 *muda* is necessary for the process, but non-value-added; type-2 *muda* is both unnecessary and non-value-added.

mura: Waste due to unevenness or variation.

muri: Waste or stress on the system due to overburdening or unreasonableness.

non-value-added: Any activity, product, or process that does not meet the value-added criteria. *See also* value-added.

OEE: *See* Overall Equipment Effectiveness (OEE).

Overall Equipment Effectiveness (OEE): The measurement of how effectively equipment is being used. It is calculated as a percentage. The formula is OEE % = Availability × Performance Rate × Quality.

overproduction: Producing more than the customer requires. One of the seven forms of waste. *See also* seven forms of waste.

pacemaker process: The operation that establishes the pace of the production of a product or service; its rate of production should be equal to or close to takt time. *See also* takt time.

Pareto Chart: A bar chart where the categories are presented in descending order of frequency. The Pareto principle states that 80 percent of the data will fall in 20 percent of the categories.

PDCA: *See* Plan-Do-Check-Act (PDCA) or Plan-Do-Study-Act (PDSA).

PDSA: *See* Plan-Do-Check-Act (PDCA) or Plan-Do-Study-Act (PDSA).

pitch: The amount of time required to make one container of product. The formula is Pitch = Takt Time × Container Quantity.

Plan-Do-Check-Act (PDCA) or Plan-Do-Study-Act (PDSA): A short-cycle iterative improvement scheme at the core of the *Kaizen* process. This four-step process includes (1) defining the objectives, issues, and potential solution; (2) carrying out the plan in a trial mode; (3) verifying and studying trial results; (4) fully implementing and standardizing the solution. It is also called the *Shewhart cycle* or *Deming cycle.*

poka-yoke: A device to prevent defect production.

policy deployment: *See hoshin.*

process: A set of activities, material, and/or information flow that transforms a set of inputs into defined outputs.

process owner: The individual who has responsibility for process performance and resources, and who provides support, resources, and functional expertise to projects. The process owner is accountable for implementing process improvements.

product family: A group of products or services that require all or a majority of the same processing steps for completion.

pull: A system of production that is activated by customer demand, which signals all the upstream activities to build to replenish what has been used. Upstream activities do not do anything until the signal from downstream is received.

QFD: _See_ Quality Function Deployment (QFD).

quality at the source: A process that ensures the quality level of a product or service before it leaves the transformation station in a process. The implementation of _poka-yoke_ and _jidoka_ are key aspects to creating quality at the source.

Quality Function Deployment (QFD): A systematic process for identifying and integrating customer requirements into every aspect of the design and delivery of products and services.

rework: Activities required to correct defects produced by a process.

Run Chart: A graphical tool for charting performance of a characteristic over time.

Scatter Plot: A chart in which one variable is plotted against another to observe or determine the relationship, if any, between the two.

sensei: Master or teacher, in this context, of Lean.

setup reduction: _See_ single minute exchange of die.

seven forms of waste: Transportation, waiting, overproduction, defects, inventory, motion, and excess processing are the seven forms of waste identified by Taiichi Ohno, one of the pioneers of the Toyota Production System, as waste normally found in mass production. Also known as the seven wastes or the seven _mudas_.

Shewhart Cycle: _See_ Plan-Do-Check-Act (PDCA) or Plan-Do-Study-Act (PDSA).

single minute exchange of die (SMED): Term used to describe the compilation of tools and techniques used to dramatically reduce the time required to complete the changeover of production and support of one "product" to another. Think Indy pit-crew tire changes.

SMED: _See_ single minute exchange of die (SMED).

smoothing: _See_ level scheduling _and heijunka_.

Spaghetti Chart: A graphical representation of the movement of materials or people in a process. It is used to eliminate wasted motion or transportation.

standardized work: The definition of a process step characterized by takt time, a set work sequence and established in-process inventory. Deviations to standardized work constitutes an abnormality, which is then an opportunity for improvement.

supermarket: The location where a predefined amount of inventory is controlled and released into a pull system by *kanban.*

supplier: An individual or entity that provides an input to a process in the form of resources or information.

takt time: *Takt* is the German word for "beat." In Lean, takt time is the pace of production based on the rate of customer consumption.

Therblig analysis: A method to analyze the motion that an operator performs within a process step based on 18 standardized elements. The analysis is then used to eliminate the waste caused by unnecessary motion.

Total Productive Maintenance (TPM): A proactive approach to maintaining equipment. It is divided into three areas: autonomous maintenance, planned maintenance, and predictive maintenance. Its aim is to maximize the overall equipment efficiency (OEE) and minimize production losses due to equipment failure or malfunction. *See also* Overall Equipment Effectiveness.

Toyota Production System (TPS): A production system developed by the Toyota Motor Corporation based on the philosophy that the ideal condition for production is created when machines, facilities, and people work together adding value without creating waste. The two pillars of the TPS are just-in-time and *jidoka. See also* just-in-time *and jidoka.*

TPM: *See* Total Productive Maintenance (TPM).

TPS: *See* Toyota Production System (TPS).

traditional manufacturing: *See* batch and queue.

transportation: Unnecessary movement of materials or other items from one place to another, usually to storage or staging areas. *See* seven forms of waste.

TWO DIME: A mnemonic device to remember the seven forms of waste: transportation, waiting, overproduction, defects, inventory, motion, and excess processing. *See also* seven forms of waste.

value: The worth placed upon goods or services, as defined by the customer. *See also* customer.

value-added: Defined by the customer and must meet the following three criteria:

- ✔ The customer must be willing to "pay" for it. Payment is generally thought of in monetary terms, but could also include time or other resources.
- ✔ The product or service must be done correctly the first time.
- ✔ The product or service must be transformed.

value stream: The flow of materials and information through a process to deliver a product or service to a customer.

Value Stream Map: A graphical representation of how all the steps in any process line up to produce a product or service, and of the flow of information that triggers the process into action.

VOC: *See* voice of the customer (VOC).

voice of the customer (VOC): The collective needs, wants, and desires of the recipient of a process output, a product, or a service, whether expressed or not. The VOC is usually expressed as specifications, requirements, or expectations.

waiting: People in a process delayed or stopped because of process waste or ineffective process design. *See* seven forms of waste.

waste: Any activity that uses resources, but creates no value for the customer.

WIP: *See* Work-In-Process (WIP).

Work-In-Process (WIP): In-process inventory.

work module: A co-location of all functional steps, in process sequence, to create a product or service. Generally, the work stations in these areas are arranged in a *U*-shape that flows counterclockwise.

Index

• I •

BUSINESS, CAREERS & PERSONAL FINANCE

0-7645-9847-3

0-7645-2431-3

Also available:
- Business Plans Kit For Dummies
  0-7645-9794-9
- Economics For Dummies
  0-7645-5726-2
- Grant Writing For Dummies
  0-7645-8416-2
- Home Buying For Dummies
  0-7645-5331-3
- Managing For Dummies
  0-7645-1771-6
- Marketing For Dummies
  0-7645-5600-2

- Personal Finance For Dummies
  0-7645-2590-5*
- Resumes For Dummies
  0-7645-5471-9
- Selling For Dummies
  0-7645-5363-1
- Six Sigma For Dummies
  0-7645-6798-5
- Small Business Kit For Dummies
  0-7645-5984-2
- Starting an eBay Business For Dummies
  0-7645-6924-4
- Your Dream Career For Dummies
  0-7645-9795-7

HOME & BUSINESS COMPUTER BASICS

0-470-05432-8

0-471-75421-8

Also available:
- Cleaning Windows Vista For Dummies
  0-471-78293-9
- Excel 2007 For Dummies
  0-470-03737-7
- Mac OS X Tiger For Dummies
  0-7645-7675-5
- MacBook For Dummies
  0-470-04859-X
- Macs For Dummies
  0-470-04849-2
- Office 2007 For Dummies
  0-470-00923-3

- Outlook 2007 For Dummies
  0-470-03830-6
- PCs For Dummies
  0-7645-8958-X
- Salesforce.com For Dummies
  0-470-04893-X
- Upgrading & Fixing Laptops For Dummies
  0-7645-8959-8
- Word 2007 For Dummies
  0-470-03658-3
- Quicken 2007 For Dummies
  0-470-04600-7

FOOD, HOME, GARDEN, HOBBIES, MUSIC & PETS

0-7645-8404-9

0-7645-9904-6

Also available:
- Candy Making For Dummies
  0-7645-9734-5
- Card Games For Dummies
  0-7645-9910-0
- Crocheting For Dummies
  0-7645-4151-X
- Dog Training For Dummies
  0-7645-8418-9
- Healthy Carb Cookbook For Dummies
  0-7645-8476-6
- Home Maintenance For Dummies
  0-7645-5215-5

- Horses For Dummies
  0-7645-9797-3
- Jewelry Making & Beading For Dummies
  0-7645-2571-9
- Orchids For Dummies
  0-7645-6759-4
- Puppies For Dummies
  0-7645-5255-4
- Rock Guitar For Dummies
  0-7645-5356-9
- Sewing For Dummies
  0-7645-6847-7
- Singing For Dummies
  0-7645-2475-5

INTERNET & DIGITAL MEDIA

0-470-04529-9

0-470-04894-8

Also available:
- Blogging For Dummies
  0-471-77084-1
- Digital Photography For Dummies
  0-7645-9802-3
- Digital Photography All-in-One Desk Reference For Dummies
  0-470-03743-1
- Digital SLR Cameras and Photography For Dummies
  0-7645-9803-1
- eBay Business All-in-One Desk Reference For Dummies
  0-7645-8438-3
- HDTV For Dummies
  0-470-09673-X

- Home Entertainment PCs For Dummies
  0-470-05523-5
- MySpace For Dummies
  0-470-09529-6
- Search Engine Optimization For Dummies
  0-471-97998-8
- Skype For Dummies
  0-470-04891-3
- The Internet For Dummies
  0-7645-8996-2
- Wiring Your Digital Home For Dummies
  0-471-91830-X

* Separate Canadian edition also available
† Separate U.K. edition also available

Available wherever books are sold. For more information or to order direct: U.S. customers visit www.dummies.com or call 1-877-762-2974.
U.K. customers visit www.wileyeurope.com or call 0800 243407. Canadian customers visit www.wiley.ca or call 1-800-567-4797.

SPORTS, FITNESS, PARENTING, RELIGION & SPIRITUALITY

0-471-76871-5

0-7645-7841-3

Also available:

- Catholicism For Dummies
  0-7645-5391-7
- Exercise Balls For Dummies
  0-7645-5623-1
- Fitness For Dummies
  0-7645-7851-0
- Football For Dummies
  0-7645-3936-1
- Judaism For Dummies
  0-7645-5299-6
- Potty Training For Dummies
  0-7645-5417-4
- Buddhism For Dummies
  0-7645-5359-3

- Pregnancy For Dummies
  0-7645-4483-7 †
- Ten Minute Tone-Ups For Dummies
  0-7645-7207-5
- NASCAR For Dummies
  0-7645-7681-X
- Religion For Dummies
  0-7645-5264-3
- Soccer For Dummies
  0-7645-5229-5
- Women in the Bible For Dummies
  0-7645-8475-8

TRAVEL

0-7645-7749-2

0-7645-6945-7

Also available:

- Alaska For Dummies
  0-7645-7746-8
- Cruise Vacations For Dummies
  0-7645-6941-4
- England For Dummies
  0-7645-4276-1
- Europe For Dummies
  0-7645-7529-5
- Germany For Dummies
  0-7645-7823-5
- Hawaii For Dummies
  0-7645-7402-7

- Italy For Dummies
  0-7645-7386-1
- Las Vegas For Dummies
  0-7645-7382-9
- London For Dummies
  0-7645-4277-X
- Paris For Dummies
  0-7645-7630-5
- RV Vacations For Dummies
  0-7645-4442-X
- Walt Disney World & Orlando
  For Dummies
  0-7645-9660-8

GRAPHICS, DESIGN & WEB DEVELOPMENT

0-7645-8815-X

0-7645-9571-7

Also available:

- 3D Game Animation For Dummies
  0-7645-8789-7
- AutoCAD 2006 For Dummies
  0-7645-8925-3
- Building a Web Site For Dummies
  0-7645-7144-3
- Creating Web Pages For Dummies
  0-470-08030-2
- Creating Web Pages All-in-One Desk
  Reference For Dummies
  0-7645-4345-8
- Dreamweaver 8 For Dummies
  0-7645-9649-7

- InDesign CS2 For Dummies
  0-7645-9572-5
- Macromedia Flash 8 For Dummies
  0-7645-9691-8
- Photoshop CS2 and Digital
  Photography For Dummies
  0-7645-9580-6
- Photoshop Elements 4 For Dummies
  0-471-77483-9
- Syndicating Web Sites with RSS Feeds
  For Dummies
  0-7645-8848-6
- Yahoo! SiteBuilder For Dummies
  0-7645-9800-7

NETWORKING, SECURITY, PROGRAMMING & DATABASES

0-7645-7728-X

0-471-74940-0

Also available:

- Access 2007 For Dummies
  0-470-04612-0
- ASP.NET 2 For Dummies
  0-7645-7907-X
- C# 2005 For Dummies
  0-7645-9704-3
- Hacking For Dummies
  0-470-05235-X
- Hacking Wireless Networks
  For Dummies
  0-7645-9730-2
- Java For Dummies
  0-470-08716-1

- Microsoft SQL Server 2005 For Dummies
  0-7645-7755-7
- Networking All-in-One Desk Reference
  For Dummies
  0-7645-9939-9
- Preventing Identity Theft For Dummies
  0-7645-7336-5
- Telecom For Dummies
  0-471-77085-X
- Visual Studio 2005 All-in-One Desk
  Reference For Dummies
  0-7645-9775-2
- XML For Dummies
  0-7645-8845-1

HEALTH & SELF-HELP

0-7645-8450-2   0-7645-4149-8

Also available:
- Bipolar Disorder For Dummies
  0-7645-8451-0
- Chemotherapy and Radiation
  For Dummies
  0-7645-7832-4
- Controlling Cholesterol For Dummies
  0-7645-5440-9
- Diabetes For Dummies
  0-7645-6820-5* †
- Divorce For Dummies
  0-7645-8417-0 †

- Fibromyalgia For Dummies
  0-7645-5441-7
- Low-Calorie Dieting For Dummies
  0-7645-9905-4
- Meditation For Dummies
  0-471-77774-9
- Osteoporosis For Dummies
  0-7645-7621-6
- Overcoming Anxiety For Dummies
  0-7645-5447-6
- Reiki For Dummies
  0-7645-9907-0
- Stress Management For Dummies
  0-7645-5144-2

EDUCATION, HISTORY, REFERENCE & TEST PREPARATION

0-7645-8381-6   0-7645-9554-7

Also available:
- The ACT For Dummies
  0-7645-9652-7
- Algebra For Dummies
  0-7645-5325-9
- Algebra Workbook For Dummies
  0-7645-8467-7
- Astronomy For Dummies
  0-7645-8465-0
- Calculus For Dummies
  0-7645-2498-4
- Chemistry For Dummies
  0-7645-5430-1
- Forensics For Dummies
  0-7645-5580-4

- Freemasons For Dummies
  0-7645-9796-5
- French For Dummies
  0-7645-5193-0
- Geometry For Dummies
  0-7645-5324-0
- Organic Chemistry I For Dummies
  0-7645-6902-3
- The SAT I For Dummies
  0-7645-7193-1
- Spanish For Dummies
  0-7645-5194-9
- Statistics For Dummies
  0-7645-5423-9

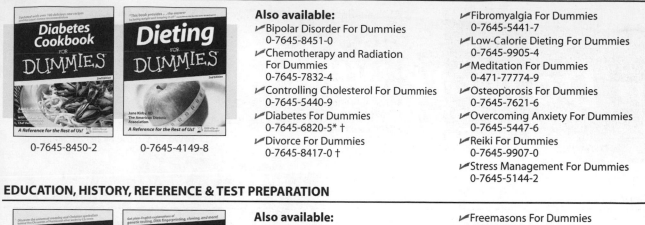

Get smart @ dummies.com®

- Find a full list of Dummies titles
- Look into loads of FREE on-site articles
- Sign up for FREE eTips e-mailed to you weekly
- See what other products carry the Dummies name
- Shop directly from the Dummies bookstore
- Enter to win new prizes every month!

* Separate Canadian edition also available
† Separate U.K. edition also available

Available wherever books are sold. For more information or to order direct: U.S. customers visit www.dummies.com or call 1-877-762-2974.
U.K. customers visit www.wileyeurope.com or call 0800 243407. Canadian customers visit www.wiley.ca or call 1-800-567-4797.